PETER
The Mature Man

PETER

The Mature Man

Terry Atkinson

Sequel to
'The Growing Pains of Peter'

Simon Peter as revealed in
the Acts of the Apostles

New Living Publishers
Manchester

Contents

*This book is dedicated to all who seek to
mature into meaningful men and women of God
and who, through many struggles,
reach their full potential.*

ABOUT THE AUTHOR

Terry Atkinson, one of ten children, came to faith in Christ in Yorkshire, England as a teenager. His early years in the ministry were spent founding churches in Perth, Western Australia. From Australia, Terry returned to England to study theology in Kenley, Surrey. He has been a minister of the gospel since the age of twenty-one, first pioneering a church in Gainsborough, Lincolnshire, England. He has been involved in Christian ministry for nearly fifty years, holding pastorates as far apart as Shrewsbury, Shropshire and Maryport in Cumbria. Now based in Manchester, England, he is at present engaged in itinerant ministry in the north-west of England and in Canada.

Terry is married to Margaret, whom he met while a theological student. She accompanies him during his ministry engagements, being used of the Lord to help and direct the lives of others who are in need. They have one daughter, two sons, and four grandchildren.

This is the author's eighth book. His writings cover many topics and include: *Dying Is Living* (on life after death); *In Sickness and in Health* and *The Growing Pains of Peter* (to which this book is the sequel). Terry is busy writing a book on the life of David, to be entitled *Diamonds in David.*

INTRODUCTION

The promise of Jesus Christ to Peter when they first met was, 'You are Simon son of Jonah: you will be called Cephas, which, by interpretation means a stone' (John 1:42). The promises of God can always be believed. In every heart, whenever there is some assurance of Christ, a promise has been received. Jesus Christ, seen in any believer, is a promise in a personality.

Another meeting between Jesus and Cephas is recorded in Matthew 16:18, but what Peter did not realise was that he was to be part of the church that Jesus would build. God builds surely and slowly for eternity. The work of the Son of God is not as the morning dew which disappears with the frost of the cold evening. God builds with big bricks, which are the lives of those who trust Him. Hence, the saying that 'man is a brick,' means some one of robust and enduring quality.

Character is developed slowly and surely through conflict
In my first book *The Growing Pains of Peter*, we see how the Lord took this young fisherman step by step, first on one pathway and then another until that stone-like character was formed in his life. Peter was as the brother of the waves of the sea, roaring, foaming, and rising only to fall back into the depths. There had to be the implantation into the character of the one chosen and called by Christ, as solid

as a rock, every bit as hard and shaped as a pebble on the beach of the Sea of Galilee. What mother nature had done with the pebble, using the sea as a tool, so the Son of God would do for the young man who would be taken from puberty to maturity, yet all the time not forgetting his humanity.

This development of character in Peter was every bit as important as any one of the five stones in David's leather pouch including the one which entered into the sling and was used to bring a giant down to earth with a bang.[1] What Jesus would do for this man in the making was as important as the first stone that the wise man used in Matthew 7:24 when building his house on a rock. It would be as important as the foundation stone of Solomon's temple built to house the glory of God. All these stones have passed away, but what Jesus put into Simon along the way through example and teaching was of eternal value. In Peter's life, we have what the devil wanted Jesus to do in the wilderness temptation to satisfy his own hunger, to turn stones into bread.[2] The reversal is true for the forthcoming apostle to the Gentiles. The bread, which could be soft and soggy, flat or hard, stale and broken, was being turned into a stone of value. The Stone of Scone that was in Westminster Abbey before it was returned to Scotland was used at the coronation ceremonies, the Kings being seated upon the stone in order to be crowned. Jesus would crown all His subjects with a stone. That stone is the work and Word of the Spirit of God, entering into the life, firm, sure and of lasting value. Peter would become a true reflection of the Stone that the builders rejected.[3] He was made into a living stone through the power of a living, loving Saviour. All that was Jesus Christ, His manner of life and disposition would become part of this volatile character called the Son of the Sea.

There is the gospel of Peter

Peter the mature man is matured throughout the gospel of Jesus Christ. Part of that gospel is the gospel of Peter: how Jesus took hold of a man, and made him into someone dependable and great; a man who would not disintegrate when the salt of the sea swept across his chest, nor be washed away when the tide came drifting in. No great wave from the centre of a storm would knock him off his feet, leaving him grovelling in the sand. He would be a man who could stick it out, see it through. Even when alone, he would be absolute and not obsolete. Remember, Jesus said, 'If any *man* will follow me let him take up his cross, daily.[4] When men do well in a war, we decorate them, placing medals of recognition for outstanding bravery on their chest. That which Jesus gave to Peter was placed within his heart. It was a character thing, not an outward show. Peter was not required to 'keep up appearances,' but simply expressed through life, lip and love all that he had learned in the presence of Jesus Christ. We display in public what we desire in private. Peter wasn't being matured to be an echo of Jesus, as a note from a trumpet, He was being trained in order to portray everything the Master taught and sought. What happened to the fisherman is what happens when the grape is turned into wine. The wine is the mature juice of the grape. Think of the process it passes through before it touches the human lip. Life is full of these processes that take us from one stage of maturity to another.

There will be development in every dilemma
Peter —The Mature Man will take you on a journey. Sometimes it will be long, and you will feel like leaving the rocky terrain. You will pass through many valleys, and move over different mountains in the human spirit. At the conclusion you will know how to walk through the Valley of the Shadow of Death, and to arrive in a Delightsome Land. There will be development in every dilemma. Your duty will be found walking in the dust of the day. Those who stay with the Galilean will become like him, a reflection of Jesus. We commence where Jesus commenced. There are insights and choice moments when we are allowed to witness the life of Christ being seen in flesh and blood. All that Jesus was as a Man you will see in Peter. The fact that he matured does not mean that the *mature* person never makes mistakes. There is in this fisherman's character so much which is appealing.

Through many experiences with Jesus Christ, whether walking along the sea shore or in a boat with a storm threatening to become your grave, or even in the quietness of the home with Peter's mother-in-law, you will understand what the Master Designer is seeking to do. A word here and there, line upon line, precept upon precept until Peter is developed into the little stone that Christ promised he would become. God finds His pearls in the pebbles that people walk all over, the pebbles that little children gather as mementoes, and then, in their forgetfulness throw away as of no consequence.

Your life is based on promises

The whole life of Peter is based on a promise. The promise of the Master and Saviour who would remain true to the man day by day, hour by hour, until something of the Ancient of Days was seen in him, until eternity became a reality in time through truth. The Galilean temperament needed controlling for it was like the wind blowing across the sea, seeking to sink every boat on the water.

Everything that happened to the son of Jonas in the Acts of the Apostles has its birth in the gospels. It is seen there sometimes in a shadowy form. In the dark areas of life God's light shines, all we need to do is to watch the Lord of Glory turn the unreal into the real and the shadow into substance. The Lord's best acts of grace are found in the human race. The Almighty's most glorious display is not in the fireworks of the heavens seen in stars and shooting stars, it is in humans. What is humanly possible is divinely acceptable. The hand of Jesus will always be there for you as it was for Peter reaching out and touching the pains and hurts of life with such tenderness. Tenderness that will turn tiredness into that which is fresh as the daisy. The Son of Man stayed with this Son of Adam because He loved him from top to toe, inside out and upside down both in faltering failures and sweet successes. Peter stayed with Jesus because he had the strong conviction that he had nowhere else to go.

The finished product, despite having passed through the finishing school does not appear in the Acts of the Apostles. There is no chapter or verse where you will see the young fisherman clothed in perfection with the sun at his head and the moon at his feet. What is happening to Peter is there in order that we might all have hope and trust. It is to make us realise that what God did with Peter, He is able to do with us. We come from the same mould. We have part of his temperament, but we can also be part of Jesus Christ. It was through Peter answering a call, that he began to be changed.[5]

Throughout the book, written by Doctor Luke, you will see a man being changed from one stage of glory to another. At no time does the work stop. The Lord is a timeless and a tireless Worker when taking hold of a man, as He seeks to turn that man into a man of God, until we exclaim with the widow woman of Zarepheth, 'Now I know you are a man of God![6]

The Lord never runs out of materials as long as we submit to Him. There was always a greater work to be done in Peter, even as there would always be more fish in the sea.

We are not always aware of our development

Education only ceases when you cease to learn. Peter was ever watching what Jesus said, how He reacted, how He performed miracles. We are influenced the most and develop the most in our unaware moments, moments when we do not think that God is at work. God rarely spoke to Peter through thunder.[7] It did although happen once. He rarely speaks in the wind, storm or an earthquake. He usually speaks in the still, small voice, the voice of a whisper.[8] He speaks to mother's sons in the mother tongue. When He does speak to us, like Elijah we wrap our faces, our personalities in a face cloth and hide them away, so that work accomplished by the Lord is fully enlarged to be seen by all.[9] The voice, the whisper ministers to your whimper and temper. When Peter had watched the Master at work, he heard a voice telling him, 'Go and do likewise.'[10] All the teachings of Jesus with Peter were an exposition of the beatitudes found in Matthew 5, and He was seeking to expand those attitudes in a life by lessons of love.

It is not enough to see Peter in the Acts of the Apostles, it is necessary to see the Acts of the Apostles in Peter. He was one of the acts. He was one that the Lord had provided and promoted. In the Book written about the Holy Spirit, one of those included from the 'first day until now'[11] is one of Christ's soldiers. He is not 'absent without leave' on an errand of mercy; he is there to 'fight the good fight of faith'. Peter, having done all, must stand in the power of His might. We are all on the Stage of Life, some are more important actors than others, but all have their part to play. None of us are puppets on a string; we have free will, and are able to make decisions for good or evil.

Sometimes in life, passing from puberty to maturity, we feel that when we express the new life found in Jesus Christ, we are part of the Amateur Dramatic Society with an inferior part to play. We are like actors who have not taken time to rehearse or read lines. We make many mistakes, and seem to give a poor performance. These are our 'growing pains'. Alas, we feel that we are but amateurs when expressing the 'perfections of Christ', W.E. Sangster's definition of sanctification.[12] We appear most of the time dramatic without fulfilling the role we have been called to fulfil in Christ Jesus.

There can be the Excellency of glory in you

Peter —The Mature Man will help you realise that God's ways are not simply with the sun, moon and stars, or that His glory is seen only in flashing lightning but also in human life. The apostle Paul depicts what we have and are in Jesus in our maturity as 'treasure in earthen vessels'.[13] The Excellency of the glory must be God's not ours. Peter is 'subject to like passions as we are,' yet the Lord enables him to overcome all things. As you read this book you will come to understand that God is doing the same work in your life and that you are in the same Kingdom. You might not literally find yourself in the Acts of the Apostles, but if you 'follow on to know the Lord' there will be countless acts of grace, numberless deeds of a Divine nature that enter into your life.

You might feel that you are only at the beginning of the Gospels, the companion of the unlettered and untutored man of Lake Tiberius. Like Thomas the twin, you appear to be the other side of Thomas, the one who always doubts. You are the 'without form and void' of a genesis that is not a genesis at all. You may feel that you belong in the Book of Judges where there was declension, and 'every man did that which was right in his own eyes,'[14] because there was no king on the throne, bringing you to the inglorious conclusion that you are but a name in the genealogy of Christ. Like the man who is being pieced together you are a wanderer on the seashore, as important as a grain of sand or a pebble on the beach. All you are gathering is driftwood, and as a token of your experience in the Lord all you have are broken pieces of a sailing ship that carried treasure fit for a palace, yet sank on its maiden voyage.

You can be one of God's radiant ones

We spend time as Peter and his brother did either cleaning, mending or casting nets, when we should be engaged in fishing and catching. Keep true to Him who is true, and you too will find yourself becoming a precise product of an unseen Hand. You will be counted among God's stars and radiant ones. It is not what you were, not what you are but what you are becoming in God. The gap between what you are and what you hope to be can appear to be very large. When nothing seems to happen, it is because you do not recognise the tools that God uses. It is only when circumstances call you to account that you respond with strength and realise that the Lord of Peter has done a glorious work in you. With this would be apostle you are going through a process, but it does not happen all at once. Be as one of the sandals on His feet, to be worn and trodden on. John Baptist saw himself as a slave that loosened sandals from the feet.[15] Sometimes you will feel that, having being touched by the hand of Jesus, you can only see men walking as trees.[16] Wait a while, let Jesus teach you a little more, and you will see trees walking as men. Those rough trees, the tough exterior, the knotted plank of wood, these twisted branches that seem to go in every direction yet go nowhere, are taken by the Carpenter of Nazareth and changed into something as delightful as a well designed human being in love with Love.

This book will help you, will give you a lift over many a gate, will open to your heart many a shut door and see you through to another glorious day where the Lord can do something new for you. If He could do it for Peter, He can do it for you. There is an overflow, a manifestation of life from His work in the life of Cephas. Just as the Syrophoenecian woman said, 'When the dogs find no place at the table, and no food is prepared for them, they find crumbs under the table.[17] It might appear that your lot in life is described as just crumbs of comfort. If you are under the table, it is where the feet of the Master are going to rest. Crumbs gathered together make full loaves.

Grace can be your teacher and you can be its scholar

When you turn the pages of the Acts of the Apostles, in each page there is new enrichment from the fingertip of Jesus into the heart of Peter. Each page can be breathtaking as it reveals another part of His riches of grace. Grace to help is found here, grace for the weary traveller, in many forms and shapes, and in times and seasons. This same soldier of the cross in his epistles writes about adding to your faith virtue; (not as an addendum or letting it be stuck on) and to virtue knowledge, patience and godliness, brotherly love and kindness.[18] For in doing so you will neither be fruitless nor barren. A whole new character will develop in you. What Jesus puts in, the devil would throw out. Jesus values His words and workings as being of eternal quality. The devil only sees them as 'dustbin waste'. Even Aaron in the Old Testament said, 'I threw this in and this came out.'[19] Jesus does not toss and throw things into a life in order for them to land as a heap of rubbish. He plants, He sows and He reaps. What He plants in the Son of Thunder is part of a plan.

You can never limit or define God's influence

When you close the Book of Acts, you do not shut out what happened to the fisherman. The Holy Spirit is more than a book of cold print. He is God's other Book called Nature. He works beyond, before and through the page. You may close the book but you cannot shut Him out. You might close your ears, but He will still speak so that you can hear, not always using words, He uses acts and deeds. As He disappears, a thousand reappear, and one of the thousand is you and the work of the Lord in your life. *Peter —The Mature Man* will never die while you live. While you allow the Holy Spirit to act, you will become one of those acts. Your whole life will become a biography of the Holy Spirit, a testimony of trusting times. The Life and Times of the Holy Spirit are in you, working out your own salvation with fear and trembling.[20] If you are afraid, 'Do yourself no harm; we are all here,'[21] said another of God's men. We are all part of the human race. Races are for running, and obstacles are placed there in order that you might overcome them. In doing so they will make you into a true Christian. It is more than a hop, skip or a jump, it is a lifelong journey. You begin with Peter as one of those whose heart the Lord has touched. We face the same difficulties. Let these words became a rallying call for you to go on and be the person, the man or woman God has called you to be. Let this be the meditation, (to chew like a cow chews the grass) the medicine of your heart. Let the words written in Acts of Peter be acted out in your life, a life of blessing and giving. Follow Jesus Christ with all your heart, mind, soul and body, and one day walking alongside of you will be Peter as revealed in another person, your brother, sister your friend. You will exclaim in a quiet corner of your soul, 'Here is where God has been at work. Here is one workman that God did not bury.' You will meet *The Mature Man* today, somewhere in your life, either in yourself or in another.

Notes

[1]   1 Samuel 17:40.

[2]   Matthew 4:3.

[3]   1 Peter 2:7.

[4]   Luke 9:23.

[5]   Matthew 4:18, 19.

[6]   1 Kings 17:18, 24.

[7]   John 12:29.

[8]   1 Kings 19:12.

[9]   1 Kings 19:13.

[10]   Luke 10:37.

[11]   Acts 1:21.

[12]   W.E.Sangster, a Methodist minister and writer from the last century.

[13]   2 Corinthians 4:7.

[14]   Judges 17:6.

[15]   Mark 1:7.

[16]   Mark 8:24.

[17] Matthew 15:27.
[18] 2 Peter 1:5.
[19] Exodus 32:24.
[20] Philippians 2:12.
[21] Acts 16:28.

Chapter One

THE MAN FIRST AMONG EQUALS

The last glimpse we have of Peter in the gospels is a Peter who lags behind others.[1] He appears as a stranger and straggler when seen at the end of the gospels. He denied his Lord, and followed afar off. When Resurrection morning dawned, John outran Cephas to the tomb.[2] It seems as if Peter is left standing on one leg. This would be disciple who followed Jesus in the shadows is left in the shadows. There is a promise that the 'last shall be first,' a promise which was completed in the character of one who had been a coward. The word 'coward' comes from a word that signifying the 'tail' because the tail is turned when the back is turned. It was not the tail that Jesus required but the truth, the whole truth and nothing but the truth with the help of God. It is very difficult to make cowards and renegades into leaders, but all things are possible with God. The man who had been the first to deny Jesus became the *first among equals.*

In Acts 1:13, Peter is mentioned first among those who had reported for duty. It was the same Peter, who had denied the Lord, but the Lord had not only risen from the dead, He had risen also in Peter's life. All we can assume is that in John 21, when he was challenged as to whether he really loved the Lord, he came through victorious!

The traitor must become a true servant
The colour that would have depicted Peter in the gospels is yellow, the colour of the traitor, the backslider, the inconsistent. In the armed

forces they painted a yellow streak across a deserter before he was dismissed. In certain paintings of Judas, he is always painted wearing a yellow garment. In some countries the Jews wore yellow because of their denial that they betrayed our Lord Jesus Christ. Christianity took the yellow, converting it into something worthy and noble, even as it converted Peter into *the mature man*. Later in Christian art Peter is depicted dressed in a robe of gold and yellow, yellow now shown as an emblem of faith, In China it is the imperial colour. What a wonderful change had been wrought in Simon! Making him the *first among equals*.

What a challenge when Jesus met Peter by the boats on the seashore. It brought such a great response from him.[3] If Acts 1 presents us with 'many infallible proofs,' that his repentance was wide and deep, it proves that the love of God follows us until we are changed. We can be taken from the bottom of the pile and brought to the top. Instead of Simon being the tail, he became the head. He had been knocked out, ready to be dismissed forever, yet somewhere and somehow he heard a fresh call from his Master and his slumbering heart was, so disturbed that it sprang into action. The man asleep in him was roused out of his sleep to faint and falter no more.

The initial evidence of maturity

The initial evidence that this man was being *matured* is found in Acts 1:4, 13. Peter was there as a man in the shadows waiting to be revealed. There was a moment when all heaven knew that the three years of training given by Christ Jesus was not in vain. It was no mistake that he was among those present in Acts 1. The marvel of it all was that when someone was needed, it was Peter who stepped forward and assumed the mantle of leadership.

Before the Holy Spirit was poured out in Acts chapter 2, maturity was being poured in. Everything that had to happen to Simon, every word, thought and deed had been tools used by Jesus Christ. He had to learn to love his circumstances because they were God's way with his soul. Peter seemed to be shoved from behind in order to take a step forward. Love that had grown in his heart took him into his position among the rest of the disciples. You might have all the letters of the alphabet, but to put them in the right order you have to find the A. Peter found that essential part, and the rest followed.

It is Jesus and His influence that can turn a fisherman into a follower, then a learner, on to be a disciple, until finally one day he is proclaimed an apostle. He had to learn to follow before he could lead. That was part of his training and his being brought into a closer walk with Christ. Leaders do not just arrive, they are skilfully made for the moment. Greater than all this is the fact that here was a leader of leaders, yet to find out if he was a leader, he had to look and see who was following. 'They only serve who stand and wait.' Peter had been in the presence of Christ which had influenced him far more than the boats, the business or the sea around him. George Bush, the President of America, when asked who had influenced his life the most, replied, 'Jesus Christ.'

Our greatest influences are our mentors

When Jesus first met Peter, he said to him, 'Follow me, and I will make you a fisher of men.[4] Meaning, I will make you an 'influence.' Jesus had to first influence this new convert before he could influence others. Peter was becoming to the world and the church what Jesus Christ had been to him.

Long before God takes a man, He makes a man. Long before He uses any person, He knits their affections together, until they become one with one purpose, so that Peter might say, 'Whose I am and whom I serve.'[5] The man had to be made whole so that he could serve with his whole heart.

What made Peter outstanding is what had happened to him in some quiet corner of Galilee. Those with him were his equals. They had all been with Jesus, but it seems as if that wild spirit in this Galilean fisherman was now being used for the best possible purpose with the best possible motives. *Maturity* will always make you stand out in a crowd. You need this rare quality of *maturity* to help you in leadership.

On other occasions you will require this cardinal virtue to take second place as you work alongside others. It is *maturity* that will help things run smoothly when you reach the difficult areas. This is the reason that a boat in a storm does not sink nor does it swim, it rides the waves and goes with the storm. The boat is made from a wood that has *matured* in winter storms which stops it from cracking or breaking and sinking. There might be those who were still running away from the influence of the gospel, but not this son of the sea. There was a race to be run, and Peter came first.

The mature person is not threatened by their past

When Peter stepped forward, all that Jesus had made of a floating wreck was stepping forward in him, and was about to speak through him. The hot head and the sudden rush of blood had gone. As calmly as he had witnessed Jesus calm the stormy sea, he stepped forward with a plan in his heart and a peace in his soul. The *mature man* is not threatened by great names or people who know about his past. When Judy Garland sang, those who were her 'minders' would invent people in the audience. They knew that the greater the name, the better she would sing. There was no one greater in the presence of Peter than the resurrected Lord. The man who has been developed to fruitfulness acts as if he is still in the presence of Jesus. For him there were no good or bad seasons, it was a matter of casting his bread upon the waters, whatever the season might be.

If fingers were pointed at him because of his past failures, he took hold of them, and shared the Good News with them. Those present in Acts 1:13, James, John, Andrew, Philip, were not there as spectators waiting to applaud a good performance or cheer a man who could tell a few smart jokes. Something had happened to each one. Each heart knows of its own evolution. They were the 'anchor men' for Peter. He was more the 'sheet anchor,' the main and heaviest of all the anchors that were thrown into the storm as a last resort. Such an anchor would be heavy, tough and reliable just like this man in the making. Doctors refer to the man treatment of a disease as 'the sheet anchor.' William Carey, as he ventured as a missionary many years ago, said, 'If you hold the ropes, I will go.'

Those around you are moulding you

Remember this, Peter would never have been what he was, or was going to be without the other disciples, even Judas. Each disciple taught him lessons as he watched and prayed. In your *maturity* you owe far more to those around you than could be written in any book.

The organised man does not just jump feet first. No more was his tongue not connected to his brain. The two worked together even as Peter and John did. Peter let his heart and head work together. How different from this same man in the gospel record who simply let his emotions rage as a fire. In his immature state, he had to be reined in and held back. Jesus had said, 'Every one who served Him would be 'perfected' even as the Master was 'perfected.'[6] This word 'perfected' suggests the training of a colt. It is the bringing of that young horse to the trainer to be 'broken in,' so that it might yield and obey the slightest movement of the reins. That spirited beast must be captivated by control so that it might use its potential for the work before it. Here, Cephas was let go, and when he went he had something to say. I guess, he, too had been to Saint Mary's Bible College at the feet of Jesus in John 11. He had sat with Mary and Martha, and oh, the teaching had been so deep. All that had been received in him was now moving through him and, like a well trained soldier he was ready for the war.

God puts His actions into us before we become a man or woman of action. I don't just want to be an 'action man,' but a man of action coming from the unction. Simon became like one of the soldiers who spoke to Jesus, and said, 'I say to one, 'do this, and I know he will do it.' I say to another, 'do that, and I know he will do it.'[7] As with the solider at the command of his Officer, everything springs to attention, feet, hands, head, so it is with the man, *first among equals.*

Time and opportunity develop us all

In one word, one act, one step forward, it was plain for all to see that the man was different. The 'shadow of a man' had been developed, and there was substance to him. He wasn't only worth hearing, but he was worth listening to. When he spoke, it was as the 'form of sound words.'[8] Much had to be taken out of him, but much more had to be put into him. The selfish and human must be replaced by the Divine nature. When God calls us, we must be ready. Peter didn't think his training was complete. It was only just beginning. There comes a moment when we realise that if we are going to see the light of God and walk in the light as He is the Light, then we must extinguish our own torch. There were many more lessons which would come to him through the circumstances of life. Those gathered around him would become hammer, chisel, saw and blade, even at the side of the Son of God what angels and promises fail to do, those around you will complete. Friends are given to us to continue His work in our lives.

There was no spirit of rivalry. There was no voice or whisper that said 'Grant that these my two sons shall have first place, one at Your right hand and one at Your left.'[9] True greatness does not require a letter of introduction. Peter did not need a character verification to tell a good story about his life. All he required is what we need, and that is a deep work of the Spirit of God in our hearts. This will ring out better and louder, longer and clearer, than church bells.

What you have experienced will tell its own story, will write its own ledger. You are what you are by the grace of God. Peter did not stand out like a sore thumb; he stood out like a General leading his troops into battle. Every group of people need a voice and Peter's is that voice. After listening to the voice of Jesus, the next voice they heard was that of Peter, who like John Baptist could be described as 'a voice crying in the wilderness.'[10]

The need to enlarge drives us to pray

Although he had moved on, in Acts 1:14 we see Simon still required prayer. Leadership will always be prayerful. Intercession is essential if we are going to give the work of God in our lives some direction. In fact the first recorded utterances of the reformed character are about prayer and the word of God. The *mature man* speaks about the Scripture being fulfilled. That fulfilment had made him into a dynamic man. The man who lacked tenacity is seen stable and wholesome by the power of God. The person who would be *first among equals* must learn to pray.

Isn't 'truth stranger than fiction?' The first man this new person deals with is a backslider named Judas. The man who had more opportunities to repent than Peter is the one who is dealt with. How Peter must have trembled, realising that he also had been tempted. The thought must have crossed his mind: There but for the grace of God go I.

Learn to stand on your own feet

After all the teaching and help he received, he stood on his own two feet. His legs must not be unequal, he must stand firm without a wobble. There was no longer a Jesus by his side smiling him into victory; he was alone except for those standing behind him, ready to catch him should he fall. When you get to the top and become the *first among equals* you will find it is a very lonely yet a lovely place. Peter was brought to that very place to continue in 'all that Jesus had began to do and teach'[11] in order that it could be seen in and through him. Some would say as they said of the blind man in John 9:20, 'Is it him? Others said, it is like him.' Some even suggested asking his parents if it was the same man. Peter became the earnest of all those who gathered in the Upper Room. He was a sort of 'first fruit'[12] unto God. Being with Jesus makes such a difference. God puts forth the best wine last, so that all may taste and see that the Lord is good.

Some are self made, and they worship their maker. Some are made by friends and they worship friends. Some are money made and they worship money. As for this man, he was like a stick of rock, the name of the place runs right through it, and wherever you commenced or concluded with the apostle who was being formed you would find Jesus Christ. That is a great testimony, that wherever you see Peter, you will see Jesus 'not far behind,' realising that the son of Jonas followed 'afar off' in his past life. When David Wilkerson in *The Cross and the Switchblade* first met one of the New York gangsters, the gangster wanted nothing to do with him, and threatened to cut him into small pieces. David Wilkerson's reply was, 'and every piece would tell you that I love you.' Jesus was in Peter just like that. It could be said of him, 'for me to live is Christ and to die is gain.'[13] It was Christ be my eyes, be my mouth, be my feet, be my hands and my understanding. Christ in my sitting and uprising. It was the full circle of life in Christ for Simon.

What you are is what you become

All those gathered together in Acts 1:14 have their natures expressed in their names. One suggests zeal, another devotion, whilst other names suggest love and God's gift. The name of Peter, because Jesus has risen from the dead, came to mean all that was promised. Jesus wanted to get the gospel and His teachings into men. In the Old Testament the teachings of the Lord had been put into a law, etched onto tablets of stone,[14] stone that was smashed, and the writings on them had to be repeated. It was only external writing that the small tablets of stone received. If the Lord could get his nature into men and women, then all would be well. Peter was one of the men that God touched in order to transform and present him with the teachings of truth in his heart and on his lips, with words as ready as soldiers to obey commands.

Here, in Acts 1:14, you have a flesh and blood Bible. A flesh and blood pulpit in a man. The Word of God would be voiced through Peter like a trumpet being blown to sound the attack to go into battle and win. Everything that Jesus 'began to do'[15] was being continued. Here was one of the 'infallible proofs,'[16] which suggests the evidence given in a court to prove a man guilty as charged or not guilty as charged. There must be enough evidence in your life to prove that you are guilty of being a Christian. If your conversations of this day were taken by forensic scientists and examined, would they find enough vocal evidence to prove that you were Christ's liege man? Circumstantial evidence is not enough. It is not only what is heard that can be used to convict; it can also be what is done and seen. This man had been developed into a full bodied man of God.

You become the person you choose to be

It wasn't just the choice of God that made Simon *first among equals*; it was also what the man chose to be. What had been so captured during the presence of Jesus had been changed, and was about to be let loose. His early kindergarten days were over, and he was entering into the university of life. He could have buried his talents and let somebody else bear the testimony of grace. He decided he would let the world see what God had wrought in the quiet moments. It was his moment to go public, not with a fit of rage, but in a controlled manner to proclaim the new beginning, a new beginning for me and for you. We can't all be the *first among equals*, but we can be the pioneer of another spirit in this age of 'dog eats dog.'

How much you have grown through groaning in the Son of God will be revealed when they knock nails into your hands and spit into your face. You might think it was easy at this moment for the son of Jonas, for everything was quite peaceful. He was about to enter into the world where lion and tiger roam ready to bite, scratch and devour. How would he react when he was called before the Council? How would he react when Paul accuses him to his face? What will be his manner of conduct when he is accused of going to the Gentiles and demeaning the gospel?[17] His life must not be what he saw in the vision at the house of the man of Joppa,[18] a white sheet let down from heaven full of all manner of wild beasts, creeping things, and birds of the air. What an inglorious mixture! (Acts 10:11, 12.)

He is still the *first among equals*. Nothing that happens to him turns him back to his fishing business. Each trial becomes the elongation of the path he has been called to walk. Every dark night moves on into the new dawn of day. In all these things he is more than conqueror, and this is what makes him into a man of honour and the *first among equals*.

You have been called to accomplish

Simon the son of Jonas was *first among equals* not only in status but in nature and action. Wherever he is in the Acts of the Apostles, you will find he is the first of many to accomplish many things. He is one of the first to be baptized in the Holy Spirit and to speak with new tongues.[19] He is the first to confirm that prophecy has been fulfilled in the death of Jesus.[20] He is the first to suggest that the painful gap left by the suicide of Judas must be dealt with. One of the qualities of his character is how to deal with an act of suicide. The *mature man* does not sweep it under the carpet, pretend it has never happened. It needs dealing with, and in a suitable manner he approaches the subject.

He is the first preacher, the first to preach Pentecost.[21] He is the first into prison, and along with John the first to see the miracle working power of God.[22] He stands with others at the front when they are persecuted for Christ's sake. His position was not one of lineage but one describing his dedication, suffering and mission. He became *first among equals* because of the trust and passion of his life. He stood head and shoulders above others because he walked tall in truth. To use some of Peter's words from one of his epistles, 'If these things be in you,' [all the persuasions of the Holy Spirit] you will 'neither be unfruitful or barren.'[23] Peter's words here help us to know that with the Holy Spirit at work in us we are meant to go on even to greater glory.

Notes
[1]   Matthew 26:58.
[2]   John 20:3, 4.
[3]   John 21:15-17.
[4]   Mark 1:17.
[5]   Acts 27:23.
[6]   Luke 6:40.
[7]   Luke 7:8.
[8]   2 Timothy 1:13.
[9]   Matthew 20:21.
[10] Mark 1:3.
[11] Acts 1:1.
[12] Exodus 34:22.
[13] Philippians 1:21.
[14] Exodus 32:15, 16.
[15] Acts 1:1.
[16] Acts 1:3.
[17] Galatians 2:11.
[18] Acts 10:11.
[19] Acts 2:4.
[20] Acts 2:17-30.
[21] Acts 2:14.
[22] Acts 5:18,19.
[23] 2 Peter 1:5.

Chapter Two

THE MAN WHO FIRST PREACHED PENTECOST

The conviction of what happened to Simon Peter and the disciples is an integral part of what Peter preached on the Day of Pentecost, as recorded in Acts chapter 2. Preaching and teaching will always be as a life poured out. People may doubt what you say, but they will always believe what you do. The first Pentecostal preacher did not take a cold text from the Bible and expound it. There was that which came from above in the form of wind and fire that drove Peter on to make the declaration he did. Each statement was in a flame of fire and a gale force wind. What had happened was suddenly released, and the people were 'pricked' in their hearts.[1] The man who preached could handle the occasion. It was what he had experienced: stormy weather; the sinking of the boat; the walking on the water; the glowing of the Person of Christ in the Mount of Transfiguration,[2] all had made an impact on this man's life. That which was buried deep within his personality would surface in the profile of his new life in God.

The wineskin and the wine must be matured
God hadn't finished with the education of Cephas. There was more to come, and preaching in Acts chapter 2 was part of the whole. Jesus told a story about the wineskin and the wine, recorded at the beginning of the Gospel of Mark. The rest of the Gospel is dedicated to the maturing of both the wineskin and the wine. This is what the God

of Abraham was doing with Peter under the picture of wind and fire and other tongues. The vessel and what it contained were being made strong enough for the purposes for which they were created.

In Acts chapter 2 it appeared as if the men were drunk. The suggestion was made that they had been drinking the new wine in an unlimited manner. The wine is another metaphor for the Holy Spirit, as are wind and flame in Acts. The wine had to mature, and it did throughout the Acts of the Apostles. To be mature is not to be quiet and self effacing; it is not to be weak, which some mistake for meekness; it is to have all your personality controlled by the Holy Spirit.

Preaching or speaking in the manner Simon did suggested the blowing of a trumpet. The trumpet sounded in order that those who heard it would prepare themselves for the forthcoming battle. The person who has been trained in music knows exactly when to sound the attack or retreat. Peter knew only how to sound the attack. That which was in his soul would be poured out through his mouth and all around would hear.

When speaking, go on to demonstrate what you mean
The Day of Pentecost had come, but also the day of Peter had been ushered in. The man from the shadows had stepped forward as a volunteer.

Peter lifted up his voice as a herald about to proclaim good news. In England, before the days of newspaper and radio, a man would go to the street corner and ring a bell to get the attention of the people. Some news would be written down, and then taken onto the stage, where actors act out the news of the day. The printed word was made public by puppets on a stage. It is not only speech, but the 'Word made flesh'[3] which demonstrates all that has been worked into a life. Many times the prophet Jeremiah had to demonstrate truth. He was told to tell the people, then to go to the potter's house. (Jeremiah, chapters 13 and 18.)

The attention of the crowd had to be gained, and the Lord did this through wind, fire and other tongues. Nothing speaks better than speech. The messenger was in the message, and the message was in the messenger. It was a pure Pentecostal message sent forth with a thick Galilean accent which had brought Peter into conflict during the trial of Jesus.[4] God is not interested which tongue you preach in, as long as your heart is flowing with the message, a message which has made an impact upon you. Let your language be your love. Let your tongue speak the truth. The tongue is the vehicle that can express all those days spent in the hands of Jesus being formed and informed. Here was one beggar, in Peter, telling another beggar where to get bread. In Acts chapter 3 the beggar is given the bread. The giving of bread to hungry people; bread from Heaven that is in a life touched by God, which in the giving to others is a true definition of Pentecostal preaching.

The Lord wants to take and use all your capacity
The Lord of Pentecost used all the capacity in Peter. We are told in the Gospels that Judas carried the bag that held the money, but there was in Peter that which required filling with Kingdom coinage. Jesus was continually putting into Cephas the riches of glory that would lead him to growth —his humour, emotion, intellect, voice, character and ability being witnessed by the known world. This was his 'baptism of fire' for he had never done this before. Jesus had promised that when the disciples stood before the people the Holy Spirit would tell them what to say.[5] There was no talent left buried when the son of Jonas came to speak. All the fellowship and sitting at the feet of Jesus was worth it. The Galilean had a story to tell and a message to preach. That which had been born in him and added to by Jesus Christ was on display when he preached. These were no empty words of a man who could say anything and do nothing. They were not the words of a politician. This was no 'worm in the tongue'[6] experience. He talked the noise of a mighty rushing wind and descending fire. It could not be said of the young Galilean, as had been said of Pharaoh, the mighty king of Egypt, 'Pharaoh is but a noise,' (Jeremiah 46:17.) He was not talking their noise.[7] It was no empty tongue in a mouth. The faculty that lets you down in private and public is the tongue. The tongue can hide, show temper, can tantalise and terrorise others. The loose tongue can be as a spark that starts a fire, such was the

old nature of Peter. Yet there was no empty head here. The 'dunce cap' had long gone, had been replaced by a crown of fire, the badge which would authenticate each of the Lord's servants.

Let your heart contain the cry of the Spirit

It is fine to stand before a crowd, but you need to have something to say that is backed by the Holy Spirit. That which is 'born of the Spirit' contains the cry of the Spirit. The One who can deliver must be with you. Promises are fine, but who is going to fulfil them? There are deep convictions in Simon's ripeness. He has been there. He has seen Jesus at work. He bears the scars of hurt, pain and misunderstanding. He is an assured man because he is convinced that he is part of a larger plan that would not only encompass Jerusalem but the whole world.

The character of Peter defined

The work, word and character of the apostle Peter are characterised both by the 'key' and by the cock that crew, causing him to go out and weep bitterly. Thus the emblem of this disciple had its origin.[8] They said of the apostle Paul, 'What will this (babbler) cock sparrow say?' 'Seed picker' says another translation. (Acts 17:18.) Peter is preaching as the cock is crowing. Can you see how every lesson taught and learned is not wasted? As he preaches like a cock crowing, it is expected that, as he went out and wept bitterly, the same thing will happen in the book of Acts, as others are released from their condition and come in weeping after repentance. What the cock crow had done for the penitent Peter it would do for others. When the cock crew, it was demonstrating its nature.

David, in Psalm 39:3, said, 'While I was 'musing' the fire burned. While I was thinking and working at it, the Almighty was accomplishing it.' Fire came and the complaint of the Psalmist disappeared. God can use complaints to build your character. While Peter and the rest tarried, the Holy Spirit descended to burn in their hearts. The metal that Jesus had put into Peter did not warp or melt but stood the test of the fire and the blowing of the wind.

Peter was teaching the crowd: you may fail to be what I am, and you may never do what I am doing as I preach this message, but aim higher than me! Go for God, make God your goal. Have a heart for the Holy Spirit, who appears here in the form of wind and fire, and you, too will be changed. Fire always changes the nature of anything it meets into its own image. Peter was reflecting the new image that Jesus had made of him. Let your closeness to the Lord be as close as the wind was to the fire, and you, too will be the *first among equals.*

So live that people will be convicted by your life

We know that what Peter preached worked because the people who heard it were 'pricked' in their hearts.[9] He had a target; he aimed at that target and struck it hard. When he spoke he expected something to happen, and what he believed for he received. In speaking to one, he was speaking to all. Peter took what the crowd didn't know, combined it with what they did know, and the result was miraculous. So live for the Almighty that you will reproduce those who are like Jesus first, and like you second. There is a sense when it is not wrong to be a 'chip off the old block.'

The first principles of development were being introduced. Commence believing, and God can start doing His work. He will work through the Holy Spirit and His word. That word which was spoken by Peter was full of maturity. The wind will not only blow away the chaff, it will reveal the essential corn that needs planting for a future harvest. The fire will not just remove the dross; it will leave you with pure gold.

Have a listening heart and a talking tongue

For his sermon notes, Peter borrows from many sources. What he has to say the Lord whispers through the wind into his ears, searing it onto the walls of his heart through the fire that fell. When Peter cannot hear what the Lord is whispering, God turns that whisper into a 'mighty rushing wind'. As Peter speaks, it is as if again, through him, Jesus is gathering together the apostles. Peter was more than fishing; as he preaches he is building the Church of Jesus Christ. One of the ways you can serve people with the fire of Pentecost is in a sermon.

From that fire of your maturity there will be many sparks, some of which will be other tongues. Other offshoots from Pentecost will be evangelism and deeds of mercy, visiting the sick and helpless, those who have been assailed by life's circumstances. *Maturity* does not end with the Pentecostal experience, but it can begin there. Before the fire falls, the altar will have to be built.

It is as you follow Christ that you become Christian
When Peter first met Jesus, the Lord did not say 'Follow me, and I will make you into a good preacher.' He said, 'Follow me, and I will make you a fisher of men.' Even there, a suggestion of 'making' is in the promise. Part of being made into a 'fisher of men' was the enriching process. If you are going to land great fish as Peter did on the Day of Pentecost, you need a mature rod and a strong net with a boat that will not be overfilled and begin to sink. The 'catch of the day' became his because he listened, and learned, then demonstrated truth. God demonstrated truth through 'other tongues' in Acts 2:4. Peter had to demonstrate that same truth through the one tongue that the Lord had given to him. The way to overcome getting too many fish into the boat is to increase your capacity. Jesus did this for Peter. When the disciples in John 1:38, 39 asked Jesus where He was staying, He took them to the Potter's House. Andrew and his brother Peter were greatly influenced by the Son of God. It began with one, then two or three, but developed into a crowd, because the Lord of Glory knew Peter was large hearted enough to cope with it all. You may not be able to speak to many, but what you are will speak to individuals, crowds, multitudes and nations. Wherever you go, you are an 'epistle read of all men.'[10] If there was any weakness in Peter, God sent the Holy Spirit in the form of wind and fire to help him. 'He 'helps' our infirmities.'[11] He takes hold of the other end of the weight, yet He is bearing the whole weight. The Lord of Pentecost wanted to push him along with a wind behind him. Even Peter with his smattering of theology on fishing knew that if you have a strong wind, you must have a mature canvas for that wind to blow into to drive the ship to its destination. He also knew that if you are going to sail in deep waters, you require a ship with timbers that have been hardened and

caulked to stand all the heaving and pushing of the sea.

The Lord is making you true to His cause

There was no form or ceremony as this first Pentecostal preacher stood to his feet. There was only a mocking crowd, and maybe some of them had been part of the crowd that had bayed for Jesus to be crucified. Through the message preached the Lord would change them, would make them into true men. Any builder must start somewhere. He has plans that he wants to execute. The things that had worked together for good for the fisherman would now work together for good in those who responded. Peter is never seen in a more mature role than the way in which he conducted himself as he expounded the 'happening' of Pentecost. For those who had their 'breath taken away' because of what was said, the wind that filled the entire house was to form their 'second wind.' Adam in the Garden of Eden had been visited by God in the 'cool' of the day. (Genesis 3:8.) The word 'cool' means 'wind'. For those who had been Adam's children and were returning to their God, here was another wind and window of opportunity.

Your graduation day will come

Simon son of Jonas was, by now, wise enough and stupid enough to use what the crowd said. 'These men are full of new wine'—he used it as a starting point for New Testament preaching. Long before the wine bars had opened, God had been at work on the bottle and the barrel as seen in the life of this Galilean. We are not here to discuss the exegesis of what was preached. The work of Christ in the Galilean must not be added to or taken away from. We are not looking to count how many references to the Old Testament are found embedded in the sermon. We want to see a reflection of the growth of the man of God. This was to be his 'graduation day,' having been in the 'school of life' for many years. The glory needed to shine through, the glory of conversion and growth.

True preaching and speaking is living

What a man says, what he preaches, will teach more than theology, which can be dry and academic. What any preacher says might be a mere whisper, and hard to hear. What a man is will shout at you louder than what he says. Character had been formed in the young apostle which was a true foundation to his preaching and teaching. This message would be contagious, would start an epidemic among those who wanted the reality of the Holy Spirit. It will teach you theology, which is the 'knowledge of God.'

The growing man of God seems to have all the ministry gifts of Ephesians chapter 4 in his message. There is part of it that is evangelical, part which is prophetical. There is room for the teacher, the pastor and the apostle, the one who is sent. How God had been working in his life, a life that could have been presented as a piece of Galilean driftwood, but the Carpenter of Nazareth had applied His tools to this piece of wood.

Long after the sermon had been preached, Peter had to live among the other apostles. How did he treat James or John, or even the apostle Paul? There could have been rivalry, there was only revelry in all that God had begun to 'do' and teach.

Growth means new dimensions

Growth of the soul will always open your heart to new dimensions. Whatever God is doing, you will be doing. There is one thing wind and fire both do: they create a greater capacity. God, whose nature is one of fire, is revealed by the one whose only trademark had been a strong impulse. Peter was always ready to go, but never knew quite where he was going. He would breeze in and out without any direction until he heard a voice speaking to him. The Lord gives us more than emotion or strong impulses, He sends to your soul fire to live and die by, until your life will be as attractive as the fire of Pentecost.

It isn't only the experiences we receive from the Lord, it is also what we do with what God has done. It can be tasted or wasted. It can burn, burn out, or be fanned into a new flame. Those 'other tongues' can magnify God or they can just be 'other tongues'. If the Eternal made your tongue your life, how would it appear?

There was no echo in this sermon of the Sermon on the Mount. It was a full explanation of what God had done, based on what they had experienced. It is, if you are called to preach, a lot easier if there is a sermon you can read that someone else has preached! The only copy Peter had was Christ. He had heard Jesus teach by parable and by precept. He had seen the light shining in Jesus. That fire Peter had received gave him many tongues, which were used to touch the many different nationalities as he began to expound the experience of Pentecost.

There will always be the evidence of God's activity
In that which is wrought by God there is a language that all understand. Make your theology matter by living it. Of the *mature man* we can say: 'How is it that we hear every man speak in our own language?' This maturity as the outpouring of the Holy Spirit touches every nation. There is nothing quite like a glowing man of God, a man who has been enriched, prepared to do and dare in the dynamic of Pentecost.

This was not the old Peter with fire, where he warmed himself on a cold night as Jesus was betrayed.[12] This was not the young man who was borne along by the winds on the lake of Galilee. In the Pentecostal experience there was a fire of new warmth and vigour. It was a new man with a new move of the Spirit of God. The crown he wore that day was not one of silver or gold but one of fire. Peter appeared as a slain beast on the altar, and the fire of God fell to consume the offering. That offering had to be mature; it had to be fully grown and acceptable in all parts. There would be nothing lame, no scurvy, no part missing; it could not have one blind eye.[13] Scriptures say that it should not be a foal or calf but a full grown beast. From this happening Peter began to preach, just as Elijah did in 1 Kings 17 when the fire of the Lord fell. Fire destroys, yet it brings new life to birth. It clears a way for new growth. It purifies and cleanses. What the wind does in the autumn, cleansing away all the old growth and dead leaves, we need to see happen in every life.

When the Holy Sprit came in the form of fire and wind, God was adding to the work already done in Peter. God was ready for the man, but was the man ready for the Lord? Noah's ark had to be prepared before the first animal entered before the flood came.

All you are in God will be confirmed

What you have accomplished, what you are in the Lord, is not lessened by raging fire and blowing wind, it is confirmed. That work of grace in Peter was so deep and long lasting that the wind could never blow it out, it could only supply fresh oxygen for the fire and flame. The fire would enhance what Cephas was as the Spirit testified of Jesus. A thousand tongues cannot express *maturity,* yet a lowly humble heart can experience it. It was his native tongue that told what the new nature had accomplished.

All the training of love was about to be poured through this first Pentecostal preacher. All that he had imbibed was being let loose to do its work. When fire takes hold of *maturity* it results in great conviction among the people, for in Acts 2:37 they were 'pricked' in their hearts. Through those holes the dirt ran out. They were 'stung' as with a wasp sting. In fact the Greek word *katanusso* given as 'pricked' can mean to 'stun' as a beast is stunned before it is offered on the altar. This man is so changed the crowd are looking for excuses because of the phenomena of speaking in other tongues, received by the Holy Spirit. *Maturity* is not a one-off experience it is the product of prolonged teaching that leads you to your goal. Learn to speak the language and live the life of those who have been trained by truth.

What a mature man both says and does is worth your attention

What a *mature* man has to say will register in the hearts of others, causing them to feel a conviction too great to be resisted. After Peter had 'done' what he should, the crowd asked the question, 'What shall we do?' The open man will open up other people's hearts to the truth he not only speaks but lives by. Any experience with the Almighty will give you something to say. Peter's previous three years of training was set alight at Pentecost, and enough light came from the fire for all to see the error of their ways. It was such a light as would never go out. From Peter's sermon all could see the light that rested on the Cross of Jesus Christ. God added the power of the Holy Spirit to the personality of the preacher. If you burn, men will come to watch you burn. In that fire and through that preaching there was melting, moulding, warming and setting free. God required a trained man to tell the truth. It was not dead religion or formal truth that sped through his lips, but that which had been set on fire by the Lord.

Maturity will make you equal to the task

Peter had been in training, waiting until there was enough in him for God to set on fire. He stands and speaks as an example to all who would minister in the Name of Jesus. From the *mature* man flowed a message connected by fire, relevant to the day in which he lived. The Lord loves to work through a heart in which He has wrought a good work.

Through the readiness of Peter, God formed new doctrine. It was the order of new things, which came about through a man who might have been considered a failure. People can get so taken up with the fire of Pentecost that they forget the misdemeanours, the mistakes, all the tantrums and the immaturity. Peter not only gave the answer to 'what does this mean?' he became the answer. You only become the 'answer' when the things in your life begin to add up to something. It had taken a long time, but when you listened to what he had to say it was worth waiting for and listening to. Throughout life he had been taught the lines to say, ready for this important day, the birth of Pentecost, and the unveiling of Cephas, the small rock.

It wasn't just the Pentecostal experience that appealed to the people, it was also the man who presented the message. Christianity is fire, yet it is more than fire. The message was the man, the man was the message. The man was a living Pentecost. There would be a *mature* man to deal with after the sermon had illuminated them because of the fire it contained.

We might all ask the question, 'What sort of man was this Peter when he had finished preaching?' Did he walk the talk? Some ministers are such good preachers, yet at home they are poor in temper and holiness. Many a preacher's wife has wished her husband could always be in the pulpit! It is of little consolation if you are only *mature* when asleep or resting in a chair. The world is looking for what the Almighty has done in your life. They are not interested in that which lasts for a day. The need of the hour requires the man of the second, minute and moment who has been well trained. He, then, goes on to trade his training in his living.

Many will have read of Smith Wigglesworth, one of the early Pentecostal pioneers in the United Kingdom, and how God used what he was to spread the fire of God worldwide. I was once watching a 'game show' on television, when a family named 'Wigglesworth' was introduced. They explained the meaning of the name, saying, 'The first part of the name, 'Wiggles', means 'warriors,' and 'worth' is the old English word for 'field.' So, the name means 'warriors of the field.' Peter was just that as he became the first man to utter words of Pentecost to the people.

There is a fullness for all who will yearn for God

The Pentecostal experience was likened to men drinking new wine, but it was wine that had matured. The fire that rested on their heads had been nothing before the Eternal answered their waiting, praying, searching and hungering hearts. It was fire of the 'full' flame, not a spark in the dark. Even the Day of Pentecost was the 'fullness' of the day and the 'fullness' of the Upper Room with the 'fullness' of the individual. There were no parts or portions, it was the full experience that all need. The fragment had become the whole in the life of Peter. What happened to the life of the preacher was what had happened at Pentecost, as the promise of Jesus was fulfilled. They had to tarry and pray, that was their part. God's part of the plan of Pentecost was to send the fire. It demanded a certain amount of new- found maturity in Peter to wait more than five minutes for anything. In the 'tarrying' was the developing. If you 'tarry' to become the total person needed, to not only preach Pentecost but minister it through your words and conduct, then you will see results. There was a man in the early Pentecostal revival in England named Lewi Pethrus, who became known worldwide as 'Mr. Pentecost.' He travelled from nation to nation teaching what the Lord had done. Like Peter, he had to be of a certain type, because he took the Pentecostal message into many denominations.

Shortly after the crucifixion, disappearance and resurrection of Jesus, in fact almost the next moment, Peter could have said, 'Look chaps, we have made a bit of a mess of things, and it hasn't worked out; I am going fishing.' It wasn't enough for him to have been brought on by degrees, it was only enough to wait where Christ had said, and to receive what He had promised. There had been a response in the young man's heart, and that brought him to his pulpit to preach Pentecost.

Pentecost will never be a cold doctrine. It will ever be an experience that will outlast all other things if it is received by those who are going on to perfection. It is an experience for those who have 'been saved,' those who are 'being saved,' and those who will be 'saved.'

Notes

[1] Acts 2:37.

[2] Mark 9:2.

[3] John 1:1.

[4] Matthew 26:73.

[5] Mark 13:11.

[6] 'Worm in the tongue' refers to people who constantly talk and say nothing. They turn the conversation this way and that way, but never really say anything worth listening to.

[7] An Americanism, meaning to just make a noise for special effect.

[8] Mark 14:30, 68, 72, 72.

[9] Acts 2:37.

[10] 2 Corinthians 3:2.

[11] Romans 8:26.

[12] John 18:25.

[13] Leviticus 21:18.

Chapter Three

THE MAN WITH A PASSIONATE LIFE OF PRAYER

Peter was part of the group of disciples who had asked Jesus to teach them to pray. (Luke 11:1.) Jesus said, in Luke 18:1, 'Men should always pray and learn not to faint.' Throughout the gospels, and into the Acts of the Apostles, Jesus taught them and us not simply to pray, but how to pray, how not to give up praying, as found in Luke 18:1, how not 'faint.' The word 'faint' means not to 'cave in'.

From the Lord's Prayer, right on to the Acts of the Apostles we see a prayer life established in Peter. It commences small, with a few stumbling words, but grows as the man grows. Our prayers grow as we *mature*. *Maturity* doesn't necessarily bring answers to prayer, but we are taught how we should pray and, also that there are certain things we do not need to pray for. Sometimes the Lord says 'no,' other times He says 'yes.' There has to be a time of trial as there was in the young fisherman's life, where there is an allowance for growth. There are occasions when we need to grow to be trusted with answers to prayer. We are not big enough to handle all that the Lord wants to give to us. It takes a discerning man such as Peter the fisherman and then the apostle to lead us on in prayer.

God does answer prayer
I like to follow an example revealed in the growing Peter as he reaches for God as a flower reaches after sunlight. Peter received answers to

prayer. Sometimes he was the subject of prayer.[1] Sometimes he was the answer to the prayers of others.

Prayer for Peter is found in Acts 1:14 as they met to make prayer and supplication. For the first time after the death and resurrection of Jesus the disciples would discover whether prayer really worked. Did God answer prayer in the absence of Jesus Christ? Was what they had been taught relevant? It was at that moment that Peter, along with the others, began to pray, and the outpouring of the Holy Spirit was based on prayers. They prayed making supplication, meaning they 'breathed heavily' into the prayers. These prayers that the fisherman of Galilee was involved in became his teachers, a part of his growing up into all things. That prayer was no indication of weakness, it was the fact that they could not stand alone, and was born out of deep conviction that the Jesus, who had performed miracles, would answer prayer again.

Prayer must be passionate and sincere
I don't think Peter prayed to be made more responsible. He expected what Jesus had done for him to shine through even in his *passionate life of prayer*. There are times when only the solid conviction of what God has done in you will drive you to prayer. It is the *mature* man who does not depend on his fishing vessel to bring fish in, but seeks the face of God to help him. The one who has been through a process knows that the Lord answers prayer in His own way and in His own time. We need to have grown enough to put into practice that which has been sent from heaven by God and put into our hearts. When the Lord began to alter the situation in the Acts of the Apostles it required a *mature* man to know what to do with the answers. A ball of wool will not turn into a knitted garment if given to a kitten. If a person is healed instantly, what must be done for that person? Real growth is not seen in praying, it is seen in what we do with the answers we receive. Will we be as the squirrel, hoard those answers, burying them away, using them for our own pleasure?

Prayers heard and answered must be shared

It is a true man or woman of God who will share equally with others
what God has done. If God meets your need, then do as Peter and
John did at the Gate Beautiful, when they shared what God had given
them. 'Silver and gold I haven't any, but what I do have, I give to
you.' It is one thing to have a praying heart; it is totally different to
have a sharing, caring heart. There is such enrichment through prayer
that they are able to share what has been shared with them.

The second time we witness Peter praying is in Acts 1:24. It
is maturity that tells us, even dictates to us, that we pray before
we appoint. We make an appointment with God before we make
appointments with men. The ointment for the appointment that you
have will cause everything to work out in healing as soothing as
prayer. The fact that the Galilean should pray on this occasion or
be part of the selection process was dictated by the growth within
his soul, growth which had produced conviction of the need and
usefulness of prayer in the life of a Christian. The instability that had
been part of the Peter nature is no benefit when making momentous
decisions. Peter needed to look to Heaven before he looked around
on earth. God looked on his heart before he could look on the heart
of another. He knew that before Jesus had appointed the twelve, He
had spent time with His Father. Peter and the rest of the disciples are
taking Christ's example in the Upper Room. The influence of Jesus
lives on in the man with a *passionate life of prayer*.

Before we pray, God knows the answer

In Acts 1:24 it is the *mature* person who acknowledges that the Lord
knows certain things, and that there are many things that we do not
know. The man with a *passionate life of prayer* trusts the Lord for
things known and unknown, for things seen and unseen. The prayer
offered was directed to the situation. They required a revelation of
the hearts of men. You might think that the Holy Spirit would have
revealed this to them without praying. Not so; the man who has
matured is always ready to acknowledge the power of God, to take
nothing for granted. On other occasions, such as Acts chapter 5, it
does not appear that Peter even prayed, but God knew he could be

trusted with the revelation of another's heart.

Sometimes God does not answer our prayers for revelation because we need to get to grips with our own hearts first. 'Man 'know' yourself,' is a good adage. In knowing yourself you will have the sure knowledge of others when you pray for them. When the physician has 'healed himself,' then he can minister that healing potential to others.

The development of the man becomes an enlargement of his prayer life as revealed in the Acts of the Apostles. There are many instances where prayer was needed. Sometimes Peter couldn't even pray for himself. When that happened, he had to be *mature* enough to take a backward step, to let others pray for him.[2] When God answered their prayers, he was delivered from prison.

We pray, and we listen to what others say in prayer. While we are looking for the answers, God is looking at us, seeing if we have moved forward in the expectations of grace. A prayer can be a question, or it can be a doubt. Be assured that God not only gives and sends the answer, but He, the Lord is the answer. If there has been no stretching of our own hearts, the El Shaddai[3] can delay until we begin to measure up to the measure of God. Hands that have been used in prayer become capable hands, the hands of Capability Brown.[4]

There has to be commitment to prayer

Acts 3:1 John and Peter were committed to the 'hour of prayer'. We attend a Prayer Meeting, treating it as just another time of prayer. Sometimes the God of Abraham, Isaac and Jacob surprises us as He surprised Peter and John. The thing they went to do was turned upside down. They never made it to that Prayer Meeting, because God met them on the way. We need *maturity* as revealed in Simon to show that we don't always have to wait for an organised time of prayer. On the way there, or on the way back, or even while we are there, God can meet a need. There was at least one extra attended that Prayer Meeting! It was the man who was healed. Be *mature* enough to go to the 'hour of prayer,' but as with Peter so with you, be prepared to take some answers into the prayer session with you.

Prayer and maturity is not ask, talk or take, it is give and give again. The promise is that if you give even in prayer 'It shall be given you, pressed down, shaken together and running over.[5] What shall we do with the 'running over'? *Maturity* will decide what is not for 'better or worse,' but what is for the good of everyone. Prayer was not meant just to satisfy you; it was introduced that you might make a measured request, and be *mature* enough, as Peter and John, to take the answer on with your self. When they saw the lame man healed they could say nothing. They looked and listened.

True *maturity* does not lay any claim to fame or greatness achieved by you. The apostles said, 'It is not by our own holiness or power that this man is seen walking.[6] It is the God of Abraham who has answered our prayer.' Be holy enough to let others know that the answer to prayer was not your own holiness. In spite of us God answers prayer. It is the one growing in grace and knowledge of our Lord Jesus Christ who points to the source of inspiration and healing.

Those who pray together stay together

Acts 4:24 —they joined with one 'accord' and prayed. There is something so magnificent when a company of people reveal their *maturity* in a common cause and make common prayers to God. These prayers come from the 'Common Prayer Book'. They lifted up their voices as one and cried to the Almighty. Every man's voice becomes as yours in prayer. Every voice becomes the echo of another voice, and the echo of another's need. There is a word used to define praying together that means 'concert pitch'. (Matthew 18:19.) As we pray as these prayed, we enter into a 'symphony of prayer'. It is when all the voices are gathered together as in one piece of music. That is *maturity*, and unity in unison.

There were many notable men among the company who were threatening the new believers, including Annas the high priest with Caiaphas and the Council of the Jews. (Acts 4.) You have to be *mature* enough to understand that God has seen it all, but He loves us to report in prayer to Him all that has happened. We sometimes come to pray as a child with a scribbled note. The writing unintelligible, the reading very difficult, as difficult as the blind man trying to read. Leave the interpretation of the need to God. That will demand *maturity* beyond your years or prayers! When we have believed the 'report' of Isaiah 53:1 we learn to 'report' in our rapport with God all the happenings of an extraordinary or ordinary day. It is essential enlargement that will accomplish this. Growth in the soul does not mark the difference between the miracle and the mundane. It all needs committing to the Lord. When you do this, you hand the power back to the Creator of the world. What others have usurped from the Almighty, you give back to Him in prayer. In your moments of ripeness you are handing back to God what is God's and to the world what belongs to them.

Prayer does not shake God, but it does shake you

Despite the apostles and the place they were gathered in being shaken, nothing of the work of Christ in Peter's life was destroyed or loosened. In fact the opposite happened, any convictions that might have been a little flimsy, were settled down. (Acts 4:31.) There is a 'shaking' that sends the seed planted deeper into the earth to make it strong and secure in its environment. That seed was the word of God in the young disciple gathered with his brethren. What happened only confirmed what God had said, what God had done, and what He was going to do. For the man going on to perfection, times of shaking become times of raking, when a large rake is passed over the soil, in preparation for fresh seeds and a new harvest. What has been brought to fruition in any life will remain fruitful whatever the circumstances. The outside may be shaken but with assurance within you can sleep like a purring cat.

For the man who has been enlarged there are times when the actual content of his prayer is not mentioned. It seems in Acts 5:17–42 as if the prison doors were opened without any reference to the prayers of Peter. There comes a moment when we add together all that God has done in the past, and almost without praying the doors of the prison swing open. God wants us to pray, but He doesn't need our prayers to meet a need. He has others lined up ready to pray, men and woman who have committed themselves under oath to pray for you. This takes some accepting and believing, but it is in believing that we receive. There are many things in life we never ask for, but

God in His wisdom and grace grants them to us: the air we breathe the food we eat, the water we drink. We might pray over them, and give thanks for them. We prayed for none of those things, yet, they are ours as gifts from the Giver. It takes large heartedness in us to accept these things. When we do, it is a sign that we are reaching out into unknown territory, as unknown as prison was to the men it caged. Through our prayers we become the recipients of the Val'lary Crown, the crown given by the Romans to the first soldier who mounted the vallum of an enemy's camp. We do this when we pray. When you pray you are the first to go into attack.

Prayer can be a whisper

When the soul is silent it is still singing and praying in its salvation. One word for 'prayer' found in Isaiah 26:16 means a 'whisper'. There is that element in growth which commends us to God because of Jesus Christ. In Acts 5:17 onwards, we have the evidence of prayer being answered almost without it being offered to God. I am quite sure that Peter and the men of faith called upon the Lord. It might not have been in a loud voice that would shake the prison, it might have been just the echo of the 'still, small voice' that Elijah heard in the cave.[7]

There is an atmosphere about those who are growing. As any growing plant will diffuse its perfume, so the Christian who is passing through hard times has an aroma that speaks of God. We are a savour of life to those who are living, and to those who are dying. *Maturity* will always surrender a 'sweet smell' before the nostril of the Lord. Even going through a dark dungeon there is that which is offered to God without a word being spoken. Diamonds send out shafts of light without speaking in dark places. The mere fact that these were incarcerated spoke volumes to the heart of God that no lips of a trained orator could utter. In our stillness we learn to 'be still and know that I am God.'[8] A modern translation puts it like this: 'Let go and let God.' The silence of a prayer not recorded is broken by the answer to that prayer when they met to rejoice and proclaim what the Almighty has achieved. He that lets you go into prison or difficulties will also bring you out of them. Our silent minutes in grief are turned into hours, days and years of rejoicing when we are expanded, and that expansion includes the silent wish which is interpreted by the full heart as prayer.

God sends healing and consolation through prayer

There are moments in enlargement when our grief is so galling, pain is so painful and hurt so hurtful that we lose our voice when coming to express the passion of our prayer. A sudden shock can snatch your voice from you as a thief might grab a handbag. Whatever happened to this young Galilean never took that from his spirit which had been lodged there through the teachings of Jesus. It is at times like this that Romans 8:26 becomes our Paper on Prayer. 'The Spirit *helps**
our infirmities: for we don't know how to pray for the need to be met, but the Spirit itself makes intercession for us with groaning that cannot be uttered.' [*My emphasis.] There are requirements in the stretching of the soul when we are as dumb animals before Him just as Peter seemed to be at this time. Grief can imprison you just as much as pain or disappointment. The secret of what to do is with the apostle who has extended his reason to conclude that God is at work when we are not. The prison door that holds us fast does not limit the Lord. He is the Sovereign Lord, the God of all races, places and faces.

Here is the remarkable thing: the man they could not shut up. The very person who seems to have a word of comment on everything done, said, seen and heard in Jesus Christ seems to be speechless. What a great work has been accomplished in him! The clay is silent before the working hand of the Potter. This is the work of grace and the word of grace that leaves us speechless, but God does not refrain from answering prayers in the dire dungeons of darkness. When we accept that God is God, He is Father and you are son and child, then everything will be rosy in the garden, or should I say dungeon!

Prayer is all we can offer when the burden seems so heavy

The man who turned and ran away could run only to the Lord in prayer. To know that He knows is a tower of refuge, where the righteous run into it and are safe. Prayer in the mature man can be the weeping of the eye, an upward look or deep sigh in the spirit. It can even be as the whimper of an animal, as in Psalm 55 when the Psalmist cried out to the Lord. Whatever was said or wasn't said worked, for all who went into that prison came out. And the fact that not one was harmed presented to them a greater opportunity to witness for the Lord Christ. When there is nothing to be said, nothing to be added to the promise, then is the time to believe the Lord, seeing Him work a work without your assistance or interference. The supreme objective of what He does is for us, in us and through us.

God came into that prison through prayer. He had no need to tear the bars of the cell away or to lift the prison doors off the hinges. He came in with the master key, the Master's key. He had whatever was required. Jesus said, 'I will build my church,'[9] and here is Peter letting Him do just that. The prisoners are part of the building process. They are set free, as free as a prayer offered, although they might have been silent. There are occasions when silence is not only golden, it is powerful enough to open a prison. The apostle Simon was *mature* enough to let God work it out. When he could pray, he would pray. When he was in any situation where he could not verbally express how he felt in prayer, then as a strong person in Jesus he would trust in the living God. When there is no sound God still works. He works in the black of the night; He operates in the stillness of the dawn. There is a need to be seasoned until we trust Him whatever is said. When you don't speak, God acts. When you forget to pray for someone, be matured enough to believe that God will still answer even that which has not been requested. It seems as if they had all the time in the world yet it is not recorded that they prayed. The time had come for God to work, and as He did so the thoughts and meditations of the heart became acceptable in His sight.

Prayer reveals your true desires and nature

In your *maturity* you may be put into difficult situations where it is nigh impossible to pray audibly. All you think you are and have will be tested, not to defeat or bend but to reveal its true nature, to discover if your nature is true to His nature. In a dark prison, are you as a true reflection of light? When this happens, and there is no recording scribe to write down what you have uttered, then believe that Jehovah has put someone else in another place to pray on your behalf. Jesus, in l John 2:1, is our Advocate. He pleads on our behalf, but it takes a certain amount of confidence to trust and believe that it is so. Be so ripe that you pray as if the whole situation depended on your prayer, and then accept that the Lord can work without you ever uttering one word. Without a syllable or a sigh, God sends out answers to prayer. In fact, if it had been the old Peter, to say or speak might have spoilt the whole event. Cephas might have put his foot in his own mouth. 'God has a thousand ways to answer every prayer', and your praying might not be one of them. If the Lord chooses to include your prayer, then be thankful and walk out of the situation even as those apostles in the making walked out of the prison.

Praying can be very lonely unless we know we are being heard
Certain demands are made of us as we *mature* in truth. Peter, in Acts 9:36–43, prayed before Dorcas was raised from the dead. There is a loneliness about prayer as seen in the man who has grown in his soul by the measure of prayer. The teaching received from this man who has been schooled by the Spirit of God, and initially by Jesus Christ, is that he put everything out before he took anything in. Some prayers are not for public consumption. There are public prayers and there are private prayers. Acts 9:40 Peter put all other influences out. There are prayers from those who understand that such prayers are for the Lord's ears only. They come from your heart to His ears.

There are certain things that you will have to disown if you are going to display a true passion in prayer. This prayer touched God then touched a dead body. Peter was willing to give his hand to an answer to prayer. It is the *mature* person who does not just pray, witnesses the answer and then goes on his merry way. There is an after ministry to be taken up. Peter, after giving his heart in prayer, gave his hand to a new life to support the answer. Some answers to prayer are partial. God just sends a portion of the whole. In John 1:16 we have the verse 'Grace for grace'. There is practical help needed after a prayer has been uttered. The ending of the prayer should not end the commitment of ensuring that the answer remains intact. There is an adversary who would knock down what the Lord has placed on its feet. That which is brought out of darkness will have its light blown out by the strong breath of Satan. The mature person lends the two hands that have been folded together in prayer in order to support the feeble body until full strength is restored, and it can walk unattended. What you are and have in Christ must be transmitted to others.

Practise not only what you preach but how you pray
The Church of Jesus Christ is seen as a Body.[10] That Body requires those who have enough rigour to call blessing upon it. When God answers a prayer, thank Him for those practical people who are as the shadow of Peter and come alongside others to comfort them[11] to push them gently along.

After the strong man has proved his strength in prayer it seems as if there is something left in that praying hand, and Peter assists the sufferer with that hand, passing on more help. Help might begin in prayer but it does not end there. You come to prayer with an empty hand, but after prayer there is something given to you to pass on. When you have been on your knees because somebody is on their back, get off your knees and begin to walk with those who might stumble. The hand held up in prayer will surely hold others. The hand that has touched the Lord will touch His human creation. If you can't give them a leg up, give your hand to help. Let them eat from the hand that was used in prayer.

The person who has *matured* never leaves the prayer chamber empty. They have given their all in prayer just as the Simon Peter had, but there is always something left after the prayer has been offered. We serve the Lord through prayer, praise and being practical. God loves practical prayers. He adores those who spend time on their knees and, also, time on their feet.

Prayer makes you look at things differently
The final look at *Peter: The Man with a Passionate Life of Prayer* leaves us with the strong conviction that as he *matured* so did his prayers and his answers to prayer. Somewhere between him and his

maturity faith was sandwiched. As the apostle moves from one area to another he never leaves prayer in a prayer book. It is not a prayer read from a scrap of paper. It is part and parcel of his yearning soul, part of his apostolic tools for building, his weapons for fighting.

The next place Peter went to was Joppa as recorded in Acts 10. One of the first things he did when entering into a new situation was to pray. That time of prayer took him out of the way and on to the top of the house. The developed person will learn to look down on the world of problems from a position of unassailability on the top of the house. If the house should fall, it would not fall on the apostle, because he was on top praying. Always leave your prayers as your calling card whichever house you enter into, whether large or small. It is lovely when God moves us out of the way. He commands and, without us even knowing He has commanded, we move out of the way. Peter moved out of the reach of people, yet remained in touch with Heaven. He left a world below in order that he might enter, in prayer, a world above. He had to go to the housetop to pray, because God had some important business to accomplish with Cornelius the Italian.

A praying heart never lacks a praying place

That which is enriched by grace never lacks a praying place. Peter converted the top of the house into a prayer platform. As he ascended, so his prayers ascended further, on into the presence of God who was building another house the Church. Simon Peter possibly thought he was getting away from it all, but in fact he was entering into a new depth because of prayer. True prayer will take us from the shallows into new depth and expanse. Prayer will make you more than what you are, and through it you will receive more than what you have. Without it you will live in the cellar: dark, damp, dismal. Through prayer you will ascend to the top of the house. The problems of life might surround you, limiting your every move, but as you go to the place of prayer so you meet with the God of prayer. As you move up, so you move into another realm and into a deeper relationship with the Master. The puzzle becomes a plan; you are the 'A' in the centre of the word 'plan'.

Even before grace is said, the tablecloth, as a white sheet was lowered from Heaven. It contained all that might have been put onto a table to give guests a good meal. It was more than 'heavenly manna'; it was the provision of heaven. That meal provided contained a message for a man of *maturity*.

God was bringing the Gentiles into the Church, and although He is the Almighty God He did not accomplish it without prayer. There had to be a man who had been developed to enact what God wanted. Someone who was weak in the head and weak in the knees would not fulfil the role that God was ready to reveal. Anyone with 'house maid's knee'[12] would not be capable of taking the strain. The reasoning was that if it was born in prayer it would live in prayer. Peter is revealing how it should be done. New converts are ready to come into the Church and be baptized in the Holy Spirit. It is prayer that united Jew and Gentile, through prayer foreigner and stranger became sons and daughters, and the prayer of the enlarged person does that. The prayer offered is developed until Peter realises there is no distinction in prayer between race and creed. A true Jew brings no converts, but praying guides all souls into the Church. You know you are *mature* when you can pray for anybody and accept everybody. Prayer knows no limits as to whom it shall bless.

Prayer can give you a new vision
For those who will allow God to stretch them to their full capacity prayer is developed into something else. From that prayer a vision is seen. A missionary is in the making. The wall between the Jew and the Gentile is broken down. Meditation is born. Prayer is never an end in itself; it is only the conception of an idea. It must develop, even as we must into what the Lord requires. Prayer must become more than platitudes and prayers, it must produce what is prayed. Small minds will discuss people in prayer. Average minds will pray about events. Great minds and hearts will discuss ideas with God. It isn't recorded that the young fisherman asked for anything, yet God took what he would recognise as a sheet that had been used as a boat sail, and filled it with all manner of things. God gives us the capacity before He fills that capacity. Have you a heart as wide and long as

a sheet that is knitted at the corners? If you have, the Almighty will fill it. He will lower the answer to where you are. There will be no necessity to run around chasing answers to prayer, tripping over the very sheet that is used to lower the answer to where you are.

The Lord did all the arranging. Peter is on the house top, awaiting a meal. The Lord became the Waiter as the meal was delivered. God is sending men to Joppa to the area where Peter resides. Who says God does not know where we reside? God did not get the address wrong, nor will He get the answer to a prayer wrong, even when He says, 'No'. All things were working together for these who loved the Lord.

There seems to have been an intermediary stage where Peter saw the white sheet lowered from Heaven. That was only part of the answer. The prayer was the beginning of the outreach, but it was not the conclusion. That which came down in prayer in a white sheet must go out, as it reaches others. What begins for the *mature* person as a few words of prayer, even as one falls asleep, becomes something larger. Every word of that prayer bore twins. Everything uttered by Peter, God doubled and quadrupled as the Gentiles were brought into the blessings given by a grown man of God.

Prayer can be so simple yet so powerful

It was just a simple prayer that might be offered last thing at night. The prayer that Jesus offered on the cross might have been that of a Jewish child. 'Father, into your hands I commit my spirit.' From that one prayer, something wonderful happened. It was like the rivers in the book of Genesis that broke into four heads, each river containing valuable things. The Holy Spirit fell on all 'them' that heard the word of Peter, and they began to speak with other tongues. Preaching must always be preceded by prayer. It commenced with a prayer and we cannot tell to this day where the end results of that prayer have gone. In fact, that prayer of a *mature* man encircles the world. There are Gentile believers throughout the world. I don't know how many gathered to hear the Word of God. All who gathered were influenced and touched by the power of God because of one man's 'dreamy' prayer on a housetop in Joppa. This sort of praying should encourage every preacher of the gospel. The sermon should commence with a prayer. The house that Peter visited when he went to see Cornelius commenced with a word of prayer. One word of prayer, as a reflection of Him who is described as the Word in John 1:1, but what a great and gracious influence He has had throughout the world. Do not listen to prayer. Do not learn to pray. Pray with all your heart, and let that prayer become your mark of *maturity*. Let prayer develop you into something else. As God loves prayer so I will love others, as an expression of my growth in God.

Notes

[1] Acts 5:18–20.; 12:7–16.

[2] Acts 12:5.

[3] Another name for God. It is used 31 times in the Book of Job.

[4] Capability Brown was the Head Gardner for Queen Victoria, England.

[5] Luke 6:38.

[6] Acts 3:12.

[7] 1 Kings 19:12.

[8] Psalm 46:10.

[9] Matthew 16:18.

[10] Ephesians 1:23; 2:16; 3:6; 4:4.

[11] Acts 5:15.

[12] A malady that house servants used to suffer from, and because of it were unable to kneel.

Chapter Four

THE MAN WHO SAW MIRACLES

Peter was part of many miracles. He himself was a miracle in the making. With the writer of Psalm 71:7 he could say, 'I am a 'wonder' (miracle) unto many.' There are many facets to the miracle of *maturity*. Each dimension contains a lustre of its own, waiting to reflect that *maturity* in the darkest night, turning it into radiant day. The greatest miracle the fisherman every received was that which was developing his character as the years passed. He began as a small rock (Cephas),[1] and that rock had to be shaped until it became a diamond. Cephas must be one of the 'living stones' framed to fit onto the Chief Cornerstone.[2]

When he responded to the call of Christ, it was not only a physical call to follow Jesus, it was a spiritual call that would command the character of the man, an irresistible force that would influence the young fisherman for the rest of his life.[3] He and his brother had learned probably from their father. Now, he was going to learn all about living in Eternal life through Jesus Christ. Peter would be taught far more by Jesus than anything learned at his mother's knee or in the home.

The miracles he witnessed

There were many miracles in the life of the man called by Christ. There are 15 obvious miracles that are witnessed in his life. Each miracle was a 'sign', a 'wonder', a 'power' and a 'good work' performed. It is one thing to receive an answer to prayer; it is a totally different aspect what we do with what God has given to us. Sometimes the Lord does not answer prayer because you are not *mature* enough to handle the answer. He will not cast His pearl before swine! There had to be much suffering, some stretching, even hurting, all necessary in order to make the man who was God's man into a holy man of God. There are things that have to be in the following of Christ which are as deep as they are wide, so that when the storms arrive, they will not wash away what Jesus has been applying to a life.

We need to be strong and to have the wisdom to realise what we should do with answers to prayer. Be wise enough to accept an answer to prayer, and with prayers that aren't answered, have the wisdom to leave them with the Father. Peter had this wisdom because he had listened to the Wise One. The vessel that contains such rarities from the hand of the Lord needs *maturing* , so that, unlike those in Hebrews 2:1 it does not become a leaking vessel, or like the apostle Paul who speaks of himself becoming a 'castaway', meaning a 'cracked pot.'[4] If the character is not right, then the gifting will be wasted. *Maturity* is music to the heart in love. When the Lord extends us, He does it through multiplying grace in our life. The Almighty, in nature, has given to us perfect balance, a combination where all things work together for good. The man of God must be wholesome and, at the heart of what he is, there is a place reserved for the glory of God. In Cephas we witness a man in the making. After the shaking there is the sharing of the deeper life of God. Where the love of God flows what it finds it changes into its own nature. Love, as water, will always find its own level. The deeper the heart the fuller the flow of love into that heart until it overflows.

He saw miracles because he was a miracle

Here we have a description of the man who could work miracles through the Holy Ghost solely because he was a miracle in the making during his life. When God is at work in your heart, you are never far from a miracle because you are being formed into one. When God is making a man into what He wants him to be, it is disastrous to touch what the Lord wants to accomplish before it is complete. If we do, it is like stepping into wet concrete or touching drying paint. There used to be a book called 'Danger, Saints at work!'; can we change it to 'Danger, God at work!'

Each miracle received by the Galilean was an act of grace. God confirmed it with 'signs following'. Ezekiel in the Old Testament was asked many times to become a sign to the people. He had to act out the message of Jehovah.[5] The *mature* man did not receive miracles as tokens of his own goodness, they came into his life as tokens of God's goodness, but he had to know how to move from A to B, what things to leave behind and what to take with him. Life handles us sometimes well and at other times as if things are going from bad to worse, and we don't know what to do. Like Simon we have been called to walk on water, yet all that happens is that we sink like a stone.

There was no mixture of dark and light in him

If there are any flaws in a man's character, there will be that which is fragmentary, containing splinters, and the whole will be lost. There can never be any mixture in Cephas of light and dark. One will expel the other. When Jesus the carpenter went to Heaven, He left the Holy Spirit on earth to work on the man of Galilee. Even as a solid block of gold was beaten into shape for use in the Old Testament Tabernacle, so this young fisherman experienced many hammer blows that would all serve a purpose, as others witnessed the glory in his life that had been in the life of Jesus.[6] He personally made a ship, and he knew how important it was to get every detail correct. If he didn't, the only thing the boat would do expertly would be to sink, its one and only voyage being to the bottom of the sea.

None of those miracles received by the apostle Peter were for him. He never turned stones into bread that he might feed himself or find aggrandizement in them for himself. There was always a pattern running right through whatever happened to him. It takes a *mature* person to handle what the Sovereign is doing. If we have not *matured*, then there will be waste and the whole loaf will be broken in the hands of a man who has not gone the way of grace. The love of God is manifest, yet at times, we don't know how to control that which has been given to us as we pass it on to others. Growth in God for Simon was more than glitter. He knew that one boat tied to the shoreline was as good as another until it was released from its moorings. Out on the sea in the middle of a storm revealed the true timbers of the boat.

Peter in trial could be trusted to triumph

In the Old Testament, Gehazi the servant of Elijah could not be trusted with miracles. He used them to obtain gifts for himself. The man's character was short by a mile![7] Simeon the Sorcerer in the Acts of the Apostles thought that the gifts of God, the miracles of the Majesty could be bought. He required more theology and then he would have known that every miracle has already been purchased by the blood of Jesus Christ.[8] Very few people are gifted equally with gift and grace. In every miracle there must be safe hands and a heart to see it through to the end. God's gifts must not be broken into small pieces by hands that do not care or reach out. The hand that reaches out must be the same hand that has taken. Peter did not simply receive grace from God or the grace of God, he gave willingly and freely. The miraculous must always be added to by being wrapped in the heart. You can receive without giving, and you can give without receiving if the motives are impure and warped.

When Peter received or saw miracles, there is nothing in him that speaks of self worth. At the Gate Beautiful he still has no 'silver or gold'.[9] He had been trained for the moment of the manifestation. The burning bush that Moses saw had spent many years growing unknown and unnoticed in the desert sands. The tree that Zachaeus climbed in order to see the Saviour had grown from seed until it was able to bear the weight of a small man. Even the rod that was held in the hand of Moses must grow from a sapling before it knew anything of the achievements of God. When God's training in truth came to this man in the making in the shape of a miracle, he knew what to do. Each miracle received was passed on with willing hands to others, to the needy followers of Jesus. Each manifestation of glory fills a deep hole in the heart of the recipient.

The maturing man experiences 'growing pains'

If you think it does not matter whether a man is *mature* or not when receiving a miracle, then let us take a further look at what happened to Peter during his 'growing pains'. What a mess the unwrought Simon, full of dash, dare and do left behind him! The man leaped, then looked, and as he looked landed awkwardly damaging himself. There seems to be a lack of tact in everything he did. If he was asked to follow, he fumbled. If he was called to obey, he went to play. If Jesus said something to teach him a lesson, he thought it thundered! If the truth, the whole truth and nothing but the truth was known, even when they fed the five thousand, it would be Peter who carried the basket upside down, so that none of the miracle bread could be saved.[10] When he tried to walk on water, was it just to step into it to wash his feet? His motives were pure but his actions were puerile. He was asked to 'walk with the Lord', not 'talk with the Lord'. Not knowing any better he was made better by the Best Man who ever lived —Jesus Christ, the Son of God. As the Son of Man, He was ever seeking to help a man into sonship.

Jesus asked Simon the son of Jonas to come and to walk on water.[11] Peter could not handle the situation. We know that he looked at the waves, and that what might have been a splendid conquest became a complete failure. There is an immature side to character that leaps before it looks, that goes before it listens. There was something in Peter that could not respond to the situation, that turned the miracle into a mirage. The reality became unreal and took him under instead of over. The final picture of what might have been never appears because of the fearful, trembling Peter. The only thing he received that day was a good soaking! If you step out of the boat, as this man in the making did, if you come out of the conformity of religion, that will be good for you and those in the same boat. You can't respond with alacrity to the Lord if you have 'lead feet'. Like Cephas, there are some things in life that we have dealt with, but we do so in a poor way. Instead of reviving some we have knocked them unconscious, because we have acted as an ass, and given them a body blow with the hoof of the ass!

Peter had the beginnings of a beautiful disposition

Peter had never walked on water. He had never crushed those situations under his feet. He had never let Jesus Christ turn a foaming cauldron into a soft, silky stretch of water to walk on. Peter had the beginning of a wonderful disposition provided by the Almighty yet because he was weak in character he could not see it through to the end. Seeing something through to the end is the glory of anything we receive from the Lord God. Look beyond your nose and see your toes. Be future-looking in your true repentance. Next time they came to the water (John 21), Simon Peter did not walk on it, he jumped into it as he proclaimed, 'It is the Lord!' If you can't walk on water where it is deep, and where whales and dolphins have their school room, then jump in where it is shallow. If you haven't any faith no one will know!

Miracles are not an end, they are a beginning. Will what God has done be so arranged that it blesses as many as the breaking of bread and fish did for the five thousand? Many times it is what we are once the show is over. We can get excited about signs and wonders, when you should be the 'wonder' after God has given the 'sign'! You can be 'the sign of the fish',[12] once ripeness has been produced in you. It is what we are after the glow has gone, when we are left to see the outworking of that which has been provided by God tells its own story, writes its own biography.

Testing times came to the young Galilean to discover whether he was capable or incapable. Each miracle in the Acts of the Apostles wrought by the Holy Spirit, in conjunction with the life of Peter brought wonderful benefits. There had to be a man to take those who were healed or brought back from the dead, to re-introduce them to their families. Those whose eyes were opened had to be shown the right path to walk. Those who were filled with the Holy Spirit needed someone to guide them in the use of spiritual gifts. The people receiving miracles through Peter were not left to grapple alone with what had been given to them. There had to be a human face, human hands and feet and a voice to help them through the difficulties. Peter, in one of his epistles includes the fact that he is a shepherd.[13] The shepherd must have certain qualities that he has learned with the sheep. He must know how to cross a swollen stream, to pass through a deep defile, to move along a narrow pathway. Your ministry as the *mature* must be with your heart in your hands, not on your sleeve!

God commences a work for us to complete

If Peter had not *matured*, then there would have been no hand to take the man at the Gate Beautiful, and lift him onto his feet. Even after a miracle has been performed it takes strength, strength of character to see it through to its completion. Miracles must not be left to fall by the wayside. God sometimes commences a miracle, and the end result is left with us. The man without feet or at least with crippled legs needed a man with hands outstretched towards him in the form of a young fisherman filled with the Holy Spirit. All manifestations of glory must have an after ministry if they are not going to degenerate into a mirage. They are given for the 'profit of all'. The word 'profit' means 'to bear together'.[14] Both the giver and the receiver have mutual benefits in these signs.

I want you to discover the Peter after the miracle had been performed. You will see him full of zeal, ensuring the work that has begun will continue through to the end. If zeal is seen as a cloak, then someone has to wear it. If it is depicted as fire, a person is needed to keep that fire burning. There is such satisfaction in a job well done, a work completed. It is the same feeling that God had in Genesis 1:10, 12, 18, 21, and 25. 'God saw that it was good.' The sun appeared, and that was God's smile on His creative acts. The after-service is sometimes more important than the miracle. In modern living, the goods may be good, the 'show room' might be excellent, but most businesses fail because of their lack of 'after care' of the customer.

Small things are important

It is this same man who sees loose ends tucked in and bits and pieces are taken hold of until the whole story is told to the glory of God. The crumbs taken up after the miracle of the feeding of the five thousand were as important as the miracle, itself! Even the number of fish, loaves of bread, the crowd and the baskets were counted.[15] It takes a *mature* person to do this. They see what others never see because they never turn a 'blind eye' to any situation. They see through things to the other side. Spend more time gazing at the horizon than the kerb edge outside your own front door! Today, the enlarged person is gazing into tomorrow. Today's map with roads going from it is in their hands. We are not dealing with meals on wheels or a service in the church when we expound *maturity*. We are entering into that which is of miraculous proportions. The miracles were safe and sure, but in unsteady hands they might fall, might not produce what the Lord intended. There are those who after lifting a man to his feet would drop him again, and his condition would be worse than it was originally. There is nothing worse than something good which goes bad because we are too *immature* to see it through to the end. We have all heard of 'The House that Jack Built'.[16]

The fact that Peter was numbered among those who gathered in the upper room is a miracle of proportions.[17] It is a miracle of *maturity*. Peter was used to sailing, coming and going like the waves of the sea, sometimes on the beach, sometimes sailing, other times walking through the water. In his nature he had been as restless as the tide coming and going. In Acts 1:13 he is numbered among those who tarried for the Holy Spirit. There was a part in the Body of Christ for this member. He was among the number that Jesus spoke to before His Ascension. Something happened in the heart of the Galilean fisherman. The storms had been taken from it, just as Jesus had stilled the raging waters of Galilee. God had been at work, and something wonderful had taken place. The instability had gone. He no longer roams. The words he spoke in John 21:3, 'I am going fishing', are not repeated. He was here to stay, going nowhere, and yet going everywhere to preach the gospel of peace. All the *maturity* of one who had travelled, had been near and far, was in his heart ready to be revealed. When we *mature* it isn't something we can declare at a certain time, it appears as if from nowhere. It hasn't always been there. The development of it is so small yet so sure. It cannot be measured in advance, but it can be seen when it is shown.

Let God develop the ability in you to wait

Having the ability to wait until the plan of God is revealed is part of *maturity*. Sometimes sitting is better than standing, even as waiting is better than going. If we try to be *mature* we are *immature*. If we try to be strong when we are weak, then we shall fall down, and never rise. We shall fall to stay; but God's method is, if you fall, then to rise again as Jesus did. There is something more to be added to the fisherman's life. The Creator has created many things in the life of this young Christian. Things that once mattered no longer matter, while those things which didn't matter now count for everything.

Waiting is wanting what you are waiting for. There comes a moment when we must let the soul catch up with the body. The fact they were told to wait in Acts chapter 1 was not because God needed to catch up with them, they needed to catch up with God. In the stillness of waiting there is such a work taking place that is not found in the loud bang or the violent voice. It is here that the eagle's flight feathers develop.

Let us note the aftercare that the enriched man applied after each miracle was performed. In Acts chapter 2 there had to be someone to calmly explain to the people what speaking in other tongues meant. There were 120 gathered together in that upper room, but it was the *mature* man who did the explaining, preaching and teaching. He had the answer to the question, 'Men and brethren what shall we do?' The blind needed a guide, and Peter became that guide. Speaking in other tongues was no measure of *maturity*. What the man did and said was the measuring rod. The tongue of *maturity* will always have a listening congregation.

The healing of the man at the Beautiful Gate

In Acts chapter 3 the healing of the crippled man sitting at the Gate Beautiful is recorded. It is not just the healing of this cripple that we are interested in, but the man who dealt with all the surrounding affairs after the man was healed. The character and conduct of a Christian man named Simon Peter shines through.

There was a time in the past that Peter would not have known what to do. His head would have been quite empty, swimming in the waters that he sank in. This is not so in Acts 3. Simon takes hold of the healing and uses it to teach the things that God is doing. As with the miracle of loaves and fishes when twelve baskets were gathered up so that there would be no waste, it is the same in this story of healing. Peter takes every aspect of it, weaving his sermon around it, as he reaches out to those who need the Lord.

Cephas could have been happy with a healing. He could have felt that his work was done when the man leaped up to praise God. That was the beginning of the work. There comes a moment to start, and God chooses that moment. As the man makes his appeal God is appealing to all the rich qualities that have been placed in the character of the Galilean. There was no 'stage fright' in Peter, only the might of the Spirit of God. There was no trembling, only trust and triumph.

Humility and holiness are part of maturity
In Acts 3:12 the humility and the holiness of Peter is brought to the fore. He includes John in his statement of faith. As Simon preaches, what he has been taught and received comes right from his heart, sounding out to those within the sound of his voice. He takes the miracle and every miracle back to its source which is Jesus Christ, the resurrected Saviour. The princely things in him came from the Prince of Life, Who paid the price for that life. Everything he had to say to those who had witnessed the crippled man and his healing was part of the heart of the man who God had used to heal. Much of the infant theology of Peter is found in his first two sermons in Acts chapter 2 and 3. He is not as the stuttering child; as a man he thinks as a man, he teaches as a man, he speaks as a man. Christianity, if believed, will make you into a man —a man of God!

How different to that which had been spoken by this same Peter at the end of the Gospels where he cursed and swore, and then went out and wept bitterly.[18] As those tears flowed down his face, so something of the work of grace flowed into his heart. The tears and the empty heart made a place for the glory of God. There is no rancour here, only the sweetness of a heart that is challenged to fall in love with the Christ of God. We have that which is positive in destiny and ardent in intensity as he opens his heart before the listening crowd. Cephas had been as much healed within as this man had been outwardly. What he said proved 'whose he was and whom he served.'

The mature man did not threaten others

In Acts 5:29 Peter, along with his fellow suffering believers, had been set free from prison. Peter as the *mature* man did not threaten them. He did not smite those who had smote him. He did not take one of the bars from the cell door and use it as a sword to threaten the authorities into submission. He had ripened enough to know only the power of God could do that. There is a reflection here from Isaiah 53:4, 7 where it suggests that Jesus gave his back to the smiters and, 'being threatened he did not threaten'. When Peter emerged there was something of the prison door, the steel bars from the prison windows that had entered into his soul. He might have gone in as sand, but he certainly came out as rock. In the darkness he had received light. All the keys hanging from the prison keeper's belt did not unlock anything in Peter's heart. It was the one key missing from those keys kept by the authorities that helped Cephas. He needed more grace. That dank atmosphere, with rats scurrying across his hands and feet in the stocks, did not get into his soul. He came forth with such a fragrance that could not be obtained in any prison cell.

All was quiet in prison. You could hear the Still, Small Voice. While rations were meagre he fed on the Bread of Life. There would be no condemnation of accusers because the apostles had to spend time in a prison cell without trial. Peter simply did what Jesus had taught him, he turned the other cheek, and by doing so others could see the smiling part of his face.

There is no bitterness in maturity

There is no bitterness in the man who has passed through the valley of the shadow of death. He has learned to 'fear no evil.' The concept of putting anyone in prison was to defeat their resistance. You cannot imprison that which is already captive, and Peter was a willing slave, a willing captive to Christ. You cannot defeat the defeated. Nothing can be spilled if what you are carrying is already empty. It can only be filled. Peter went into that dark, dank cell as a negative to be developed into the full photograph. What gracious words he speaks when he comes out of prison. He is as one who has been through the wine press alone. There was no prison cell with bars and doors surrounding him. He was in a palace with Christ on the throne. There is the light of revelation that can never be shut out or blown out.

This man became their spokesperson. He did not jump in where devils or angels fear to tread. He simply made statements that were the overflow of an overflowing heart. There are so many aspects to having gone through 'thick and thin'. The theme that was preached on being released from prison was 'obedience to God rather than men.' The obedient servant is speaking from his heart of obedience. True enrichment will be fully seen in obedience. It was not a matter of following the letter of the law but following love to the length, depth, breadth and height —Ephesians 3:18.

Obedience is the heart of obeisance

Obedience is the next best thing to obeisance. It was an act of worship to obey God. The *maturing* and *mature* man did not lack in his duty, the duty which obeyed every word that Christ had spoken into his heart. He became an echo of what Jesus had begun to do and teach an echo of Christianity. There has to be submission to the authority of God that proves our *maturity*. Peter was doing what he had been created to do. If you want to know what the doctrines of the early church were, then look at Peter. This enlargement in him was to display the Kingly nature of Jesus Christ. Christ in flesh and blood in feet and hands will win far more converts than any message preached. You can preach and be remote, totally divorced from what you are saying. The *mature* man will be an expression of the character of Christ.

Peter was the initial evidence of all that he was saying and would say about Jesus Christ. It worked and was worth believing because it worked in Peter. He was part of all that Jesus 'began to do and teach.' *Maturity* is what we have allowed the Potter to do with the clay. This apostle had been so unpromising when he first ventured to follow Jesus.

There was a process to follow and a life to be stretched from pole to pole. As Peter preached, in Acts 3, he taught: 'Don't look on us,' but do look deeper and see the qualities within us that have been developed by the grace of God. There is grace for every race and there is glory for every goal as we follow.

Peter and John were sent to Samaria

In Acts 8:14, Peter is one of the two chosen as *mature* men to send on a mission. *Maturity* was recognised by brethren. *Maturity* does not grow on trees but finds a home in the heart. Peter did not only grow publicly, but, also privately among his fellow believers. There are people you can trust such as the men sent to help others. You recognise what has happened in a believer when the hand grows larger as he gives and smaller as he takes from others. They knew that in sending Peter they were sending a man who would not only teach and preach the truth but would live the truth. Truth in action and unction has an attraction; all are drawn to it. When *maturity* steps in through the front door, adolescence and puberty go out the back door. There was no place for petulance or partiality when dealing with those in Samaria. There is such richness in that which is fully developed that can never be found in the seed before it is planted. These were people of strong convictions, but the man who brought the Gentiles into the faith could be trusted in all circumstances. Whichever way you have gone through, a process will always stand on its feet even in a rocky place. When the road became broad and crooked you could trust Cephas to remain as true as the proverbial die. You make your mark by keeping that mark and aiming for it. This Galilean fisherman could be trusted to see the matter through to the end. That which has grown is not an end in itself, but it takes others to where it has been.

Peter developed a great 'aftercare' service

In Acts 9:33, 34, a crippled man was healed. This man called 'the rock' who had been re-arranged by Jesus Christ went to Lydia. The miracle was important to the man who required healing, but was only important to Peter in the sense that he is revealing how to deal with one who has been healed. It is this mark of Christ in Peter that arranges everything around the Person of Jesus. When sickness is taken out of a life, then God sends health that will help us to venture forward. That malady was not covered with a cloth, but it was healed. Peter, as the dispenser of the medicine, stayed long enough to see the power of God at work. There is something very practical about the advice that the apostle gave to the man. First things first and last things last. Everything else in between can work together for our good.

The first thing Peter suggested to Aeneas, the healed man, was for him to make his bed. Further development would arrive if the healed man not only found work to do, but carried out the necessities of life. That which has been touched by Christ and taken further is able to command lives. Once the man had made the bed he could lay on it. There is something so practical about maturity. It does not simply seek to get itself warm, it lights the fire before inviting others to be warmed at its coals. When people are not convinced about a healing, they will be convinced when they witness an untidy man, a man without any sense of law or obedience, making his bed. The life that has been 'made' by Jesus will reach out and influence all around. The bed is for sleeping on, but *maturity* is to define us as those who have received the new wine, a wine mature in all its aspects. It was such a simple thing that Cephas advised. 'Go and make your bed.' That is your first mission. We have only been prepared when we begin to affect those around us. That which has been ministered into must reach out and minister to another. If you are not sure about helping another in your *maturity*, then try making a bed. Do something practical, and when men see it they will glorify your Father which is in heaven.

You must develop the ability to deal with your own problems
Peter could never deal with the problems of others if he couldn't deal with his own. If you can't make a bed, then what can you do? What was invested in the life of Simon always opens doors for others. If you do well in small things others will believe in you and your Saviour. Holiness and obedience sleep well together in such a bed as this man made. All it meant was that he rolled up his bed and tucked it under

his arm to walk away into a new day. *Maturity* will never leave us asleep while there is work to be done. Peter went to work on the man's circumstances and he re-arranged everything. There was not one sleeping wink in the man when he had been healed. The days of sleeping and dreaming had come to an end. In a very practical way he needed to demonstrate the power that had healed him by doing a very ordinary thing. It was not a call to go to the other side of the world but to make a bed. The darkness of the night and the sickness had gone. The fisherman knew where the local man would have the greatest impact, and that was locally. Home-bred is always knowledgeable when it comes to influence in the locality. There must not be a vacuum for the man to enter into. One of the first signs of *maturity* is obedience and then service. Make the bed but don't lie on it! Service where it matters is service that matters. The man of the night was going to be a man of the day. What had been a burden and an anchor was taken and lifted up by him to be carried away. I believe in *maturity* that is able to handle every burden. Service to the bed that you slept on needs to be fully carried out until the bed is made, as proof that the sickness has gone. One thing *maturity* will always do is remove the pillars you are leaning upon.

Leadership must lead by example and maturity

Peter was simply asking that the healed Aeneas would demonstrate what had happened. Those in leadership will always be able to help others through their own development. Can you see the fisherman as the father encouraging his son to take the first few steps? He had been there; he knew what it felt like. Aeneas would depend no longer on that same bed. He would be an independent man, yet always depending on God. As we depend on the Lord, so we become independent of others. We do not need to lean constantly, but we must find time to do some loving and reaching in our teaching. See if the power of God will stretch to him *maturing* into making a bed. The 'form' of things would be changed. What had been bed-shaped was destroyed forever. Notice, it wasn't a heavier burden that Peter placed on the shoulders or under the arm of the healed person, it was something so light —light enough to act as wings in the winds of change, whatever might come against him. *Mature* men are pleased to display the healing power of Christ in their completeness.

Maturity can break down religious barriers

When Simon Peter went to the house of Simon the tanner another chapter was written in the life of a *mature* man.[19] A miracle took place, the miracle of speaking with other tongues and prophesying. This miracle that Simon witnessed was greater than the manifestation of spiritual gifts, was in the fact that the Gentiles were being brought into the covenants and promises of God. In all this, a wise man's conduct: 'The words of the wise are as goads in a sure place'. This wisdom manifest in the life of the apostle was as the word 'wisdom' suggests: skill, right balance, teaching, prudence, intelligence and thoughtfulness, all words translated 'wisdom' in the King James Version of the Bible. These things are in the growing Peter. The fruitfulness that he wrote of in his epistles is seen in the abundance of his life's work of teaching, preaching and praying. He could not be left outside or in prison forever. There had to be a moment when he was sent to do something for the Jesus who had done so much for him. All he said and did was an act of worship. The son of Simon has grown into a son of God. He becomes a reflection of his Lord and Master. The character of Christ is seen in him, not as a one-off happening but as a permanent feature of what and who he is. That *maturity* becomes an integral part of the young man who was trained by Jesus. He had closely watched and listened as Jesus taught many parables. He was now to reveal the 'facts of life' in Jesus.

The mature man will always give Jesus the worship

A lesser man might have accepted the worship of Cornelius, but Peter stands him on his feet. A *mature* man will always direct worship to the Son of God. The things offered to him in Acts 10:24, 25 were given to Christ. Peter would not share the glory that didn't belong to him with another. The prepared person is not only fit for a king, he is a king moving and working in his domain. That domain had been given to Jesus Christ. What had happened to Cornelius and all he had influenced was the Lord's doing and he must receive all the praise, honour and worship. When you can take a back seat as men bow in worship, then you know you have done your work. Not many preachers leave their congregations worshipping and speaking in other tongues, while others prophesy.

Simon leaves with this lodged in our hearts: we must not accept thanks or praise for what we have not done. The lesser person would have sought to take the crown from the head of Christ. When one minister was thanked too much, he simply bowed forward; to let the thanks go over his shoulder to be received by Jesus Christ Who was standing behind him. The under developed would take the words of Jesus and claim them for their own. The life enriched by grace will not rob God of tithes or praise. If we, like Peter, tell it as it is, then it will reveal us as we are. In his report we have a heart that is being poured out. Even as Jesus built with wood as a carpenter, this man was building that which God had done. It left a deep impression of Jesus, not of Peter. We must not add everything that happens in the church to our programme, and make it appear as if the programme has arranged it. As in Acts 10, there will always be words of wisdom, a true testimony to the availability of God's power. The preaching and teaching of the visitor took on a very natural role. Peter began to tell of all that had happened to him. He was simply taking and talking his development in God. Preaching and teaching should be the result of your *maturing*. This was no textbook sermon. Peter was not quoting from other sources, what he had to say was the echo from his heart. It was a life being poured out. Those who listened began to drink deeply.

Maturity is developed as we sit at Jesus' feet
Maturity will always command the attention of the restless and the resisting. The preacher knew what to say and what to do as he entered into the house of a Gentile soldier. The young apostle stood and spoke like a general in an army seeking to muster the troops and give a report of a previous battle. He had been the pioneer into Pentecostal experience. What had happened in Acts 2, and every other part of Peter's life, was taken and used. To that one who is going on to perfection nothing is wasted, nothing is wanting, nothing is left to

speculation. When we have been enlarged we have something to say. We never come to the experience of the dumb. When we sit at the feet of Jesus for a time, then what we have to say will be timeless truth. At His feet *immaturity* is trodden under foot, and *maturity* rises from the ashes. We open the mouth that God has filled with such fullness that what we say is complete. The circle or the square does not need any addition. You cannot add to that which is ripe and wholesome. It required no attention to what Peter preached, and nothing could be taken away. It wasn't a meal lacking salt, pepper or relish. Peter was *mature* enough to lead them into the baptism of the Holy Spirit and Baptism in Water.

Maturity can always deal with contention

In Acts chapter 11 this full-grown man had to deal with a contentious issue. It was whether he should have preached to the Gentiles, when under the law this was forbidden. They had sent him to Samaria with John, but they were not sure why he had gone to the house of Cornelius. He dealt with it in the same spirit he dealt with those in the house of Cornelius. Peter simply told an old story and applied it to those who were listening. There was nothing added or taken away, the simple facts were given as a child might repeat a story. There was no curse invoked as those will be cursed who add or take away from the Word of God. *Maturity* will always tell what God has done. In everything he had to report, Peter simply fitted into what the Lord was doing. He had gone there as God's errand boy, not to catch fish but to confirm what had happened to men. This discipline of quality is not interested in the works of men or of the flesh but has invested itself in the Word of God. Dead religion has no future in this region. Real prepared people make no distinction between high and low, rich or poor, Gentile or Jew. The content of his heart saw no distinction in colour, creed or climate. All was one and would become one as he was one with the Lord. Cephas went to the house of Cornelius just as he had gone to stay with Jesus in John 1:39. He was prepared to be a string coming from the heart of God.

Experience will always give you something to say

What the ripe man had to say before the brethren in Jerusalem was simply a repeat of what he had told Cornelius. One false word or one false step might have shattered years of preparation. He was sure footed; there was no patch of oil where he trod. What he said fitted together neatly as those 'other tongues' had in Acts 2. When men are blowing glass, one false move, or, if the breath is too great, can mean disaster. The heat of the moment has to be the right heat. God in His Sovereign will arranges everything, to ensure that we do not enter into things before we are well prepared for them. Peter would not shrink or wobble. He would not be turned on one side as a deceitful bow. After passing through many experiences here is a man ready for both friend and enemy. When Simon had finished speaking, any enemy became his friend, and his friendships grew. What might have been a suspicion became select, for the people he spoke to had been chosen by God. If he had worked the works of Christ, he must now speak the words of Christ, words that came from a *mature* heart. Love that came from a life devoted shone right through into the brethren as they gathered together. *Maturity* does not hide facts; it simply helps them by telling all who will listen. There was nothing 'sheepish' about this shepherd.

It was because Cephas took his stand that others stood. When he had finished speaking all were on his side. The enriched life is a winner of doubters. Those who were opposed are brought to his side to stand with him. They were not conscripted, they were called by a silent voice which came to them as Peter gave a word of explanation. He is *mature* who, through his words and deeds, can develop a rabble into a crowd, a crowd into Christians, and Christians into Christian soldiers. *Maturity* witnessed in a way of life as seen in Peter is the essence of discipleship.

Notes
[1] John 1:42.
[2] 1 Peter 2:6,7.
[3] Matthew 4:19.
[4] 1 Corinthians 9:27.

[5] Ezekiel 3,4,5,8,12.

[6] Exodus 25:18.

[7] 2 Kings 5.

[8] Acts 13:6,8.

[9] Acts 3:6.

[10] Luke 9.

[11] Matthew 14:29.

[12] The sign used by the early Christians which meant Jesus Christ God's Son and Saviour.

[13] 1 Peter 5:1–3.

[14] 1 Corinthians 12:7.

[15] Mark 6:43,44.

[16] The 'House that Jack Built' refers to anything done badly. Nothing was in its right place, everything was disjointed.

[17] Acts 1:13,15.

[18] Luke 22:62.

[19] Acts 10.

Chapter Five

THE MAN WHO GAVE WHAT HE POSSESSED

The man in training possessed more than silver or gold. The essentials of the heart are the expressions of the Holy Spirit as He begins to work in a life. The early chapters of the Book of Acts are a picture of Peter portrayed in all the fullness that Jesus had poured into him. Jesus, through His teachings, was the Teacher. We are called to witness all that Christ as an artisan said and did in this man of Galilee, not only in Holy Ghost dimensions in the gifts of the Holy Spirit, but in making the character of a man. When you heard Peter preach you were listening to the heart of the man. He was saying what Jesus had put into his life. His life was the meaning of the word 'parable' in reverse. Peter is an earthly man with a heavenly meaning. Within his character is the truth, the whole truth and nothing but the truth. He was more than an excellent preacher, what he said came from experience. There was breadth, length and depth in the person who had been with Jesus Christ as an extension of the love of God. In his public speaking he wasn't only laying a foundation, he was a foundation stone, hard, squared, worked upon and ready for others to build on what he had to say. This man was no fool, only a tool of truth.

Don't hold back what you have been given
Cephas could never be accused of holding back that which had taken place in his heart. His words contain rich themes from the teachings

of Christ. That which has been developed by Christ is not for the self-centred, it is for the help and mutual development of others. Simon was made into some one who would count in the lives of listeners, changing them from listening into doing and then into becoming all that they were called to be. He was 'saved to serve'. When we are least aware, our life is calling out to those around us.

Peter is a man with a mission and is totally committed to that mission. He has a message and manhood that has been enlarged in a life that had previously only experienced the fullness of boats, the sea, fishing nets and the fishing business. God had a greater plan for him —greater than all his past years, seen in those few special moments as he stood before the crowd and presented Christ, the Son of the living God. He preached what he had declared earlier in the ministry of Jesus.[1] We are sometimes called upon to expound what we mean. When Peter said, 'You are the Christ, the Son of the living God,' he might have thought that was the total sum of his theology. Growth came during the following years, growth that goaded him into declaring publicly what he had said privately.

It is easy to give everything and yet give nothing

When the young fisherman said to the man at the Beautiful Gate 'Silver and gold I have none, but what I have I will give to you,' there were no strings attached. It is easy to give, yet give nothing because what you give has cost you very little. It is much more difficult to give your all, as Cephas did to this man. It was as if he said to the beggar, 'All within my heart is yours.' No wonder the man leaped and danced his way into worship. Something from the apostle, via the Holy Spirit, had entered into him . That 'dash and dare' was still in Peter, and it entered into the man as part of 'such as I have, I will give you.' 'Such as I am, I am giving it to you. I am giving what I cannot keep to receive what I cannot lose. All there is of me for all there is of you.' What dedication! What a supreme offering! Nothing was kept back that would take a man forward. If what you have and are can give a crippled man new legs, a mute person praise, then it must be given. It was given in the scriptural order that Jesus suggested, 'Pressed down, shaken together and running over.'[2] Gifts that some people have are worth sharing. Peter was referring to the healing that God was going to give to this cripple. There were other things in the life of the preacher that were there to help. Peter did not call in an organisation or someone who was more qualified to meet the need. He went into the situation and gave what he had. The young zealot gave more than his hand. He handed to the man all that he needed, an unmeasured miracle on a wonderful scale. The need of the moment was to be met there and then. When God takes qualities to a heart, He does so swiftly and surely right to the source of the sore.

You can give without giving yourself

You can give and witness a miracle without giving yourself. The greater miracle might be in what the person does alongside the miracle of God. You must be more than a miracle worker. The miracle is directly from God, the Ancient of Days, but *maturity* is a child of the years, the enlargement of a heart that is longer lasting than any physical manifestation. Peter had obviously passed by this man many times, yet had never stopped to help him in this way. There comes a moment when we have developed enough to respond to a call, turning away from that which could be defined as 'clamour'. There was more of God in the miracle and less of Simon because of the work of grace in the space that the Lord was given. With a heart touched by truth and filled with faith, he stops to demonstrate the dynamics of God. When God would use a man, He takes that man, teaches, trains and transforms him making him totally triumphant. Remember, Peter once had that crippled element himself within his spirit but Jesus had dealt with it. God has to perform in us what we would see Him do in others. The healing and enlargement in Cephas was not as a 'bolt from the blue' as it was for this man at the Beautiful Gate. Peter's *maturity* was performed over a period of time. *Maturity* comes as we let the Lord do what He longs to do. What was spiritual to one was physical to the other. When God re-draws a life, He makes it complete with good legs, arms, voice and speech. The person who is 'going on to perfection'[3] must 'go on' to achieve that perfection.

You have the potential for helping another

Within every heart there is the potential for helping others onto their feet. You can help a person to stand who has been on the 'wobble'. Whether it comes via miracle power or the *maturity* wrought by Christ Jesus does not matter. We all have a thousand qualities that we are not aware of. The very air we breathe can be sanctified by the presence of God.

Peter had the capability to realise that this crippled man did not want a long sermon. He needed lifting into a new realm. He needed new legs to walk on. He needed someone rich enough in grace to grant new legs and a new way to walk. It is quite useless giving a man with crippled feet new shoes unless you are prepared to believe God for new legs and feet. You can present a new way and pathway to walk, but if the person is crippled it will result in confusion and consternation. You will make him more of a cripple than when you first met with him. You have to freely give what you have been given.[4] If you have a full purse, and that purse is the hand of God, then giving will never empty it. There was something so complete about that which God allowed in a life.

That quality of enlargement in you will help others to walk and dance and praise the Lord God. That which has been given by the Holy Spirit was given to you in order that you might give it away. When we call upon the Lord, He is always at home. If God has given you something, give it away, and if you do, it will be a token of the fact that you are growing large enough to give and to receive. As with the apostle, you are not made poorer by helping someone out of your experience, you are rich beyond all riches, because in you are the 'unsearchable riches of Christ.'[5] Out of His poverty He made many rich;[6] from your riches you can make many who are poor in spirit rich beyond gold. What has been built into you is for the help of another. If you have extra blessing and God has been so good to you, do not let it stay with you. 'Love your neighbour as yourself'[7] is the finest declaration of spirituality that I know. However large or small the work of grace in the heart, it should be ready to overflow. When that which is based on *maturity* in the Holy Ghost is given it will make room for many. Once Peter and John had witnessed the lame man healed, they were ready for their next 'acts of service'. We are not ready for acts of service or active service until we have passed on what has been given to us. It is in helping others that we help ourselves. In giving to another you give to yourself. We don't seem able to get our minds around things like this. The benefits were not only for the beggar but for the believer. Both beggars and believers become receivers.

Surrender to the promptings of the Holy Spirit

When God has done His work, and we have surrendered to the promptings of the Holy Spirit, we have that within us which can bring light where there is darkness. You in your *maturity* can bring hope where there is fear. You can be the bringer of good news, the good news that has been enriching your life. Better than talking or taking theology to this man was the actuality of him being healed. That spoke volumes to those who witnessed the healing. You, in reaching out after God, confirm to the unbeliever that there is a God. At the same time you reveal a God so large that, if believers don't receive from Him, then they do not have the ability to reach and take through a touch. Only what was in Peter, via the Holy Spirit, could be given to the man who was crippled. Have much, have plenty, but be prepared to be emptied as you meet the longings of others. Their requirements can become your ministry of maturity. There are situations that are awash with doubt, fear and the inability to praise God. Christ has given you the ability to be able to re-arrange aching hearts.

Your life can be made effectual

Peter the apostle was totally assured of what he had, otherwise he could not have said, 'Silver and gold I haven't any, but such as I have I give it to you.' It is total confidence in God which brings that assurance. In every situation you can be assured that what has happened in your life can be made to count. The man who has nothing is nothing, can do nothing. He concludes where he started with nothing. The person with something from God has everything. Adonai is able to fill up, and make complete, those things you require. Simon bar Jona wasn't simply referring to spiritual gifts but 'grace gifts' in the words 'silver and gold have I none, but what I have I give to you.' Gifting and grace work together as Peter and John. The crippled man needed a miracle but he also required a hand to lift him. Here is where the spiritual meets the natural, and go hand in hand, singing along life's way.

It is this enlargement of heart that will see others being brought into worship. It will add to your numbers. The greatest evangelist is the person who has a conviction brought by Jesus Christ into their life. They work on the basis that God, who has performed great wonders in their life, can do it in the life of another, one who might be a cripple who can become not just 'another' but a brother.

What Peter had was worth having and sharing

That which was in the young apostle was worth having. It was worth keeping, but it was also worth passing on to another. You cannot divorce Peter and the work of the Spirit of God in his life. The two go hand in hand, until one hand is large enough and strong enough to lift the lame man to his feet. There must be some 'lift' about our love. There must be some 'lift' in the life that God has given. *Maturity* will always bring others to your level. If you are unable to help, then question whether or how much you have been assisted by the Holy Spirit. If 'growing up in all things'[8] means anything, it means that you can reach out into other lives, leaving with them what the Lord has given you. Cephas could not give coins of the realm, but he could and did give the currency of the Kingdom.

The gap between yourself and someone you might think is a cripple must not remain. You must have enough of the work of grace within your own heart to bridge the gap. If you are whole, spiritually healthy and rejoicing in the Lord, then show it by reaching out to those you think are cripples. If you don't, you become as disjointed as they are; when you reach out to them, you will be amazed to find that they are as whole as you. By doing what you do, you take another alongside, to pray with you, to grow with you and to learn with you. One becomes two, and two becomes three. If we are going on with the Lord, we gladly take others with us. We make our goals and glory their goals and glory. We shall not be happy until the unfortunate are travelling with us. The man who is a miracle, and we all are, must witness that same miracle and miraculous power working in others. You must never give an empty hand when you seek to lift others by that work of the Spirit which is in your own life. The empty hand becomes a mockery when you have been promised the fullness of Pentecost.

You require training to help one another
There is an inner work as you follow Christ that needs to reach out and touch the untouchable, reach the unreachable and teach the unteachable. There was no great gap that Cephas could not bridge, when he reached out and gave to the man who was healed. Hadn't he stepped out of the boat, and covered the gap between the boat and the sea?[9] That had been good training for helping. Your growing character and new nature will never be secluded or sectarian. No one you minister to needs to be a beggar or a cripple. You can give fullness of life because you have life in Jesus Christ. 'If any man is in Christ, he is a new creation,[10] and new things keep bursting out all over.' What Peter saw was one of those 'new things'. That which happened was different because the Christian worker was different. You can only give what you have received. You can tell only what you have heard. You can go where you are sent.

I have mentioned earlier in this chapter that Peter and John when going to the temple would have noticed this man before. Why wasn't he healed the first time they looked upon him? The answer is that the time was not yet ready. Peter had more work to be accomplished in him. The Carpenter of Nazareth makes sure that joint is ready for joint before the two can dovetail together. Peter wasn't quite ready to give what he possessed. He had to have something more. The man required more than sympathy, more than wishing him well or telling him to be warmed and filled but not at Simon's expense. Words are only wishes and empty dishes if they are not attested by creative acts of faith. The man who follows Christ will do what he has to do where and when the opportunity arises.

God gives to you that you might bless others

When God gives something, when He develops anything in your heart, it is so that you can reach out, crossing every barrier and giving what has been given to you. There was no requirement to cut corners or trim the message to the situation. Just give what you have, but make sure you have something to give, and something that is worth receiving. Don't just give yourself once; give time and time again as illustrated by Peter and John continuing with the man into the temple. Anything was better to the man at the Beautiful Gate than what he had. It doesn't take much to make such a beggar happy, to see him seated among princes. We sometimes think that what is required is far beyond what we can give, when the answer to the problem is in our assurance. You are being trained for such moments as these. Within the son of Galilee was that which could and did make a difference to a man in need. What the young preacher had was measured to the need of the beggar. The man needed the light of healing, and that is what he received. God gives us what we need, not what we expect. He gives those things we are not necessarily looking for. The beggar was not expecting his healing. If what you are in God, and what you have in the Holy Spirit, does not make a difference it is not the real thing. The real thing brings about health and help to another. It does for others what they cannot do for themselves.

What Simon had is what God used

The Lord God took Peter to where there was a great need. It was just another visit to the temple yet it saw Peter reaching out to the true temple in the shape of a man. If this man was a temple of the Holy Ghost, somewhere in that temple there must be an altar. Simon Jonas offered what he had and what he was on that altar as he spoke to the man. The disciple had to simply pour into the need what Christ had poured into him during those years of ministry spent at the feet of Jesus. Simon had no need to learn all about cripples, and institutions that deal with medical conditions. All he required is what he had, and that was a life shaped to share in the Holy Ghost. You are a bundle, a package of life, waiting to be opened to others.

Everything God has created, from sparrows to stars, was created for a purpose. The lame man was as much a part of the plan of God as Peter and John, even though he had not yet been made conscious of that arrangement. It is that growth in the heart that brings what the Lord has planned to fruition. Not one blade of grass, not one grain of sand is unnecessary in carrying out the will of God. Nothing is wasted. No experience you have in the Lord, whether some great miracle or God just walking with you, is wasted. Everything that has happened to you is for a purpose far greater than the purpose you were involved in when it happened. What we would consider as wasted fragments left after the miracle of the feeding of the five thousand[11] were taken and counted held ready in reserve for future days of hunger and trial.

Reveal what you are and what you have

Peter did not stay in the Upper Room. The disciples did not go into some holy huddle; they were not even in the temple when this miracle took place. The best of Simon is seen out in the open, not simply in a church building. Your development in the Lord will be seen most on the high street or amongst your own family. If what you are is not worth much in the world, rubbing shoulders with the milling crowd, it will not be worth much among the angels of Heaven. Where we walk and talk, that is where people want the evidence of Christ likeness until it is said, 'They perceived they had been with Jesus.' If they were going to retain what they had and add to it, then it needed to be given away in order that the Divine Architect might do more character building. We never lose by giving away what the Almighty has given to us. If we keep it, we lose it; if we give it away it returns to abide with us forever. Peter was not made poorer by giving what he had, but richer, wiser, taller and greater. In your ministry you can grow suddenly even as this preacher and bringer of miracles did, as the healed man walked with them. The man was not given a crutch but a character to believe in. They now had a living testimony to the grace of God with them.

You must be convinced of your intrinsic worth

'Such as I have, I give it to you,' is a conviction that there is something you have in God that is worth having. That which is abounding in me can abound in you, can change your life. There was no religious institution in this miracle worker, just a heart full of hope, healing, blessing and helping, exactly what the man required. Cephas, as with the other apostles, had a commission to go into the entire world and preach the gospel. He became a 'living epistle' to be read of all men.

When Peter first met Jesus, and learned the first A B C lessons, his heart received that which would be of lasting value. Here was something that went from the Gospels into the Acts of the Apostles. *Maturity* is added, and leads us because we have been with Someone. With the lame man in mind, God did His work in the heart of Cephas. Character is forever; charter is what we do in our service, here and now. Life in the Spirit of God is worth having. Walk in the Spirit, talk in the Spirit, receive and give what you have received in the Spirit of the Lord. Speak a word, as Job did, to him that is weary. It was healing given, but there was more to God's workmen than healing. What was given through the hands and words of the disciples working together was more than a thought, it was found in a deed. We have a message that tells us to 'do it', not 'what to do' or even 'how to do it'. We must be balanced enough to know when to speak and when to act, and then when to act and speak together. Miracles are there, but there is a healed man within the worker as he sought to establish the kingdom of God.

There must be miracles in your own heart

The miracle that Simon was responsible for had to be applied to his own heart. There was a requirement for an inner miracle for this estranged man. The heart and not the head of the man had been dealt with. The physician does not need to heal himself. What the servant has he will serve. What he receives is reserved for another not for himself.

When we are in the infancy of our faith, God is in the adulthood of His power. The Lord does things for, in and through us, so that we can reach out and pass on what has been given to us. No gift is given for your own joy or peace. God always gives more because we must remember a friend, go to him, and share what has been surrendered to us. What you are being made into and have been made into is to have some help for another. There was enough in the man to meet the need of the cripple. God does not send us to war at our own charges.[12] If we put Him in charge, then we have somewhere to go, something to say and something to do.

You must have a heart large enough to contain miracles

The evidence of your *maturity* will be where you are in witnessing cripples healed, blind seeing and the deaf hearing. There is a need for the large heart in the smallness of the minds you will come to. There can be more than enough in you to meet the need. You can't measure your influence when dealing with those who do not have integrity, who constantly lie, or think that God closes one eye, and cannot hear. This miracle can mean physical healing, but it can also point to what your ministry produces. If we have grown up in God we will not compile or complicate misery with our ministry. As Peter and John did, we shall move people from where they are to nearer to where we are, and the Jehovah that we serve. We are saved to serve, yet we serve to save others, helping them out of their particular situation. Simon did not leave the man where he found him. Successful ministry expressed in the Holy Ghost and revealed through *maturity* makes a difference to the servant and the served. The one who gives and the one who takes are made into better people.

There are many people who cannot walk where you walk, who cannot pray as you pray. They have no eyes to see, no mouth to speak, no ears to hear. They need all the attention you can give to them. They require the wholeness that is in you to be given to them. We who are 'strong' should 'bear the infirmities of the weak.'[13] Peter gave what he had, but it was not surrendered because of a threat, it was surrendered to an opportunity. The man was asking for something, he knew how to beg. Simon the son of Jonas knew how to give lavishly, as Christ had given to him. Those who require your ability are walking through the valley of the shadow of death. They are waiting, and each day as you pass if you are attuned to the Holy Spirit you will hear their cry. The eye turned towards you is full of need. The hand stretched out is not as a physical hand, but can be seen in a look or a furrowed brow. The still form is crying out for you to use what has been implanted and is growing in your heart. There are babes in Christ who need you, out of your *maturity* and fullness to feed them. They wait as those dogs under the table that Jesus spoke of,[14] who get the bits and pieces that fall from the master's table. Life had served the cripple with an awful hand-out, but it was this worshipper who brought what new life had to offer in Christ.

Believe and receive to reach for others
Some are unbelievers who don't seem able to believe, yet who want you to believe for them. As you come alongside them as Peter came alongside the crippled man, they long for your companionship, because the work of Christ in you can reach out and turn atheism into assurance, blindness into blessing. Must they be left waiting generation after generation? As you pass them, they think the Almighty has turned His back upon them. When it would be too much to comprehend if Jehovah sent an angel to meet their need, He sends a man or woman. People need a miracle but they need a human voice. Most miracles are served by human hands.

The missionary for Christ would not forget about the need and aspirations of others as illustrated in the parable of the Good Samaritan.[15] There must be no 'passing by on the other side of the road'. Going into the temple would only meet the need of Peter and John. Meeting the needs of the beggar would meet the need of an individual, of family, friends, people and on into the nation. It proved what God can do with one, He can do with any man, and He can deal with 'as many as the Lord our God shall call'. The man did not require a service; he needed a warm hand that had been in contact with Jesus Christ. He required, as we all do, a *mature* man full of the Holy Spirit. From the Holy Spirit came the healing, kindness, longsuffering, joy and peace —all from the same Source. A miracle can be seen for a few hours, a few years, even a lifetime, but that which is complete as a circle, called character, will last forever. When the Pharisees wanted a sign, the only sign that Jesus offered was the sign of the Son of Man.[16] They were not looking where God was performing His best works. What they required was in a man, but they were too blind to see it. What the cripple required was in the man called Peter, who introduced him to another Man, the Son of God.

The Lord will grant you what you desire and require

The man required life. Not human life, he already had that. He required life for his legs, even as some need hope for their heart. It was within the remit and capability of the fisherman to give him what he required. Peter didn't even pray; he just looked the man in the eye, and gave him the outstretched hand of fellowship, welcoming him into the fellowship of the Holy Spirit. The fisherman gave what he had, and did what he did, with what he had. There was no call on him to be a John or another disciple. He had to be what God had made him. He was not the finished article, what he did was part of the work of Christ in his heart. There was enough of the work of God in his life to share with this man, and with every person he came into contact with.

The wonderful aspect of *maturity* is that it is not diminished when under pressure. Sharing does not diminish it. As we reach out, so does what we are. What we are called to do, and the situations we enter into, causes what we are to glow and grow. You become larger by becoming smaller as you give something away. We need challenges like the cripple at the Beautiful Gate to enlarge us, to cause us to grow. It is only as we face challenges that we grow. Difficulties do not take from they add to us. Crooked legs or a crooked heart are a challenge. Do not join those crippled in heart and blighted in spirit. Stand up and reach out, believing the situation to be changed in a moment in the twinkling of an eye.

The challenges we meet and master change us

It is not the challenges we meet that change us, but the challenges we meet and master that make us into masters. We have to get those things functioning in the order they were created to function. As we do, we shall witness holiness and sainthood. Do the right thing. Give what you have, whether healing, money, wisdom, your ability to bake —just give it! Don't count what you give; if you do you will never give it. What is given is not wasted but is wanted. There is a crippled disposition in the nature of another that is waiting for healing hands to come through the Holy Spirit and your *maturity*.

The big fisherman was *mature* enough to let God use him, and found a new friend in the man at the Gate. He did not join Peter and John as a cripple, but as one made whole by the power of God. Without Peter giving what he gave and doing what he did, they would have joined a cripple associate to the band of brothers. *Maturity* sorted it out before it was brought in. You must know what to do. You must have grown enough to know how to act and react to the tear stained face.

How much have you to give?
If you give what you have, how much would that be? If you are empty, you pass on that emptiness. If you are hurting, you will pass on your hurt by hurting others. If you are full of the Holy Spirit, and *maturity* is the wealth that you possess, then you will have all things by giving all things. You will be rich indeed, making many rich because of your disposition that has been worked upon by the carpenter of Nazareth. It would have been of little use Peter passing on his rough edges or his uncouth manner, his failings and impetuous nature. He had to have something greater than all he had through a natural birth, and he freely helped the crippled man with it.

'Such as I have, I want to give it to you.' If you have a dream, share it. If you have a vision of what the Lord is going to do, share it. If you have leadership qualities, then take training and prepare for serving. By becoming one thing to the Almighty, you become 'all things to all men'. If you have something from the Holy Sprit, share it. If you have wealth and health, share it. If you have the ability to evangelise or teach, share it, for in so doing you will be neither unfruitful or barren —a word taken from Peter's advice when writing to the early Church

Notes

1. Matthew 16:17.
2. Luke 6:38.
3. Hebrews 6:1.
4. Matthew 10:8.
5. Ephesians 3:8.
6. 2 Corinthians 6:10.
7. Luke 10:27.
8. Ephesians 4:15.
9. Matthew 14:29–31.
10. 2 Corinthians 5:17.
11. Mark 6:43.
12. 1 Corinthians 9:7.
13. Romans 15:1.
14. Matthew 15:27.
15. Luke 10:33.
16. John 4:48.

Chapter Six

THE MAN FILLED WITH THE HOLY GHOST

When any man is filled with the Holy Spirit, a Divine guest has come to live within a personality. Your body is described as a temple and a home,[1] and into that area the Holy Ghost comes to reside as part of the Bride of Christ. 'The Englishman's home is his castle', but it has to become the home of the Holy Spirit. He comes to bring you to birth, to turn filling into fullness. The Holy Spirit needs to live at your address. Not in a home made of bricks,[2] wood or straw; not just in one small corner of the cellar, but as light fills the home, so does the Holy Spirit when He comes in. Every part needs to be filled enlarging every faculty, to become one of faith. All life needs to be interrelated and intertwined with the Holy Spirit. What He is you need to become, and what you are requires to become His true likeness. Every part of you needs to become an extension of Him. He does not come just to visit, He comes to stay, to take up residence, as One born in that home, and He brings His gifts with Him.

God takes and shapes each vessel
Peter had been with Jesus for three years during which time his life had been as clay, formed by the Potter into a vessel, a maturing disciple. Even as Jesus, the Carpenter, had worked on pieces of wood, developing them into shafts, spokes, and wheels, so this same Jesus had worked on Peter. The power of Christ had been at work in his life, and now, through a Pentecostal experience, that same power

was to fill his existence. The service of Christ's ministry had been received, making a new man into that which was wholly acceptable to the Lord. The 'infilling' of the Holy Spirit puts a new spirit within a man. In John 14:16, 17, Christ had informed the disciples that the Comforter would be 'with' them and 'in' them. The Comforter alongside would, also come 'inside'. This infilling recorded in Acts 2:4 and Acts 4:8, 31 turned a runaway and a renegade in John 21 into a resplendent Christian man. The weak became strong, the defeated brave, and the shadow became substance because what he received was real. The Holy Ghost will make you holy, i.e. different. When you have lost your reasons, finding them again results in the infilling of the Holy Ghost. Peter might have walked off the pages of Holy Writ, but he walked into the arms of the Saviour. All those broken pieces were brought together again. What might have been wasted was wrought upon by the Spirit of God. Everything that happened to make Simon into an apostle was found in the Holy Spirit. All the loose ends of his life were taken and tied to the purposes of the Lord. When the sacrifice was offered in the Old Testament system of worship, the beast to be offered was tied to the altar with cords until the fire entered into its bones. From an offering it became a sacrifice, on the altar. The lost were brought in, even as the sheep that had wandered from the ninety and nine. Cephas was a sheep before he became a shepherd, then a chief shepherd.

God crowns His children with an anointing

God crowns all those who believe with such an anointing. What they receive, and what makes Peter into a man filled with the Spirit, was part of a promise. The promises of God have to get inside of you before they make any difference. A promise to be filled with the Holy Ghost is not worth the paper it is written on unless you are prepared to believe and receive it. The Holy Spirit will bring power and new dimensions to your living, speaking, working, praying and witnessing. He is the Holy Spirit —the fullness of the Spirit for the fullness of the man, entering into every realm. There must be no door shut or gate fastened, with a sign that says 'Do not enter.' The attitude that says 'I will be filled with the Spirit but not today,' makes your

God the God of tomorrow, and today is as vacant as an unthinking mind. You might read about the Promise of the Father, but you can never measure that promise being fulfilled in a human heart. You can never measure that influence, because it spread to all the known languages. (Acts 2:7–11.)

The stronger the thirst the deeper we drink

As you follow the Acts of the Holy Ghost, you will find that some of those 'acts' are centred in Peter. As a finely tuned instrument he became an inspiration. This is what made him outstanding! The Spirit of God takes the ordinary and ordains it into the extraordinary. The small becomes large, the poor become rich, and that which was empty is filled with all the fullness of capacity. The larger the heart, the deeper the work, yet greater the filling, as we are filled to bursting, in spiritual gifts with languages and songs. The stronger the thirst the deeper we drink and drink again, until, as recorded in the Acts of the Apostles we are accounted as those being drunk. 'These men are wine bibbers, they are full of new wine,' will be said of you. Simon did not lose his capacity to communicate. His tongue was set free to speak to the fraternal who had gathered at Jerusalem. His tongue for a time was displaced by the cloven tongues of fire that became the emblem of the Holy Spirit. They knew the stories of when the fire fell in the Old Testament to consume the offering on the altar,[3] but this was a new fire and a new dispensation. We haven't been called to simply know about the Spirit. There isn't just a limited calling to walk in the Spirit; it is to be filled to overflowing. Saturation by the Spirit was Peter's goal and resulted in God's glory.

We are sealed by the Spirit

The book of Ephesians refers to receiving the Holy Spirit as a seal, a stamp of approval. (Ephesians 1:13; 4:30.) God is sealing His sons in a fuller, different way. A seal is a sign of acceptance. It was used to declare part of an inheritance, as the ring placed onto the prodigal's finger on his return could signify an engagement ring. Now it is used to make an impress into the wax to confirm whom we belong to, making us acceptable as authentic. It was used as a signature on a letter. The seal was the end of an argument. The one who had been writing concluded with a seal of approval. It guarantees delivery and the contents of the package. When this happened to Peter as he waited to receive the promise, God was sealing the work of Christ in his life. These signs shall follow them that believe they shall be filled with the Spirit of God. Simon the son of Jonas did not lose control. He did what he had done so often with his fishing vessel. He turned it so that the wind might take it to its destination. As the wind blew, he simply gave the boat more sailing material to enable the wind to act upon the fully raised sails. The ship went swiftly from port to destination.

The Spirit is given in floods
The vessel that God has formed He longs to fill. There had to be obedience to the arrangements made by the Resurrected One. When the Holy Spirit comes into a life, the effect of that coming is not like a raindrop, but rather a flood, a river. In Acts 2:18 this is described as a pouring. That is, without sides, top or bottom —an immeasurable fullness. This was Divine giving and pouring. After He had 'poured' out His soul unto death, the Almighty could 'pour out' the Holy Spirit. He comes to fill to overflowing. The vessel and all that it is can be lost in the overflow. The vessel itself only will be seen when it ceases to be filled. The disciples became vessels unto honour, fit for the Master's use.

There are many 'overflows' in the life of Peter that we need to note, if only we can catch something from his life and heart. Peter was 'filled' with the Holy Ghost as a man filled with new wine. Note how a drunken man acts: there you have a picture and a definition what being 'filled' with the Holy Spirit can do. God fills what we are. Serving follows filling, walking, and working together as Peter and John. When Peter was 'filled', he was influenced and supplied the need. When the Master said to Cephas and the others, 'Follow me and I will 'make' you fishers of men,' He was making them into an 'influence'. The infilling of the Spirit is God influencing you, so that you might influence others. The word 'influence' means 'to flow into and with.' It is to operate as Simon in that 'outpouring'. He was enabled with that which is from Heaven. The Holy Ghost came from the Father's heart to the hearts of men. The Lord will not ask you to dig a field, plant seed, or look for a harvest without giving you the tools to work with.

God does not dwell in buildings made by hands

God no longer dwells in buildings made by men; He dwells in men made by God. What He saves He keeps, what He keeps He fills and what He fills He uses to its capacity. The Holy Spirit will stretch you to the full. There are many things we require in service. All are found in this pouring into and pouring out of. They are resident in this work that God wants to perform. It wasn't a work which had been in process for a number of years. It was that which had been poured, and had found its way within the apostles, the floodgate of spiritual gifts. They were entering into another dimension of life in Jesus Christ. In the Gospel of John, Jesus said, 'Out of his belly shall flow rivers of water.'[4] Water that had been poured out, and poured in, would flow as a mighty river. Water means influence; it suggests going on with fullness and width.

We can and need to be filled again and again

There is a thought in the word 'fill' of 'replenishing'. It is the figure of the dry desert that needs the rain to be poured into it, to create new streams that run everywhere. It can be an act in the present that points to the future. God sends His men but He also fills those men.

The word 'fill' as used of the Baptism in the Holy Spirit is the same word used in Matthew 13:38 of a net full of fish. In John 12:3 it describes the ointment that Mary freed from the broken pot to 'fill' the house. It is the same Greek word *pleroo* used in Acts 2:2, describing the Holy Spirit in wind and fire filling the house where they were sitting. In Acts 2 it was the 'fullness' of a day-Pentecost, the fullness of a house and the fullness of the individual. When God fills He fills to the brim, to saturation point. They spat on Jesus,[5] but God turns that spit into a pouring out of His Spirit. All that men offered to God's Son was spittle from their mouth. God gives wind, fire and water from His heart, from His inner being to your inner man.

You can receive power from on high

Jesus had promised they would receive 'power' from on high when the Holy Spirit came. (Acts 1:8.) They would receive the *dunamis*, the Greek word for 'power'. It is to have an ability passed on. The word 'power' means 'to be able'. From the Greek word *dunamis* we obtain the words 'dynamo' and 'dynamite'. Peter surely was more than able. 'Dynamics' the science of force, along with 'dynamometer' the work of a machine and the measure of power, all come from the same New Testament word *dunamis*. All these attributes are in the *man who was filled with the Holy Ghost*. Cephas had a God-given ability. He used all the might given in the Holy Spirit with all his natural might. Human will and Divine purpose came together in a man.

The Holy Ghost is a guest

It is from the word 'ghost' as in the Holy Ghost that we obtain the English word 'guest'. When the Holy Spirit comes into a life, that life counts for something and everything; it ceases to count for nothing. Another dynamic, which comes from the Greek word *dumamis*, is translated 'power' when referring to the operations of the Holy Spirit. No matter how much power or personality your will, intellect and emotions possess, there is an 'extra' which the Spirit of God brings into a life. The terms Holy Spirit and Holy Ghost are used interchangeably in the Acts of the Apostles, and both refer to the personality and power of the Holy Spirit. 'Wind' and 'Spirit' are from the same source. The Old Testament word for Spirit is *ruach*, translated as 'wind'.[6] The Holy Spirit will always bring extra wind to the life and heart as He did to the apostle Peter. Whatever he lacked, the Holy Spirit complemented with that 'extra', allowing him to go the extra mile.

The Holy Ghost puts God in control

The fisherman had been used to controlling nets and fish. He knew all about the squally sea, the tides, the breakers, what to avoid and what to challenge. Suddenly he is asked to give up his self-control and to surrender to the control of the Holy Ghost. He is magnanimous enough to do what God required of him, to pass on the captaincy of the vessel to Christ, to learn to do as he was told. It is difficult for a man to become an obedient child of God. Those who would be leaders must first learn to be led. If you are to have a following, then you must become an example. What the Spirit suggested, Simon had to be man enough to follow and to obey. The Holy Spirit comes into the life not to be the servant but the Master. Remember, you are son, He is father. Jesus said 'If any man will follow Me, let him take up his cross.' Grow up enough to obey the promptings of the Spirit. Let Him do the talking while you do the walking. You must operate along the same lines as the Spirit. Where you see His footprints there plant your own. When the Spirit of the Lord prompts, learn to obey that prompting.

When Peter required inspiration, the wind began to blow upon his life. The disciples had come to the end of themselves. Jesus had gone, and they were left as 'orphans'. In John 16:7 the Master had promised they would not be left 'comfortless', i.e. as 'orphans'.

The Holy Ghost becomes the driving force within
When Peter needed direction, the wind of the Spirit blew him on the right pathway. When there was a need for a 'time of refreshing' it was promised in the Holy Ghost. When he required new strength, or stability and length of endurance, he found it in this outpouring of God. The word 'refreshing' refers to that which is overheated being cooled by a soft wind. In Fremantle, Western Australia, at the end of a very hot day a soft wind begins to blow that is called 'The Fremantle Doctor'. The disciples had been promised 'another comforter', and they found this to be true of the Spirit of God. The full meaning of 'comforter' is the Spirit alongside Peter to help him in time of need. The word 'comforter' suggests 'to make strong and brave,' especially when facing tremendous odds.

The fire will fall on the sacrifice offered
In the Old Testament, the altar and the sacrifice was prepared; it was then that the fire fell on the offering.[7] The *maturity* developed in the fisherman was attested to by the wind and the fire. The wind will blow the fire along. We are not filled with the Holy Spirit because

we are *mature* but because we are obedient, thirsty, willing to tarry until the Spirit is given and received. The Spirit of the Lord will take what we are and use it to the glory of God. It might only be a dry old stick, but if it is set on fire it becomes a burning branch.

You can become Christ's ambassador

When comparing scriptures we find the first instance of Peter being related to the Holy Spirit was when they were given power against unclean spirits. (Matthew 10:1; Luke 10:9,10.) The Holy Spirit granted them the authority, ability, and the right to act on behalf of Jesus. They had the 'right of disposal' because they were given the goods belonging to Jesus Christ. Any healing, or spiritual gift is part of the riches of His glory. Part of the disposal of what Jesus had in riches and wealth was the power over demons. He who was rich became poor for us, that through His poverty we might make many rich.

Jesus was always willing to grant freedom to sons and daughters. Peter was one of those sons, but unlike the Prodigal Son, he did not go into a 'far country' to waste Father's 'goods' on wrong living. He took what Father gave, and used it in the Kingdom to set people free. 'Whom the Son sets free is free indeed.'

Later, in John 20:22, Jesus breathed upon them and said, 'Receive the Holy Ghost.' The Greek word used for 'breathed' is used in the Septuagint Version of the Scriptures to describe God breathing into Adam, the 'breath of lives' (plural) in Genesis 2:7. In Acts 2:1-4 we have the infilling of Simon Peter with accompanying manifestations of the Holy Spirit. Peter had to be humble enough and wise enough to wait on God until the promise of the Spirit was fulfilled in his life. Peter had often seen a boat beached, waiting for the fullness of the tide before going on a fishing trip.

This baptism produced a new Peter, a new man appearing as one clad in armour. Jesus had declared when the Spirit 'comes upon' you —to be clothed as with a garment, you shall be my witnesses. (Acts 1:8.) You will be prepared to die. The meaning of 'witness' is 'martyr'.

Simon son of Jonas, filled with the Holy Spirit, entered into a new realm, the realm of the spiritual. He requires that growth in his heart to be taken and used by the Spirit of God. All the workings of Jesus in his life were taken and heightened by the baptism in the Spirit. He was baptised to be made more strong. This keeps a man from self glory and gratification.

The gifts of the Holy Spirit are not toys for children
The gifts of the Holy Spirit are not toys for children, to be hung in a cot or pram to keep the child's attention and to stop it from crying. These sacred things are not for use in the night to give us confidence to shout in the dark, or enable us to turn on the light. They are weapons of the warfare that Peter found himself engaged in. They are the weapons of our warfare also. We must be as fully equipped as this man ever was in the New Testament. These things must be to 'as many as the Lord our God shall call.' It is beyond Scriptures or the Acts of the Apostles; it is into all generations, into this modern generation. Here are the 'rations' and 'armaments' for future generations of Christian soldiers.

Following Acts chapter 2 there are two other distinct occasions when Peter was filled with the Holy Spirit. He might have been full all the time, but there are special seasons when we need to be filled again with the Holy Ghost. When He abides He brings back all the previous convictions that we might have lost on the way. If we have been as the man who fell among thieves in the Parable of the Good Samaritan, then the Holy Spirit comes to pour in the oil and the wine, manifestations of Himself.

Peter was filled with the Holy Ghost
(Acts 4:8, 31) Cephas was 'filled with the Holy Ghost' before he began to communicate to the outsider. What filled the house must fill the world, and must be powerful enough to turn the world upside down. The Holy Ghost brought conviction to the listeners, and as in Acts 2:37 they were 'pricked' in their hearts. When Cephas was filled with the Spirit, as he preached the Word of God, it was as if he was holding a sword, which seemed to stab the people's conscience. As stabs were made, so light flowed into their hearts. This was Simon's

finest hour, standing and using what God had put within his grasp. When any person is filled with the Holy Spirit it will result in others being pricked in their conscience, and, being convicted they will 'go out one by one' to come in one by one. The ministry of fullness is to enable others to know they need to be empty of self, in order to be filled with what God has promised.

Peter was in the house were they where all filled, and the place was shaken. It seems in Acts 4:31 as if it is a repetition of Acts 2. God will repeat an action again and again until He has a man immersed in the Holy Spirit. It suggests one filling needs repeating as we tend to let those things that have been sent to us leak away. It suggests that as we are used by the Holy Spirit we need a 'top up'. The Holy Spirit becomes as armour, a cloak of zeal, a weapon in the hand of a mighty man.

Filled with the Holy Ghost we shall do exploits

There were other occasions when Peter was filled with the Holy Spirit, he saw the Spirit of God operate, as the devil and his demons were sent on their way in full flight. A man filled with the Holy Spirit is not running, but chasing. He does not walk with a limp; he is a well trained athlete, running the race before him with great joy. He is declared the winner even before the start of the race. As you are filled with the Holy Spirit, God is not sending you but calling you to where He stands.

The man baptised in the Holy Spirit is no mean spirited man. He is one who will do *exploits*. In the King James Version of Daniel 11:32 the word *exploits* is in italics, because it has been supplied by the translators. It should read, 'They that know their God shall do.... What will you do? Where will you go? What will you accomplish? The answers are in our obedience to the Holy Ghost. The word exploits means 'that which is done'. The mountain is conquered, the stream crossed, the city taken. A person filled with the Holy Spirit will, like Cephas be involved in acts of power. He became a pioneer in the power of the Lord, a forerunner who took messages from God to the people.

Meet Mr. Pentecost as seen in Peter

The *maturity* of Peter was seen in his sincerity, in the fact that he did not try to control the Holy Ghost, when he first spoke in 'other tongues,' it was not his own, that would be used later. While speaking in other tongues, his native tongue that had brought him into conflict was silent. It is in our rest that God sometimes speaks and accomplishes far more than we could if we were in the zenith of youth. The Holy Spirit controlled the man, and the man became an ambassador of the Spirit. We might call this disciple Mr. Pentecost. He was involved in the Pentecostal experience, submerged in what he was given. He gave a perfect exposition of what had happened. When you sink into deep waters you enter another world. When you are 'filled' with the Holy Spirit you enter into another sphere —the God area.

Cephas had to take the initial step

The *mature* man was filled with the Holy Ghost and, because he experienced many infillings, he knew he had to take that initial step. There was no A B C to follow. Others would follow in his footsteps, steps that led to and from the depths of the Holy Spirit being poured out. After he was filled he was able to operate fully in the gifts of the Holy Spirit. He allowed the Holy Ghost to operate in areas that he himself could never enter. On any mission, when he arrived he realised that the Spirit of God had been there before him, working it all out. It was rather like the women in Mark 16:3 who said, 'Who will roll the stone away for us?' When they arrived, the stone had been rolled away. It was the fulfilment of the text 'Before you call I will answer.' All things had to succumb to the man who has a relationship with the Spirit of God. 'The pen is mightier than the sword,' but the Spirit of God is mightier than both pen and sword.

When we are filled with the Spirit, we can move into the realms of seeing people not only prayed for but delivered by the power of God. The 'stayer' and the prayer became the saturated servant of Christ. He had things to say which were not only worth saying but worth listening to. Even when Peter along with the other apostles, stood before the 'authorities', the real authority was in the fisherman because he was filled with the Holy Ghost. He had rights and privileges they knew nothing of. In their religion they only had deserts without streams. He was as full as the waters that cover the sea. In such an hour that you think not, the Holy Spirit will work it all out, bring it all in, and bring to pass what God has promised. Even in prison this man is still filled with the Holy Ghost.

To be filled with the Holy Ghost is not a one-off experience

This is not a 'one-off' experience. We are commanded to 'be being filled with the Holy Spirit' (Ephesians 5:18); the Greek tense is continuous, describing a past action repeated in both the present and the future. Another day, another challenge mean we need to be soaked in the Spirit to counter whatever we encounter. Cephas would never be a deserter again. He would be a disciple of the first order because he obeyed orders. He knew how to take orders and how to give orders. The man under the influence of the Holy Spirit is 'under' orders, and because of this can be so powerful. When you subject yourself to authority you become one of authority. You become the finisher of the command, while God becomes the Author.

Simon was a 'trail blazer' in Pentecostal enrichment

Simon the son of Jonah blazed a trail right through the Acts of the Apostles. He was not a 'trail blazer' in name only, but also in word and deed. If what Cephas wrote, said, thought or did meant anything, it only added up because he was mindful of the Master's promise to fill him with the Holy Spirit. If He fills you with the Holy Spirit cannot He do all things?

This filling cannot be defined as being like water poured into a vase for flowers. All that water in the vase does is keep the flowers alive and brighten their colours magnificently a little longer. This infilling of the Spirit in Simon's life meant that what was within him affected everything that was seen in his life and all around him felt the impact. There had to be an in-flow and an overflow of the Spirit. There was and is nothing outward alone about the infilling of the Spirit. It is both within and without, to the right and to the left, above and below. Every realm is challenged to be changed.

The work of the Spirit was to take the talent and truth in Simon and fully use them. He adds what you are and connects it to what He is and has. At the end of Peter's life he was a man fully used by the Holy Ghost. The whole of the man was used by the whole of the Holy Spirit. If you follow his life, as a biography, it reads as the biography of the Holy Ghost. The Spirit said, the Spirit prompted. the Spirit led and said. His 'daily reading' was the Holy Spirit. Simon spoke out because he was filled with the Prompter. He testified because he had a testimony within him. It is possible to walk in the spirit, and not to fulfil the lusts of the flesh. It takes one *mature* man filled with the Spirit of Jehovah to accomplish great things for God. Peter became an example of all things large and small, great, good and glorious because of his infilling of the Holy Ghost.

Notes

[1] 1 Corinthians 3:16. Ephesians 2:21.

[2] Acts 7:48.

[3] Exodus 19:18. Leviticus 9:24.

[4] John 7:38.

[5] Matthew 26:67; 27:30.

[6] Genesis 1:2; 6:3. Judges 11:29.

[7] Exodus 19:18. Leviticus 9:24.

Chapter Seven

THE MAN WHO WAS BOLD

In his infant years of Christianity Peter the apostle could never be accused of being backward or shy. He was totally unlike the first king of Israel who had to be searched for as he hid under the 'stuff'.[1] The man of Pentecostal experience appears as the boats he sailed, surging forward into the deep in the face of hurricane winds without a thought of danger or the possibility of sinking. At times Simon appears as someone totally unrestrained, almost as a boat going where the tide takes it. There was no thought in his mind of rocks or shallow depths that would result in the boat sinking or thrown onto a sandbank. Life, to the fisherman had to be lived to its full capacity in a 'hop, skip and a jump.' He didn't see the need to 'look before you leap.' There were no 'half measures' or 'small beer' in his reckoning! It was quick thinking dashing here and there even if nothing was accomplished. The Word of God declares, 'How shall they go if they are not sent?' Peter was ever going without the 'sending', full of dash and dare. One of the early Pentecostal pioneers was known as 'The Dasher Forth' and his emblem was a running dog. Even when he was a great age he would cycle around the area of missionary enterprise on his bicycle. William Burton established many pioneer churches in what was then known as the Belgian Congo. He went where the Lord directed to establish what the Lord encouraged.[2]

You have to be strong in order to face storms
This Galilean fisherman had to be strong and resolute when he facing

the storms at sea as he fished in deep and perilous waters. Part of him was of the Galilean nature, ready to fight for any cause, even if he had as much chance of winning as a snowflake in a fire. There was something so daring, so unrestrained in his nature. He went with an easy tread 'where angels fear to tread.' It was part of his natural make-up. If there was great danger, Cephas would be there as the protagonist —the leading player. He wasn't one for being on the perimeter; he had to be at the centre. The Book of Proverbs states 'The legs of the lame are unequal'.[3] We never find this man standing on one leg letting life drift idly by. If a volunteer was needed this son of Jonah would be that volunteer, and he was better than any 'ten pressed men'. The word 'eccentric' which some would consider this man to be, means 'to have another centre'. If anyone needed rescuing from the sea, out went this young fisherman with his boat. If the disciples wanted a spokesman to say what they were thinking it was to Simon they turned. Peter who was so 'out spoken' even deaf ears heard what he had to say! Jesus never gained disciples under false pretences. He never hid His scars, but rather declared, 'Behold My hands and feet.'[4]

'Time and tide wait for no man'
Cephas had some noble qualities related to his natural birth, which had been developed in him as he faced the storms and situations of life. When no one dared to even think it, Peter dared not only to say it but to do it in his own way in his own time, and his time was 'now or never'. He believed that 'time and tide wait for no man.' He was a 'man's man' physically but he needed spiritual application to his arithmetic when measuring any situation. He measured things with a large hand. His 'yardstick' measured miles, and he seemed to be far out until the Lord brought him into the fold. He always appeared to act 'on the spur of the moment', to have a nature that 'spurred him on'. There was always something goading him, and he found that it was 'hard to kick against the pricks.'[5]

If you are trained well you will triumph
Anyone who is in leadership or who stands out in any performance

whether in music or sport will tell you that the most important part of everything they do is practise, practise, and more practise. You become in public what you are in private. If there is a lack of training in private there will be a loss in public. If a musician does not practise for a day it shows in his poor performance, if he does not practise for a week then the whole audience are instantly aware of it and he becomes self-conscious. If he continues without real training he will become immune to his failings and faltering. Before you can become the master of the instrument you must become the instrument of the Master. Before you teach you must be taught. Even the instrument is aware when you haven't been in the secret place of practise, where the seeds of greatness are sown. The instrumentalist loses his fine touch, and light approach. The secret of success is in the training. Training leads to reigning. It is the preparation and the training that draws out the best of this young, bold fisherman. He had been with Christ Who 'set His face as a flint.'[6] You cannot be more bold than that! See Christ, copy Christ, be Christ to those around you.

The Lord is preparing you for works of service

Peter lived in the presence of Jesus for more than three years. In those three years what happened to him became part of the practise session. In 1 Kings 17:4, 9 twice in the King James Version of the Bible it says God 'commanded' the ravens and the widow woman. The Message Bible translates the word 'commanded' as 'prepared'. Twice it says that God prepared those two things. If that is all we see being prepared we miss the whole lesson. The widow woman and the ravens were but pawns being prepared in the larger game of life. Elijah was the third one being 'prepared' by God just as much as when God 'prepared' a whale, in the Book of Jonah.[7] Jehovah prepared a whale; it looked like a whale, swam and functioned like a whale. Peter was part of this programme of preparation for demonstration. The word 'prepare' means 'before' 'to make ready'. 'Before you call I will answer.' Before you need it I will prepare it. Before Cephas was called upon to be made 'bold', the Lord was making him as ready as any star to twinkle in the night sky.

We all require balance to keep us on an even keel

It is very rare zeal and knowledge are twinned in the work of grace. If all you have is zeal then that can result in being a fanatic. If all you have is knowledge the result is you become formal or fatalistic. One must not be more than the other. The two must combine, perfectly balanced in the life of Simon. It is the work of the Holy Spirit to bring such balance and to accomplish much in our lives. In the Acts of the Apostles in Peter the working together of wisdom, knowledge, zeal and boldness is for a cause. In fact you will witness as you read it, the combination of both wisdom and boldness in Peter as a *maturing* man with so many good qualities. Through the inspiration of the Holy Spirit good becomes great, ordinary becomes extra ordinary, normal becomes the abnormal as many are spoken to about Jesus Christ. Cephas is seen as the old public-house signs were depicted in England. As the 'Five Alls'. The king in his regalia with the motto: 'I govern all.' A bishop in his robes and mitre with the motto: 'I pray for all.' A lawyer in his gown with the motto: 'I plead for all.' A soldier in his regimental uniform with the motto: 'I fight for all.' A labourer with tools and the motto: I pay for all.' We see all these things in the boldness of the apostle Peter in the Acts of the Apostles.

The untrained must be trained in order to fulfil a role

The *maturing* of the young man from Galilee meant that all the natural forces born in him and developed during his young life had to be taken, harnessed, and used by the Holy Ghost. In the word 'perfect'[8] you have the suggestion of a young colt being 'broken in' until anyone can put a saddle on its back. All its wild unrestrained nature is harnessed by a process, brought to the defining moment when anyone can sit on its back. It can pull a plough or be put into shafts to draw a cart. In the processes of nature the Lord God Almighty has declared 'winter, summer, autumn and spring'[9] shall not cease as long as the earth endures. We have to pass through all these times of life until we are married to *maturity*, until not even a man with a hammer can knock it out of us. All this had happened to the man with the strong Galilean accent in order to make him into God's man for the ministry. Peter's 'accent' had been on action, now it was on obeying. The sugar lump given for encouragement when training a horse is better and more suitable than a rod to its flank.

When Peter came to Christ, part of the old things which passed away was not this natural ability to be a spokesperson. God sanctifies all that we are when we come to Him. If we have largeness of heart and a quick wit, it is those precious commodities that Christ takes and uses. God leaves no stone unturned, not even the Resurrection stone that He rolled away, when seeking to excavate a talent. What was seen as weakness in the natural man became strength and dynamic in the spiritual man. He takes the rough and the ready, and sanctifies it fit for the Master's use.[10] When the Master Potter makes a vessel part of the clay used is from broken bits of former cracked pots. We all bring what we have to Christ. He destroys the unusable material, but also heightens our potential. There was potential for great service in the life of Peter. What was required in the Acts of the Apostles was already in this young fisherman. When 'push came to shove' it was this same disciple who would be doing the 'pushing' and the 'shoving'.

Part of growing up in all things is boldness
Part of Simon growing up in Christ was his boldness. He had mixed with men who had 'hazarded' their lives for the gospel. (Acts 15:26.) The word used for 'hazard' means 'to throw the dice'. They were willing for their lives to be thrown to the winds as a dice cube, and to depend on God for the correct number to fall face up. Whatever the situation, threatened by the authorities or threatened by being in a prison, this man stood forward and said what he had to say.

Boldness is seen many times from Acts chapter 2 right through to chapter 10. This 'boldness as a quality of the 'new birth' is not actually mentioned but is seen in all its fullness from the first moment Peter stands to his feet in Acts 2:14 to explain the phenomena of speaking with other tongues. Boldness is when caution is thrown to the winds, and the wind of Pentecost replaces it. It is when we rise up and take hold of the authority that Elohim has invested in us. It is the God-given face of brass, the will of steel and the silver tongue of the orator, when you are not afraid to make a declaration of your faith. It is not always witnessed in words. Sometimes it is seen in a smile, a prayer, in the way you live. A demonstration of the life of Christ is better than a decree from a palace.

Boldness is an enabling quality of new life

The 'boldness' in the New Testament Church is seen in Acts 4:13, 29, 31, the quintessence – the highest and purest of all the elements – of Christianity. This boldness did not 'discourage' anybody, unlike the ten spies in the land of Canaan. It says they 'discouraged' the people.[11] The meaning is that they 'melted' the hearts of the people. What had been rock-solid oozed out like water. Having nowhere to run, their hearts simply ran to ground and buried deep where no one could find them. They were told it was a 'lost cause'. Peter in his boldness was the very opposite to a heart made to melt. It is not describing water that flows away under bridges. It is describing rock-like qualities that do not change when a storm comes. Simon through Christ had received the promise that he would be a stone as seen in the word Cephas.[12] The very term bold means to jut out like a rock. Because he was part of the Rock of Ages, he stood out in the crowd. Even as speaking with other tongues in a language they had not learned stood out. Boldness makes you different. He stood like the Rock he loved and served. He stood strong, defiant, and reliable, someone to be trusted not to be washed away or rubbed out during the time of storm. Boldness is being there when all the others have gone. It is to hold our head up high, or, as the English say, 'Chin, chin.'

Be as bold as brass in your endeavours

This young preacher said to the man at the Beautiful Gate, 'Silver and gold I haven't any,'[13] but he still had some 'brass' for, as he stood before the people, he was as 'bold as brass'. There is nothing soft or breakable about this quality of boldness. Had he not been as bold as a lion, Simon Peter would never have chased anyone. He took the promise to his own heart, 'Fear not their faces.'[14]

The term boldness was used to describe Peter, John and all the followers of Jesus in the Acts of the Apostles. They became known as the people of the 'way'.[15] They stood out like the proverbial 'sore thumb,' in boldness to bring the 'words of this life'. To be bold in this 'way' is to be so caring when dealing with the weak, but uncaring when standing and having 'to do what a man has to do.' He had not only to 'do what a man has to do,' he had 'to be as a man has to be.' Not 'heady' or just plain foolish but transformed into something else as Peter *matured* in the grace of God, with enough to enable him to run the race of God. Boldness is to 'tell it as it is'. The word boldness in many scriptures means 'freedom of speech'.[16] It doesn't suggest just speaking for a gossip can do that! It does mean that when we speak we have precious things to say, and like this disciple we command the attention of great and small. God said, 'Open your mouth wide and I will fill it.'[17] This is taken from the custom of putting precious jewels in the mouth of a dead corpse as part of the decoration for the funeral and after-life. We carry our convictions with us in our heart.

Do not be 'tongue tied' or 'mealy mouthed'

Boldness is to see those convictions revealed as we speak with passion. There was nothing limp or lost, nothing easy or soft in Peter as he stood before the crowds in the Acts of the Apostles, not 'tongue tied' or 'mealy mouthed'. There is nothing 'tongue in cheek' about this quality of *maturity* and new life. It was this rarity that led them to take liberty and exhibit freedom. It is 'free utterance' because Christ had made them free. The first thing mentioned of the experience of the apostle Paul was 'Behold, he is praying.'[18] Before coming to Christ we have nothing to say. Once we fall in love with Him we have pages to write, sketch books to fill, and songs to sing so much so that all the libraries in the world cannot contain the volumes. It is the very heart of 'free speech'. Christ gives the freedom to speak freely about His love and kingdom. His empire is an empire that is built on boldness. It is to say what God has communicated. It happened as with the healing of the dumb man in the New Testament 'The strings of his tongue were loosed.'[19] It is the experience of the child, no longer babbling but speaking coherent language for the first time. The letters of the alphabet put into words, and now spoken. The person engaged in boldness has gone from the abacus, the elementary teaching of language to something deeper, more broad. They become a linguist of love as they express their faith. You can be bright and bold anywhere in the world. Peter was never bold in prayer then weak in public. What he was in private was made known in public. There is not a stutter to be found, it goes straight to the heart of those listening when a man acts in a bold manner. This boldness is to speak the language of the heart freely; as if a vow of silence has been broken as the person erupts into speech.

It was the father of John Baptist who had been struck dumb.[20] Once that period had finished and his term of office completed he began to magnify the Lord. Peter in the Acts of the Apostles was the opposite to silence. It was unbelief that forced Zacharias in Luke 1:20 into the opposite of boldness. (Luke 1:64) his tongue was loosed, as if he had been loosed from a debt. The experience that gripped Peter means you can speak by the power of the Holy Spirit, lucidly and clearly. Courage, bravery, confidence with assurance was all part of the *maturity* of the man.

The Comforter has come to make us strong and brave

Jesus said that He would send the *Paraclete*, the *Comforter* to assist them in their speaking.[21] The very word Jesus used to describe the *Paraclete* was the name given to the man the Greeks called in to assist when an army was defeated, disunited and dispirited. It was his sole purpose to encourage the troops and to make brave soldiers from cowards. He did it by reminding them of the past glorious of their country and king. He would excite them by telling them they could do whatever they were challenged to do. The root meaning of the word 'comfort' as used in the name Comforter given to the Holy Spirit is 'to make strong and brave.' It is by the power of the Holy Ghost that we live, move and have our being. Something of the Divine nature is required to get us to quit ourselves and stand like men. That which has been on the wobble needs to stand firm and true.

Within the word boldness is the element of courage. Courage comes from the heart; it is when we stand after being knocked down, the element of surprise that wins the day. It is bravery gone mad. David was 'a man after God's own heart.' We have to be God's own heart in acts of courage. I have seen many a mother bird attack a cat with no chance of winning; they have managed to frighten the cat away. Love is courage when we feel we have to do what is presented to us. It manifests itself in all manner of service for the Lord. In any battle there are many manoeuvres that an army has to complete. The one that suggests courage and boldness is the 'charge'. Courage is boldness with assurance that all will be well even before we begin. It says what the apostle Paul said to the Philippian jailer, 'Do yourself no harm, we are all here.'[22] In Acts 28:15 the word courage is used and is akin to the words 'Be of good cheer.' Courage can laugh at fear. It did so as Cephas stood before the leaders of the people. There is molecule courage in a frown or sad look. This courage is the act of getting boldness into others. The holy work is in getting other timorous people to be bold as you share what you are with the fearful and the timid and by doing this bring them a step higher in grace.

Don't be timorous and trembling, be a tiger!

We have a West Highland terrier dog. It stands about six inches in height, and about a foot in length. It is so timid; it just loves everybody, and is so gentle. We wanted to give it a prophetical name, just like the Lord gave to Peter, saying to him, 'You are Simon (hearing) but you will be called Cephas' (rock). With 'tongue in cheek' we called this small white dog 'Tiger'!!

'We are 'confident' that He Who has begun a good work in you will perform it until the day of Jesus Christ.'[23] Confidence comes out of complete trust. When Great Britain was at war with Germany in the 1940s, during a radio speech Sir Winston Churchill describes what he intends to say when he meets with the President of America. 'Give us the tools and we will finish the job.' The young fisherman was given courage by the Holy Spirit. Courage is the first of human qualities; it is the quality which guarantees all others. When John Huss the Puritan preacher, as he was about to be burned to death was asked to deny what he had taught, he answered, 'What I have taught with my lips I now seal with my blood.' If you meet danger promptly and without flinching, you will reduce it by half. Never run away, give chase.

Be strong and brave in every aspect of life

To be a 'Brave' the American Indians meant you had passed through all the schooling and had been more than a conqueror in every quest. The term 'Brave' was used because whatever situation the man had been placed in he had proven he was taller than the mountains and trees, his spirit was deeper than the flowing river. As he overcame the difficulties around him, so he over came the difficulties in himself. The Indian youth is adorned with the feathers he has taken from the eagle on the highest mountain. His tent displays his prowess with the skins of wild animals he has slain, fighting and overcoming some of them with bare hands. Even the paint on his face was from the blood of a slain animal. He has passed from being a mere young Indian into being that defined as a 'Brave'. He has been tested and found to be triumphant in all manner of ways. He has been tested like Peter, and not found wanting.

Let some of the Resurrection stone enter into your heart

Cephas was bold because he had certain convictions. He knew that Christ could never fail. Some of the Resurrection stone that Jesus had rolled away from the tomb had entered into his personality. All his preaching, doing, serving, praying and consoling came from the assurances that he had in Christ Jesus. This boldness was a product of the cross. It was through being 'in' Jesus, 'with' Jesus and 'for' Jesus that gave him this steely approach to others and to difficult situations. If only we could get the nails from his cross into our hearts we would be strong enough to be brave. We have not been called, and neither was Simon to cling on, to just hope for the best. In English history we have ships with great names: 'Endeavour' 'Dreadnought' 'Ark Royal' 'Enterprise' 'Victory'. These names describe the nature of the vessel. 'Ironsides' was not just a fancy name given to Oliver Cromwell's troops. What a contrast between the name of his troops and those belonging to the king— 'Cavaliers'! That word has become synonymous with gaiety and easy living. You can be 'rock hard' or 'clay soft'. Those who are bold make a claim for all that is Christ's. When I was quite a small boy, I had many older brothers. Many times, as the local bully passed by, I would hide behind the legs of my brother and poke my tongue out! It was the confidence of my brother that made me bold. Peter could not do it simply by himself. He had a source of inspiration that made him 'battle bold'. You always feel safer if there is a wall of protection between you and the enemy.

Look to previous battles and victories for comfort

Many years ago soldiers entered the Armed Forces and went to war for the first time carrying their virgin shield. This shield was called 'The Shield of Expectation'. Whenever they conquered an opponent or won a battle, they etched the name of the battle or the conquered person onto the shield. When they faced other enemies they did so with great confidence. This is the purpose of the flag or the 'colours' of any regiment, to enable the soldier to recognise something that creates a sense of well-being in his heart. The Christian is 'looking unto Jesus the Author and Finisher of our faith.'[24] In the Acts of the Apostles they gathered together to report all that the Lord had done.[25] The natives of South Africa gathered at night by the camp fire to tell of their exploits. In so doing they caused a burning sensation in the hearts of the young listener. The old 'sea dog' did the same as he told stories of piracy to a young man with 'salt in his blood'. Boldness was born out of relationship. Simon son of Jonas was a man of 'expectation'. He expected the Lord to help him, and the Lord did what Cephas 'expected'. He was looking for the 'unexpected'. If this boldness is holy boldness then nothing will stand before you all the days of your life. You will not be the mouse chased by the cat; you will be the dog chasing both cat and mouse. One shall chase a thousand. Many may fall to your right and left, but it shall not come nigh your dwelling.[26] You will live in the land of the free, and in the home of the bold.

Let the small be tall and strong

The humming bird is the smallest bird in the world. There are about 488 different species. One such humming bird measures only just one fourth of an inch long, and is found in Cuba. What makes them hum their happiness, as they go along? Nearer to the truth and our expectation is what makes them so bold? The bird is so small yet so bold that it will attack much larger creatures and drive them away because of its ferocity and meanness of spirit. It can hum but it can also fight, it is bold and stands up for its rights and the rights of others. You can sing but can you stand? What a lesson to you in your small corner and I in mine! Be a Daniel in the lions den. Be a Jonah in the whale. Be a Peter who was so bold in the Acts of the Apostles.

Notes

[1] 1 Samuel 10:22.

[2] William Burton based at Preston went with James Salter to pioneer churches in what was known as the Belgian Congo.

[3] Proverbs 26:7.

[4] John 20:27.

[5] Acts 9:5;26:14

[6] Isaiah 50:7.

[7] Jonah 1:17.

[8] Luke 6:40.

[9] Genesis 8:22.

[10] 2 Timothy 2:21.

[11] Deuteronomy 1:21, 28.

[12] John 1:42.

[13] Acts 3:6.

[14] Jeremiah 1:8.

[15] Acts 9:2; 19:23; 22:4.

[16] Acts 4:13, 29, 31. 1 Timothy 3:13.

[17] Psalm 81:10.

[18] Acts 9:11.

[19] Mark 7:35.

[20] Luke 1:20.

[21] John 14:17, 18.

[22] Acts 16:28.

[23] Philippians 1:6.

[24] Hebrews 12:2.

[25] Acts 4:23.

[26] Psalm 91:10.

Chapter Eight

THE MAN WHO HAD A SECOND OPPORTUNITY

The opportunities for service and forgiveness are many in the life Simon Peter. They are more than the days of his life. Jesus was the Carpenter and Peter the object that Christ chose to refashion and in so doing made him different. There is a glory about anything that is changed. That which has been unacceptable was now acceptable, the rejected received, the lost found, 'star qualities' were added. Peter had been as rough and as coarse as the sea on which he sailed his boat or the rocks he clambered over and there was certainly plenty of salt in his disposition. Throughout the ministry of the Master, Peter was granted more grace than most. There is no limit or measure to the heights or depths that the love of Christ will go. God's tools reach to where we are. There were many opportunities and new challenges that changed Peter, seen in the open hand, the soft word, the encouragement, the forgiveness, an occasional miracle, and the healings that were taking place, in the spirit of a man who was desperately in need.

The letter 'A' of the English alphabet opens the door to the rest of the English language. The middle 'C' in music is the very centre of the 'food of love,' for that note leads on to every piece of music, whistled by schoolboys or sung by world famous tenors. A molecule is the beginning of the building no matter how small or great, cottage or palace. Each of these things is seen in the life of Peter, as God granted him another opportunity to be good, kind, wholesome, helpful and prayerful.

Opportunities abound in Simon Peter

That element in Cephas that seems small grows until he becomes *mature* enough to stand before crowds to proclaim Jesus, and Him crucified. Spiritual *maturity* is 'growing up into Him in all things.'[1] The man called to be a rock had to be shaped to meet the need,[2] completed only when the need of his own heart was *mature*. There was something soft and yet unyielding in the young Galilean. His moods were as many as the tides of the sea, and all had to be dealt with.

God will grant golden opportunities, and He will make the man ready for the favoured time. One thing about Simon, son of Jonas, was that he never came to a standstill. Even when he failed to respond, he picked himself up, dusted himself down, and journeyed towards the next vista opening up before him. As a fisherman he went from one wave to another, and port to port going on to new things which are part of God's kingdom. The Eternal is never ending. This area of destination for Peter in the Lord takes him on and, like Peter, to ensure we are men and woman not just for today but of the future. Our hope is now and in the future. The life of Cephas is a glorious exposition of hope. As the 'dying thief' on the cross gave everyone hope in death-bed repentance and acceptance in the final hour of life, so Simon grants us hope in our forlorn state.

God not only provides opportunities, He prolongs them

The opportunities for forgiveness in Peter's life are as many as the grains of sand on the seashore. Who can number them? There were many broken bits, many unfinished tasks in his life. When Peter heard Jesus cry from the cross 'It is finished,' he knew everything left unfinished would be made complete. The partial would become plenty. It was as when someone still believes in us, is willing to trust us again, and then make us into what we are. If you want to see a person growing into full *maturity* trust them. Jesus did this when He sent them out two by two.[3]

If we are not given another exploit, we become discouraged; our service is sterile and only half-hearted. This belief takes us through the open door. We cannot number the times Jesus stepped into Peter's life to help him. As many as the waves of the sea, but that which Christ provided was not meant to sink Simon, but to help him even to walk on water, to swim, and to become the *mature* man as seen in the Acts of the Apostles. If you want to see the *maturity* of Simon Peter, it is written within every chapter verse and line of the Acts of the Apostles.

When opportunity knocks don't 'knock it'

When opportunity knocks we need to run to the door and open it. Your future is in its hands. Don't 'knock' opportunity. Welcome it! Don't waste it! Don't spend it in riotous living in the far country.[4] Don't be afraid to wait God's time. If you, like Simon, are not sure when the first knock comes, then wait for the second and the third. God's moment will always be found in God's hour. What He sends, He times to perfection. The Book Ecclesiastes says, 'Everything is beautiful in its time' (Ecclesiastes 3:11). Famous men have grabbed opportunity with both hands, and bound it closely to them as a friend. When the challenge is presented to Andrew's brother (John 1:41), he takes it, and his acceptance made him acceptable. Through a process of suffering and triumph he was disciplined and defined as a *mature* believer.

Each hour of each day presented new ideals and new goals. In the Acts of the Apostles, many opportunities were given to him to preach and teach, and because of this he became a true witness. On other occasions when he became the spokesman on behalf of the rest of the disciples. *Maturity* is not a product of the mind. Peter did not shrink into something less when he was challenged by the Lord. He did not stand in the shadows, but came into the fullness of light for all to see what the Lord had done. He said what he had heard from the lips of Jesus. He became as the Thessalonians, who allowed the word of God to 'sound out from them', as a blown trumpet.

Peter became what opportunity made him

On the first occasion Simon Peter preached in Acts chapter 2, certain things happened for uncertain people and great conviction came upon them. Peter accepted the avenue presented to him to preach the Word of the Lord. He had only one role model, the Christ of God. He simply did what Jesus did. The emphasis for us is not on the preaching, or the content with the exegesis of what was said, but the fact that he stood boldly before them and presented Christ, the Saviour of the world. This was his first opportunity, and all the training and teaching was seen in all its glory. Peter stood as a man among men. Cephas did not sink as when he stepped out of the boat onto the sea.[5] He could have closed his mind to what the Spirit was telling him to say. This was a golden moment, and the man from Galilee took it, and used it to further what the Lord required. He used his opportunities as he would have used the net to catch a shoal of fish.

We are not told, but there might have been some fear and trembling in the heart of this disciple. We can be full of dash and dare, but when we are really challenged to take a step into the future we become the world's greatest coward. He might have felt that he had more control over the sea he fished in than the human hearts that were before him. We 'back off' instead of going forward, trying to hide behind others, but the preacher did not. He had been schooled for this moment. Opportunities, if they are not taken, can make cowards of us all. Break the coward mould by committing yourself to the opportunities at hand. He didn't simply get 'hot under the collar,' he had a heart that was white hot with love and devotion.

Opportune moments are part of a plan

Simon's sermon was used, for three thousand converts were added to the Church in Acts 2:41. We preach three thousand sermons and see one added to the Church. It was the right man in the right place doing the right thing that produced the right results. Peter preached once and three thousand were added. That is success by anyone's standards. It would have been an increase if only one or two were added, but Scriptures record there were 'daily added' to the Church. Peter is seen as a scholar, builder, preacher, fisherman counsellor and helper. This opportune moment is part of the plan of God for a life. A life given to God is taken and distributed into the Kingdom of God on earth; His will being done as it is in Heaven. The young preacher could have been totally satisfied. He might have felt that he would never have to do this again, but the first step is never the last step. The convenient time is now and it will always be now or never. One thing led to another. If you succeed once, new avenues will be presented to you. If you can do it once you can do it again and again. This seasonable time can come to you in a dream, a thought, a word or a night vision. Happy is that man who can see light in the night. Simon did not settle for what he had. Much more will be presented to you as you present your body a living sacrifice.[6] It is when you put your life on the altar of sacrifice that you see the sacrifice of others. There was a thirsting and a longing within Peter to reach out and touch others with this truth so dear to his heart.

Opportunity was not meant to be found and feared

He did not 'rush in where angels fear to tread'. He was that angel treading where the Eternal was leading. He was still sailing, but this time it was on dry land into uncharted areas with a new message. The man with a calling has heard a voice, has seen the agony on the Face of Jesus shaped as a map with the world at its centre. He must go because there is an irresistible force calling him, changing him, taking him into his 'destiny' —the purpose for which anything was designed. It means 'to cause to stand'. Here was destiny's child in a man, a *mature* man. If you are the master of one trade and that is to serve the purposes of Jesus in your generation you will become the 'Jack'[7] of all trades. You will be successful in the serene and in the sour. No matter where you go, openings will come, and you must be prepared to accept them with many tongues. The 'Man' in you in the Person of Christ Jesus will appeal to the 'men and brethren' that the schooled disciple appealed to in the Acts of the Apostles.

There will always be a second opportunity

In Acts, chapter 3:12–26 Peter accepted the second opportunity to preach to the people. He preached the ways of God into the hearts of those present. If you preach with a broken heart to people with broken hearts, then you will find the wholeness of Jesus Christ. Those times of refreshing will be sent to those who are pricked in their hearts (Acts 2:37). These listeners and learners were stung in their hearts and some violent emotion took hold of them as they listened to a dying man preach to dying men. When the way opens up before you preach any sermon, carry out any deed, smile as if these are the last things you will ever do on earth. Your opportune moment will lead from earth to Heaven, and include all the promises of the Lord connected with life after death.[8]

Acts 4:4 tells us that five thousand were added to the Church as Peter preached. That was a glorious increase on the number who responded the first time. The 'path of the just is as a shining light, shining brighter until the Perfect Day.'[9] Doing the same thing the second time brings a different result. The preaching was the same, the preacher was the same, but there was an expansion of influence as the words fell as that good seed in the parable into good ground (Matthew 13:8). What we are and what we have will grow. The Church grew and the men leading that Church grew. The whole purpose behind a second opportunity is that we might finish unfinished business. The work of God might be complete in you, so that you might complete the work of Jehovah for your life. They grew as they ventured forth in the King's name.

Your opportunity is here and now

Opportunity is more than vocation. We can be called, chosen, sanctified and glorified, but we all require a season in our life to gather together in God what we have been promised. The young fisherman took them out of unbelief and into belief. This was his favourable time to expound the Favourable Year of the Lord referring to the Day of Jubilee by Jesus Christ.[10] Again we are not interested in the content or even the conduct, the character of the crusader. Opportunity makes you open and opulent as you march onward to your destiny. This son of Jonas accepted the challenge of a second favour; there would be many more occasions to honour Jesus Christ. If you think the first chance was good, read how many more were won to Christ. The second attempt can be more real because the first attempt was unsure and unreal. It reveals that the Lord had more opportunities for him, more avenues than the number of fish that had ever been seen in his fishing nets! Even more success awaited him.

Simon Cephas the brother of Andrew, was weak, wayward, and found in the balances wanting. Jesus tipped the scales in his favour by using the finger of one hand. The Spirit of God in him took him from stumbling and uncertainty to running, to *maturing* and, as part of his salvation presented him as a winner. Before Pentecost this Peter ran away from the Lord. After Pentecost he ran for the Lord.

Opportunity can make all the difference

Simon by name and nature is related to that Old Testament prophet called Jonah. (Jonah 3:1) 'The word of the Lord came unto Jonah a second time.' Before that second opportunity the word 'down' is seen quite often. (Jonah 1:3, 3, 5; 2:16.) After that word had come 'a second time' Jonah began to grow up and go up. (Jonah 3:2) 'arise'. He 'arose', 'went up' (Jonah 3:2, 3). Twice in John 1, the first disciples were told to 'Behold the Lamb of God'. (John 1:29, 36.) There is something which cannot equal the second time, because it can repair all the damage done the first time. It brings grace from the throne to rule the heart. When the head has failed the heart takes over, and instead of going under we go over and out to where we belong. It is not how many avenues are opened, nor is it the many callings or promises we receive. The importance of it all is what we do with them. Robert the Bruce of Scotland was a defeated man hiding in a cave when he saw a spider make many attempts to bridge a gap. It tried again and again until it finally managed to get where it wanted to go. Robert took this as a good omen, went out and defeated the English.

Will we allow what is asked of us to help us into deeper grace? Will we constantly gaze at His face with just one eye, or listen with only one ear? When you are humble you bend low, and 'he who is down need fear no fall.' Is your ear to the ground listening for that still, small voice?

When the door opened, Simon discovered that although he was

surrounded by a crowd, he stood alone yet he had the insight, the confidence to know that the Lord stood with him. If that same Lord provides the fitting occasion, he will enable us to enter into its fullness. If you want the Lord to be with you in a special way, then accept the challenge and go further and deeper. Journey on to arrive. If you never go on you will never arrive. If you do not know where you are going you might arrive and not even realise it! What a waste that will be! More wasteful than the broken nets suffered by Cephas.[11] Peter did not become a Master Preacher because he kept to himself what the Lord required; he let it go in order to gain, scattered that we might gather together. He wanted to be fully used. It took as much faith for him to grasp this as it took for any of the miracles recorded in his ministry. He was simply a man but he was a willing man.

Opportunity is tomorrow calling today to join with it
Cephas built on that first chance and saw the greater second opportunity. To this disciple opportunity was tomorrow calling today to its side. Hope and opportunity are indispensably linked in a man's heart, forged by forces that surround him. The difference between an opportunity and no opportunity is the difference between a brick wall, or a wall with a door leading into the Land of Beulah. God never stops providing; we stop believing and receiving. Cephas was neither tongue tied, tongue twisted, nor tongue in cheek when it came to speaking the truth, the whole truth and nothing but the truth. God was pleased to have someone who had obviously *matured*, a man who knew when to lead and when to be led, a man who knew not only when to speak but also what to say. In quietness Peter received confidence and strength. Channels are presented when we have something worth saying and worth listening to. He was full of the words and works of Jesus. What you are will fit into your ministry, helping others out of their misery, and resulting in destiny.

Success can be unmeasured
If you take chances as Cephas did, success will be beyond the centimetre, metre, or furlong. God commences where and when you commence and stops where and when you stop. The God who

is served by Peter and you is everlasting. When we come to the last rung of the ladder, the Lord is the first rung. Conclusion gets mixed up with commencement. We must commence again. It is easy to prove God in the fishing boat or in the Upper Room. Will your God remain the same, stable and true as you stand before a great crowd? It was not the crowd that was on trial it was Peter, the man in the making. How would he respond? Would he say and do the wrong thing? He did not speak 'off the hoof'—*ad hoc*, but each word had wisdom as its mother, brother and sister. *Maturity* adds weight and circumference. His words are as weighty as the anchor used to secure the boat. There is trust as deep as any sea when the Almighty grants us the second time. Would that impetuous nature take hold of Simon Peter again? It did not, it would not, and it dare not. Peter did not simply use a 'figure of speech', he was the 'figure in the speech.' Preaching has been defined as 'using your opportunity.' Simon spoke, and it was like water being poured out of the Rock as he presented Christ. He had been in the School of Christ for three years, joining with Mary who sat at the feet of Jesus.[12] If you are to look upon many faces as Cephas did, you must first look upon one Face —that Beautiful Face. Take what you see in His face and relate it to others. As you preach you are an artist, sketching Christ. Peter touched so many lives. The end of one opportunity might well lead to a greater one. You can begin as Simon the fisherman, until that which is developed in you trains you to become a fisher of men. You might recognise what is there at the commencement, but as it grows so you also grow, and begin to understand all that there is between the commencement and the conclusion.

You can have a 'golden opportunity'

Opportunity is only 'golden' when we extract all the openings presented to us. It can be the goose that 'laid the golden egg'. Every time you read of the exploits of Peter in the Book of Acts, each one is an opportunity presented to a man who turned his back on God. The look from Jesus and the tears of the penitent were to turn this traitor to face forward and accept his responsibilities.[13] The Almighty only provides us with what He knows we will respond to.

We only correspond with God when we say yes to the Lord. In your *maturity* you can become a living 'amen' to all the Almighty has said. These openings seem more than the colours of the rainbow given as a promise of no further flood, when everything seems to be out of control in a storm.[14] To see an opportunity is good, to listen and hear about one is better, but best of all is when you accept it. You walk the talk, and go to what you have seen. It is what you see in that which is presented to you, that sends you to where you should go. 'Go and preach all the word of this Life.'

Achievement only comes when we go forward. Fullness is not a visit to 'Memory Lane'; it is brought to your heart to inflame it with desire. 'Chance' is the world's definition. 'Chance' is brought to us by gambling and betting. I love that opportunity that speaks of men 'who hazarded their lives for the gospel's sake.'[15] 'Chance' refers to the throwing of the dice but it is God's Hand that throws and turns until we receive the confirmation. What was presented to Peter was God ordained, God sustained and God arranged. There are no ways outside of the Almighty that we would want to travel. Those other ways are shrouded in darkness, and fear is found on every corner. No matter how loud the voice that is calling you, if it is not the voice of God, be as someone deaf and dumb, neither hearing or repeating the words. Even wiser, be as one born without ears!

If you miss your opportunity, you can miss it forever

Each opportunity usually comes once in a lifetime. If it happens more than once, then the grace of God is being multiplied in and for you. We miss the obvious as we move into the oblivious. The Greeks represented opportunity as a man with a bald head, just a tuft of hair at the front. The rest of the head was greased. If, as it came towards you, you missed that tuft, that opportunity, then there was no possibility of grabbing it again. Do not wait for opportunity to come to you, take it as an expected gift. Run with it, walk with it, and talk with it and, as you do, you will discover that what you thought was an opportunity is actually Christ himself drawing near. As we reach out after Him we release our possibilities.

Each avenue to which Peter responded provided a miracle. If you are given more than one favourable time then you are most blessed. The list of what happened to Cephas is endless. In Acts 1 he was granted an open door as he shared in the Upper Room. In Acts 2, he preached, and again in Acts chapter 3. It was as if there was a strand running through his life with the Hand of God holding the strings of his heart, arranging Peter's ministry and destiny.

Your destiny is in your opportunity

In Acts chapter 3, the Galilean and John went to the Beautiful Gate and, because of that simple fact, a man was able to walk again. Every avenue granted by God is a beautiful gate. Destiny's child is tomorrow's *mature* leader. Simon had the opportunity to see a man walk, leap and praise God. In Acts 4 this same fisherman stood, full of the Holy Ghost and boldness, speaking to the people, high priest and the relatives of the high priest. The Lord made the path of Peter and the high priest to cross at a certain point and place. Whatever the hand of the Almighty brings to you, part of it contains deliverance and an open door into something greater. That greatness must be birthed in you.

When the Red Sea or the River Jordan, opens for you in your circumstances, pass through on dry land. The Lord will not leave you in the mud or the deepest part of the river. God brings you in your moment of need to your hour of triumph. Cephas never did anything that was wasted. He did not gaze at the horizon, but looked to the furthest point and went towards it. A compass has points, yet they are not the measure of the compass, they are but 'pointers' to the direction which we should travel!

There are as many openings for Peter in the Acts of the Apostles as the Children of Israel had in the land of Canaan. Each city conquered was the fulfilment of the Word of God. As they overcame one area another was presented to them. God followers become men chasers as they displace doubt and fear. They do not chase chance they follow after Christ Jesus. If you run towards the Lord you will find all you are seeking and will join with others who said, 'Sirs, we would see Jesus.' If you falter or fall, it will be where He is —where the healing, ointment and soothing are found. God followers do not become men pleasers. When opportunity knocks, unbelief must not be allowed to open the door.

Zeal and opportunity belong together

Acts chapter 5 presented Simon with the opportunity to ensure that the new converts stayed sincere and holy. Part of your calling is to be in the 'nick of time' when dealing with a growing menace or evil. Would Cephas deal with the lies of Ananias and Sapphira with as much zeal as he dealt with the man at the Beautiful Gate? There was great zeal as he dealt with the lies of Satan. To see what God is opening up before you can bring you into springtime after a 'winter of discontent'. Peter gave himself, body soul and spirit, for every opportunity was to be as an altar on which to offer himself to the Lord. As we walk in the revelation we have, the Lord will grant further manifestations. Each day we need just enough light for the next step tomorrow. We do not obtain light today for tomorrow. If Simon in Acts chapter 5 had failed he would have failed totally, tumbling down like a bulging wall when leaned on. We move from opportunity to opportunity as and when the Lord chooses. How lost we become when we create our own vistas, without hope and frustrated. These are not the marks of the *mature* man. Each Divine happening, makes us the man or woman He wants us to be. We become part of all we meet. The 'lessons of life' await us behind the door of opportunity.

Opportunity can mean an 'open harbour'

The word 'opportunity' can mean 'open harbour'. In Genesis 49:13 Zebulun, the child of Israel is seen as a harbour for ships. There is such a need for people to become harbours, so that ships might come and find rest. You can become as a harbour unto others, even as Paul the apostle became an open door to the Gentiles.

When the word 'opportunity' appears in the New Testament, it means a 'season'—the season to plant, grow or harvest. It is the picture of the spring; the farmer going into the field to plant growing seed. It corresponds with the Book of Ecclesiastes, chapter 3 — 'There is a 'time' for....' A special time for a special purpose, when the will of God develops into more than a quote from the Bible.

This word 'opportunity can mean 'well timed'. Suggesting the 'time of need,' just in the 'nick of time,' as in Hebrews 4:16.

In Acts 5:19 the son of Jonas was released from prison. As the prison door opened, so the Lord gave him another prime moment to go and preach His Word. Opportunity can mean the difference between being imprisoned or being set free. The dead-end became an open door, a new beginning. Each prison bar represented another opportunity. Paul and Silas were put into the inner prison and when God set them free, the jailer called for 'lights' so that he could see. (Acts 16:29.) Each light presented Paul and Silas with opportunity to go into a dark world with a light that would never go out. Opportunity gives us light in dark places, even in prisons. No wind can ever blow out the light of that presented to you in the Almighty. The authorities might sentence you to be flogged or put to death, but they cannot put out your light, your opportunity. It will never diminish, or be fully extinguished. If you want to see opportunity dressed in gold, remember words spoken during the ministry of Jesus, 'A bruised reed he will not break, and a smoking flax he will not extinguish.'[16]

God will give you opportune moments one step at a time

In Acts chapter 8 and chapter 10, opportunities abounded. In one incident Simon the Sorcerer was dealt a mortal blow. In the other the Gentiles received the Holy Ghost. All are in the line of duty. There is such and much diversity in this devotee. Things happen when we tread where God is calling. When the Lord opens up the way, He will reveal it a step at a time. Before you take the next step make sure the footprint of the Master is alongside your own. If not then you are walking alone, carrying your own burden. When we enter into His choice we become choice. It is the diversity of the opportunity that comes to us through the diversity and adversity of the operations of the Holy Spirit. You need to be the echo of His voice, and the result of choice. There are as many opportunities as there are tongues of men and of angels. There is something different each time the Lord provides a way. When the Sovereign Lord provides an opportunity, there is a door that no man can open or close. Jesus has the key to lock and to unlock. Those things opened by the Lord stay open for as long as is necessary.

The door to Noah's ark and the mouth of Jonah's whale did not close until the purposes of the Eternal were fulfilled. The mouth of the whale stayed open until Jonah was not only on the menu, but had become part of the meal! All the animals were in the ark before God closed the door. When Jehovah closes a door you will find as many directions opening up as you can manage. If you pass through a 'cat flap' you are forcing your way in, entering into territory that has not been assigned to you.

In none of the occasions presented to Peter, was he weighed in the balances and found wanting. Each Divine arrangement did something for the man. God is watching to see how the man will develop. He sees the end from the beginning; that is why this clay in the hands of the Potter trusted Him. The young fisherman was not prepared to go to Heaven never having gone anywhere, or seen or done anything in the Name of the Lord. Simon left his footprints all over the known world, so that people who worshipped the 'unknown god' might know Him.

Simon never let obstacles obliterate opportunities

The emblems of the Holy Spirit were a spreading flame and other tongues. Fire and forceful eloquence, tongues of fire and of men. By the grace of God Peter had spread even as that flame, and his avenues of service came to others of different tongues. Simon never let the mountains or valleys obliterate the fullness of time. In what he did, he became the interpretation of those tongues of men and of angels. He never felt inadequate. In the word 'adequate' we have the suggestion of 'God being involved'. Wherever Simon went, whatever he was called to do, the Lord had been there before him. It is good to respond in 'the nick of time'. If you delay to obey, the time you delay will be taken from you, for in the word 'opportunity' is the thought of 'time', a limited time and opportunity. The Lord God was watching out for him. He makes the necessary arrangements that would bring the fulfilment of everything promised, and the achievement that came through the open door of opportunity. When you see the beautiful primrose or the first rose, you have what was promised in the embryo, and what you see in Peter is what Jesus said would happen.

When we travel God's way there are no fees! Simon never went to war having to pay his own wages. When Jonah ran away from God, he had to pay his own fare to Tarshish! (Jonah 1:3.) You could travel to the moon, doing your 'own thing' but on arrival you might find it is just a lump of green cheese! To cross the street, if that is the next step arranged by Alpha for you, will bring far more fulfilment than travelling to the moon! Peter never went beyond what the Eternal had promised. His needs were met by a many handed God having the ability to open and close doors in every nation. 'Seize the day' before the day seizes you never to release you again. You will never be lost for opportunity if you develop your life and become majestic in *maturity*.

Notes
[1] 1 Peter 2:2. 2 Peter 3:18. Ephesians 4:15.
[2] John 1:42. Cephas meaning 'the rock'.
[3] Mark 6:7.
[4] Luke 15:13.
[5] Matthew 14:30.
[6] Romans 12:1.
[7] 'Jack of all trades' is part of an English proverb. It means we can do many different jobs, but we complete none. We are never successful whatever we do.
[8] See author's book *Dying is Living*.
[9] Proverbs 4:18.
[10] Luke 4:18.
[11] Luke 5:6.
[12] John 11:20, 32.
[13] Luke 22:61, 62.
[14] Genesis 9:13, 14.
[15] Acts 15:26.
[16] Matthew 12:20.

Chapter Nine

THE MAN WHO WOULDN'T TAKE 'NO' FOR AN ANSWER

God answered prayer many times in the life of Peter the young Galilean fisherman. Some times answers came via other people, at other times the answers were sent directly to the man. Petition will always be the most direct route to the heart of God. There are seven occasions when Peter prayed or was involved in prayer in the Acts of the Apostles. Each time the Lord graciously answered the call and met the need. Prayers can be answered without a word being spoken. The Eternal feels the needs of our petition before we speak, the answer sometimes arriving before we pray. Part of the *maturity* of this growing convert was in the way he received answers from the Answer. He received that which was 'pressed down, shaken together and running over'. The prayers of Peter are as welcome in the presence of the Lord as the angels who stand and wait to serve. Heaven rejoices when we pray, even as angels do when a prodigal returns to God. Peter seems to have every prayer answered, uttered or unuttered. There are no limits to prayer; what is good for one is good for all. He lived in an atmosphere of the presence of the Lord. Some people in their *maturity* speak, breathe eat and sleep prayer.

One prayer answered means all prayers can be answered
Receiving an answer was as simple as breathing. One answered prayer meant there was a precedent for all utterances to be answered.

The Lord never sent the answer to the wrong man or wrong address. If the need is in the street called 'Straight', then Ananias must go to that street.[1] It is one thing to pray but an entirely different thing to receive an answer.

When Simon the son of Jonas threw a net into the sea, he expected fish to be caught in that net. On one occasion they laboured all night yet caught nothing.[2] He received a word from Jesus telling him to cast the net on the 'right side', and as he did so it was filled with many fish.[3]

We must learn to pray and not to faint

In Luke 11:1 the disciples asked Jesus to teach them to pray. He said they should 'pray and not "faint",' i.e. 'cave in'. From that moment Cephas watched, listened and learned the discipleship of prayer. Part of his *maturity* was learning how to pray, when to pray, when to be silent and to let his heart do the talking to the Lord. God can interpret all our emotions. That which is uttered, stuttered or unuttered is never unheard. Prayer never comes without an identity before the Sovereign. Cephas had heard and seen the Master not only pray, but receive answers that were multiplied in the feeding of the four thousand and the five thousand.[4] Solicitations that came from the lips and love of Christ were answered with 'bread enough and to spare'. Jesus was the Master Teacher, and Cephas learned as he watched the Master at work. Many of the prayers he uttered were based on the intercession of Jesus. He did these things that the Teacher had taught. Part of the life of Peter was to beg as Jesus had taught him.

Become part of maturity and destiny as you pray

We must be taught by Jesus, and as we are that becomes part of our *maturity* and destiny. Simon saw the ease with which Jesus pleaded to the Father.[5] He began to understand that answers to supplication were based on a relationship, not simply on the time spent praying, or quoting promises. The answers came as the echo from a voice in a valley when Jesus cried to His Father. A proposition that is wrapped in the will of the Eternal bearing the Son's image will always be delivered. We get much more out of it than we put into it. Prayer was never offered for themselves. Intercession by its very nature means we stand on behalf of another. The 'no' of the Lord is better than the 'yes' of men. Men have not the means to grant the answer. Their funds are inadequate, while God's resources are in the 'unsearchable riches of Christ.'[6]

Let your petitions be large in content not words

Peter made large petitions when he prayed. We never read that he spent time with the trivial. He spoke about matters of life and death, and each time it is recorded that the Lord granted his request. The word 'request' means 'away' and to 'seek'. Seeking that which is away from you as a Prodigal son or daughter, and seeing that which the locust and cankerworm has eaten being restored. It is seeking the Lord for the things 'far away' to be brought near. Part of your *maturity* is not only to pray it is in what to ask for. It is having such a confidence that the Lord does what you would do in that situation. *Maturity* is giving to the Almighty, and leaving it with Him to work in, work out and work through until you receive the answer. The answer is always larger than the question.

Cephas had a heart that was ready to ask and to receive. That heart had been worked upon and made ready for what the Lord wanted it to receive. A prepared heart is a heart that can be trusted with the answers to prayer. All that comes our way is not sent from the Lord. The Lord, through training and *maturity* developed a capacity in Peter not only to ask, but to give and to receive. Cephas had been as empty as a boat before entering into the sea. Many can call upon the Lord; few can listen to what He is saying. The important thing about *maturity*, the very fabric of it, is not what we pray but what we receive. It isn't the length of words; it is the fullness of acceptance and deliverance. There are no 'long winded' prayers the New Testament that take the glory from the Wind of God in the Holy Ghost, in Acts 2:3, 4. Many times an entreaty has been cut short because in the middle of the utterance, they have received the interpretation in an answer sent from God.

What a wonderful surprise for the apostles when in the midst of their prayers the answer came! He uses the unexpected to provide the expected. Each answer to prayer beautifies and beatifies any situation. The New Testament speaks of 'adorning' the gospel of Christ.[7] The figure is that of putting something on bare boards to make it more beautiful. An artist does this when adding paint to canvas. Many times the sacrifice that is found in prayer comes not when the intercession is offered but when the answer is received. The need met demands consecration. The Lord will occasionally answer a prayer, and leave you to fulfil the rest.

The Lord expects us to use the answers to prayer
When my wife and I were pioneering a church in Gainsborough, Lincolnshire, England, I needed some bookshelves. I prayed for God to meet my need. While I was praying, I heard a loud bang outside the flat where we resided. God said, 'There are your bookshelves!' I looked through the window to see a pile of floor boards unceremoniously tipped onto the pavement, that had been brought out of a building that was being refurbished. I went outside and asked the workmen if I could take some of the floor boards. They agreed; I took my plane, hammer and nails, and within a few hours I had my first set of bookshelves! God had partially answered the prayer, and I had to supply the rest. Many times this happened in the life of the young Galilean. The New Testament records they had to take the grave clothes from a resurrected body, and on another occasion, had to set food before those who were hungry. God did not put the food into their mouth.

Something is added when a petition is answered. That which would reach out and touch another is itself touched by an unseen hand. It becomes what the Almighty created it to be. Many of our petitions ask the Eternal to let things be as He created them.

We can be weighed in the balances and found wanting; prayer and the answer brings those balances to equilibrium. Cephas had within him a faith that believed things would happen even if he did not seek the face of the Lord. He believed in a God who was in every area of life —that is *maturity*! The Lord would seek him and help him and that 'right early'.[8]

Expect great things from God as you pray

In Acts 2:42 the early Church continued in prayer alongside the other necessities of eternal life. These were prayers that were meant to be answered. We live in a day when unanswered prayers seem to be the 'norm', but when we get to heaven we shall fully understand all that God did, all the petitions that He honoured, and which we, in our ignorance, knew nothing of.

When the word 'prayer' 'prayed' or 'prayers' are used of Peter and the early disciples we have the suggestion of the beggar not only asking for bread but taking that bread as the Bread of Life and using it for the glory of God. If you want to witness the full import of not accepting 'no' for an answer, look at the beggar at the Beautiful Gate, listen to what was said and what he received. Not silver or gold, for both can be spent or lost, but a miracle of healing.[9] Every answer to prayer is as much a miracle as a blind man having his eyes opened, because eyes are opened to see the answer. The basic meaning of prayer is to 'ask'. The Greek tense in Matthew 7:7 'Ask and it shall be given unto you,' is 'keep on asking'. In the telling of the contents of the heart is the receiving of that contained in the heart of your Father. Along with Cephas in prayer, we receive far more than what we request. The net that he threw into the sea was filled with many fish. God sometimes adds to what Peter said on other occasions, He deducts from it. The answer was always measured to the need. The answer was something the young fisherman could handle with care and grace.

The promise for Peter and for all who pray is 'Ask, seek, knock and it shall be given to you, pressed down, shaken together and running over.'

Every prayer uttered should be the out-flowing of the heart

Prayer was not in flowery words or long sentences, nor in textbook presentation, but in the out-flowing of a full heart. The heart in need prays that need. The heart in pain prays that pain. The bruised heart prays with those bruises as part of the pleading. It is praying what you are, from the heart and on behalf of the heart. Peter came to pray with his heart as empty as a beached boat, but when the intercession was finished, was that as full as the sea the boat sailed on. What was narrow and restricted became wide and deep. Each prayer brought more success to the believer.

In Acts 4:31 the word used for 'prayer' is to 'have a want'. Peter's 'want' was swallowed up in the will of the Lord. Want can be turned into desire that becomes a fire on the altar of God. In Acts 1:24 the meaning of 'prayer' is to 'wish for'. Prayer in the Old Testament could be a 'whisper',[10] a 'groan'[11] or a 'meditation'.[12] The full gamut of human emotion was entered into by the apostle. The word used for prayer can mean to 'call for' or 'call alongside'. It is to call another source of strength alongside. The other half sent from the Lord came to the aid of Peter. There was a sense in which he was only complete when the prayer was answered. Without this sort of pleading we are only half the person we can and should be.

In Acts 1:14 prayer is defined as a 'pouring out' not only of words but of all that is in the heart in order that God might fill it with new things. Peter 'poured out' in prayer as much as his eyes poured out tears of repentance when Jesus turned and look on him in Luke 22:61. When he 'poured out' God poured in. Our eyes might be moist with tears, but when God answers that petition there is a whole river that runs to where we are. Asking the Lord for a favour can be just the upward turn of the eye to the heavens. It can be a plea, intercession, even just a wish. God hears, God understands and God answers. The One we pray to gives the interpretation to what we might feel, as we ask in an unknown tongue. God interprets our deepest desires and our dream. The Holy Spirit interprets our groaning. That which is dormant becomes dynamic as we seek His face.

Will you know what to do with the answers to prayer?
Some of our prayers are not answered because we would not know what to do with the answers. Peter took the answers and used them as a faithful servant doing the King's business. He never succumbed to the devil's temptation when Satan said to Jesus 'Command that these stones be turned into bread.'[13] If through prayer stones are going to be turned into bread then that bread is for the hungry, not the self-seeking. If the Lord fills the bread basket, He has done it

that you might feed the poor. We need to pray for hands and arms strong enough to dole it out, breaking the pieces small enough for the child's mouth and large enough for the mouth of the adult. Prayer was answered for the son of Jonas so that he might attend to the sick and needy. He was a royal physician with more than tablets and bottles. He had something given to him from Heaven.

As you search through the Acts of the Apostles you begin to realise that at times Peter believed God, and at other times it was as if prayers were answered without even uttering a word. This kind of prayer does not come forth but by prayer and fasting. As we know, so we grow. Peter appeared as the cup of a flower with petals turned upwards to receive wind, rain and sunshine. He did not fast and pray every time he wanted an answer from the Almighty. It is good to live, speak and think in the power of prayer. It can be a disposition of life and living. The apostle Paul speaks of 'praying always'.[14] We do not read of one occasion when the Lord did not answer his prayer one way or another. God sent the correct answer. He never sent anything which was short of expectations. He never sends angels with only one wing! God sends answers quickly but He never cuts corners.

God has many ways in which to answer your prayers
The vehicles used to send answers are so many, almost like an army waiting, standing to attention just for the occasion of delivering answers to prayer. God has nearly as many ways of answering our pleadings as He has to get us to pray. Acts 1 records that they 'prayed together,' and were with 'one accord' in 'one place'. There was tremendous unity in what was said. In that chapter they prayed for someone to take the place of Judas when it seemed as if that prayer was not answered, they made the choice. You can make the choice in your heart, and then pray for direction after you have made up your mind. You can ask the Lord if He wants you to go to America after you have bought your air ticket! We never read much of Matthias after the lot was cast, yet they had prayed!

The Lord gives complete answers to our prayers
As they waited on the Lord in Acts 2, the answer came in wind and

fire. The answer was so 'full' it filled the house where they were sitting, received in wind and fire. Natural elements were taken and used to express eternal truth. As Peter preached, I am quite sure that the prayers of the heart were answered. Many a soul has been brought to Christ, not through the message preached but by the prayer offered and the life lived for the Lord. It is not recorded that they prayed for souls to repent, because the Word was strong enough to bring conviction, but God added to the church about three thousand souls. This was surely an answer to prayer, even though that prayer was not recorded. What could happen if three thousand gathered to earnestly pray for the lost!

In Acts 3 the man at the Beautiful Gate was healed without Peter uttering one word of prayer. It was a complete and instant healing. They were on their way to the place of prayer, but before they arrived God sent the answer. Needs are not tied to our begging or asking. God will answer whenever the need arises, whether you have prayed or not. If you pray, you will be part of the process. You will not be the process because the answer to our pleading does not come from our reasoning but from Jehovah. They expected the promises of God to be fulfilled on their behalf. If they witnessed, then God would work. If they did their part, the Lord would do His. God will always meet us half way, and when we come half way we shall find that the Lord was even involved in that.

The smile of God is in each answer received
The worker for the Lord received so many answers to prayer, and in each answer was the smile of God, a gift of the Lord. Grace answered and grace made people whole. There were no wasted prayers in the Book of Acts. Each prayer was spacious and gracious, directed to a purpose, never falling by the wayside like the seed in the parable. What was said was meant, and what was meant was answered with abundance. Each answer was the 'yes' of God. When God answers our request He is placing His personal stamp and seal on the event. He displays the fact that in the realm of sickness, need, world affairs or family affairs He is Sovereign. As the answer came via many ministries it was the Lord's way of saying 'Amen' at the end of every

prayer. Have you received an 'amen' recently? We can all enter this 'conclave' which means 'to enter through one door, and one key.' The master key is prayer that can unlock all that binds, shuts in or shuts out.

When they prayed the place was shaken

Cephas was part of those in Acts 4:31 where the place they were gathered was shaken. Seeking God can shake those things around us, but can also shake us until all that is out of place finds a new place and pasture in the Lord. Another prayer had been answered. Peter would not take 'no' as an answer. There was a visible manifestation of the power of the Eternal Omnipotence, when they met together and called on His Name. This became the one doctrine of the day. God waved His hand as a sign of acceptance of their prayer, and the whole building shook. Something had to happen when Peter began pleading, from a *mature* heart. This man did not waste his time praying about things that were already in operation. He did not waste time going round the world when it was Jerusalem that was in need. What was dear to his heart found its way into his prayers. He supplicated and expected the God of intercession to answer just with the same conviction when God spoke in Genesis 1:3 and said, 'Let there be light!' Just as the physician will give a prognosis or the accountant will total figures correctly, so God will answer prayers for it is His nature to do so.

In Acts 5, when he dealt with the lie of Ananias and Sapphira, prayer was not offered. God will move in judgment on account of His own holiness without us even interceding. This is what will happen at the end of the world. The Holy Ghost moved independently of anything that was said. There is something so sovereign about that which the Lord will do. He will act swiftly and decisively to keep the young Church clean. Alongside the prayers and penance of Peter we see God at work, in His kingdom.

What is believable is achievable

Without any recorded intercession, great signs and wonders were wrought in Acts 5:12, 15. The shadow of Peter had more substance than the substantial! They believed the Lord. Each time they prayed they went back to the very thing that anchored them to Christ. They had learned to talk to God about it. Sometimes it was heard, sometimes unheard, there as just a whisper of love from the heart. There is a tenderness which is unspoken that moves the heart of God.

In Acts 5:20–22, an angel opened the prison door for them to go and preach the 'words of this life'. The prayers they uttered are not recorded. Sometimes angels attend our asking, begging, pleading, and at other times angels are our prayers. The Lord sends the answer in the shape of an angel or a donkey! The angel had the keys to the prison. The answer comes via a mediator, as the angel fits the key into the prison lock. It was an answer to prayer that carried further action as the angel commanded the doors to open. The Lord could have swung the gates wide open, but He wanted angels to come into their ministry. He must find these willing servants work to do. God did what He had to do, and Peter is set free as a direct result of God's intervention. A word as a desire, telling God about it, leads to many words being preached to the people. One word of prayer resulted in many words spoken. Prayer is the gurgle of a child that the Lord takes and arranges so it is understood. In intercession we can utter anything, but it is the grace of God that makes sense of all that is said. He is not only the God of the English but of the French, German, Chinese, and all nations. We might ask in weakness, but He replies in strength. You can come in as a kitten and go out as a lion.

Prayer can be uttered and expressed in one word
Sometimes they expressed all they felt and needed in one word, such as 'help', and the Almighty answered with one word. Peter was surrounded by those who would not take 'no' for an answer. They came in the Name of Jesus that means 'Yes'; they received far more than they prayed for, even more than they bargained for! A little prayer received a great answer. My mind might be so small and my prayer so weak. Once the asking goes into the telling or begging it is translated through believing into receiving. If he came to the Almighty begging, he had to come with a large heart to receive what

146

the Eternal would give. One of the prayers of the early disciples was expressed in the following when going to sea: 'My boat is so small and the sea is so large.'

Sometimes, the provision of the Lord is as it was for Abraham, as 'many as the stars of heaven and the sand by the seashore.'[15] It can include many nations. This is one of the neglected weapons that we see being fully used in the Acts of the Apostles.

Many understand what the word Cupid means. In Greek mythology, Cupid shoots arrows and people fall in love. Cupid would wet his grindstone with blood, and sharpen his arrows on that which had been bathed in blood. We need the blood of God's Son Jesus Christ to help us sharpen our prayers, and to realise that He provides the answers through this shed blood on the Cross.

Pray in the Holy Ghost and God will answer

(Acts 8:14, 15) Peter and John prayed that the believers might receive the Holy Spirit. When we pray 'in' the Holy Ghost we pray 'along the same lines' as the Holy Spirit. It means we are willing to stop and start at His command, travelling the same way as our Master. They were simply asking the Lord to provide what He had promised. God loves it when you break off part of the promise and kneel upon it as you open your Bible to intercede. God loves you to ask with a full heart, a heart filled with the promises, so as you pray they tumble out of your heart to be taken hold of by the One who will answer. They had great confidence because of their experiences in Acts 2 when they had witnessed such things before. If God can answer one prayer He can answer all prayers.

There was so much power left with the Lord, that He wanted to share the overflow. The asking was in line with all that God was saying, giving, doing and was willing to do for the native Church. There was no disappointment in the Divine appointment. Prayer was answered fully as those who were waiting received the Holy Spirit. When intercession is accounted we receive something. We are not left as orphans without a father. God is not the 'bread winner' but the 'bread Giver'. Cephas received what he asked for. We do not receive because we do not ask. When we do plead we have hidden motives, or an agenda of our own. If the Lord multiplied bread and fish for some, they would consume it, and leave the crowd hungry. God looks at the motives in the heart, and assesses the outcome. What these disciples received happened as a direct result of the prayers of the two who came from Jerusalem. Pleading was translated into the Baptism of the Holy Spirit, it was not terminated.

Get used to receiving answer to prayer

In Act 8:24 another requested Peter to pray for him. As he was used to catching fish, so he became used to seeing prayers answered. Why pray if there is no help? Why pray if nothing ever happens? When it seems as if there is no help and nothing is happening, then we need to pray that the Almighty will blow with His wind, and things will be re-arranged for the mutual benefit of all. The fire of Pentecost sees all our problems burned up.

A veil is placed between us and the workings of the Lord. What He is seeking to accomplish is revealed little by little. The answer can commence as the ray of the dawn of a new day until it becomes full light. Even the human eye does not take everything in all at one glance. Repeated looks as repeated prayers give the fuller picture.

Sometimes God answers the supplication as we are changed. When we pour out of our own hearts, we leave room for the Eternal to do His work. Jehovah was changing Simon constantly. Every prayer was a challenge to his own heart before it received an answer that was to result in his *maturity*. If the Almighty can do nothing good for Cephas, He cannot do well for others. He works on them after He has worked in you. What the outcome is we are not always sure. At times we are left not knowing the outcome. Heaven will reveal all the answers. Many prayers that you feel were not answered have in fact been fully demonstrated, but your vision was too small to see what the Lord has done. The infinite mind is far above the finite mind. You are looking at the situation, even when God has moved, and you have not moved on. We want answers here and now. The Lord sometimes sends the answers a little later when the time is right. When that happens we have moved into another area, and have forgotten that we ever prayed that prayer. Our memories are so short when the response of the Almighty seems to take such a long time. If He sent you the result of your asking today it might be just water, but await God's time and it will be water turned into wine! It was not a prayer instigated by the fisherman, but by a man who wanted to be set free from judgement. There was confidence in what Peter said to God shown in the request of the man who was in need. That need was parcelled into a prayer, wrapped in grace and presented to God as a gift. It became wholly acceptable to God. The Eternal can respond to an ungodly man if a godly man utters the request.

Expect the answer before you pray
In Acts 9:33, 34 Peter prayed for Aeneas. He expected the answer before he prayed. Simon spoke the answer, and they had no need to wait. The Lord's time was now; He is always in season even out of season. It might be out of reason what you are asking, but it is within God's season of answering prayer. We are not told that he uttered any prayer for the sick. He simply commanded the man in the power of the Holy Ghost, to get up and walk. Peter would not take 'no' for an answer. 'No' would not bring about the man's healing. In the dictionary of prayer there is no place for the word 'no'. 'No' needs converting to 'yes' brought about by intercession. We stoop to pray, and even as we do it is as though the Almighty is saying, 'The answer is not on the way, it is with you already but you are not ready.' Your arm and hand can be too short to reach out and take what the Almighty has given. It is not what we pray, it is what we don't say which are the soft breathings of the heart. He believed that his Lord would effect a change in a man even without one word of asking. He was there to take what was on offer. In the power of the Holy Spirit we simply have to pray over a situation and see it resolved before our eyes. There was a source in the Name of Jesus Christ, a surrender and a supply of those parts that were missing. The Lord is waiting and willing to answer the prayers that do not even go to Him. As we utter them we release a power to re-create and resolve. Just as God 'said' in Genesis, chapter 1, we need to 'say' and 'see' what the Lord will do. We spend too much time asking God for what He has already given. That can be a token of our unbelief. He is waiting for the next

request and we are still grovelling for the first. Let asking be followed by taking. Let praying be followed by doing. God loves you to ask, but He loves it better when you take as He undertakes.

No one can question what the Lord has done

The answer for Simon son of Jonas was in the man being healed. No one could question what the Lord had done. This wasn't an answer to prayer written in a diary of years ago, it was of the moment, up to date and sparkling fresh as fish that had just come out of the water. It is so good to receive a 'yes' from the Eternal, to see answers around you, in you, and because of you. God could get birds to pray, but He reserves them as ravens to carry the answers as they flew to Elijah by Brook Cherith.[16] He doesn't deny you, He wants you to show your intensity of love by praying, talking to Father and taking from Father's bountiful nature. Prayer gave Cephas an extra dimension; it will do the same for you. The answer was an extension of the power of God in human affairs, the Bible calls it Kingdom.

God answered the need of the day, and changed the course of history, fulfilling what He had promised to Abraham. 'In you shall 'all the nations' of the earth be blessed.'[17] Simon went to rest before a meal in Acts 10:9. Peter went to plead, and God answered in such an unusual way. In saying 'grace' before a meal, he found the grace of the Lord. No two prayers are answered in the same way. In our human capacity, we think that the Lord is going to grant an answer in the same way each time, but the Eternal even steps outside of Bible ways when choosing the best way to reply in modern living. With Elijah it is two ravens, while with Elisha he has to dig ditches in a valley, and the Lord filled them with water (2 Kings 3). Jehovah created the snowflake and the grain of sand, and no two are the same. Consider the feathers in the different wings of birds, yet no two are the same. Shall He not reveal His diversity in answers to prayer?

Let prayer be like saying 'grace' before a meal

The prayer offered was grace before the meal. The answer was in the shape of the largest meal Simon had ever seen, many beasts and birds of all sizes coming down from Heaven. You can see the meal before you say grace. Can you see the answer before you pray? God can make birds fly down as well as up to heaven. The size of the table cloth was huge. What Cephas prayed about we are not informed. His asking was not as large as the receiving. God always out-gives us, even as He out-loves. We ask for small things, and He gives large things. We ask for foolish things, and He gives wise things. We ask for hurtful things, and He gives healing.

What Peter saw in a vision is fully explained and understood. God moved from what Peter said to what he saw. Words come to an end, dreams and visions become the order of the day. The word for 'prayer' is *proseuchomal*. It is the most used word for prayer in the New Testament. Prayer should be as common as every day speech. God has given us speech so that we might express ourselves to one another. He has given us prayer that we might express ourselves to Him. We speak to the Lord in His own language when we pray. We intercede in the language of intensity and inspiration resulting in revelation. The heart of the servant of Christ became the prayer book. It was 'need' that created a desire to pray. Asking the Almighty is simply to 'call upon the Name of the Lord'. This must have been a private silent prayer. God, in the Acts of the Apostles, answered one prayer, and the place was shaken. Here the answer is seen in a gentle, soft, floating sheet of material. Those who make the most noise do not receive the largest answers. Those who say the best prayers do not always receive the best answers. Those who pray long prayers do not get fish as an answer that cannot be counted. You know you have a great desire for prayer when it gets into your sleep and dreams, as it did with Simon. The Lord answered in a silent way, as silent as a sheet being lowered, as silent as the folded wing of a bird. The result of that petition went throughout the known world, for the Gentiles were included in God's plan of salvation. It was from the platform of prayer that God brought this new plan to fruition.

Take time to ask, and take time to let the Lord answer

The Eternal did not leave Peter with a prayer or in a prayer. God answered him as he interceded. Take time to ask, but also take time to work out the answer when it is received. Talking became praying as wishing became interceding. 'Freely you have received,' therefore freely give as you pray. The Lord took him a step further and deeper in that He added to his prayer a vision of something new. The small prayer, when God answers, can become many beasts and wild fowl. It can grow into a large sheet that contains everything the Lord has for us. You need a large receptacle to take away what the Lord gives to you. It has to be as large as the veil that Ruth presented to Boaz that was filled with the corn of the harvest.[18] God's 'yes' is always larger than God's 'no'. He grants something larger than our prayer. If you are not strong enough to call upon the Lord, how can He trust you to be strong enough with the communication received? Seeking His face in weakness and trembling we can rise strong and fierce, baptized in the Holy Spirit in prayer. If you want your prayers to mean something as they did to Cephas, get them filled with the Holy Spirit. Let your very words be baptised.

Make instant and earnest prayer

The final recorded answer to prayer for Simon was when he was cast into prison for a second time in Acts 12:3–5. Prayer was made for him. 'Telling' prayers are prayers that are told in pain and suffering as we tell the Lord. We receive nothing if we pray nothing. We can ask 'amiss' – 'badly' or 'diseased'. (James 4:3.) We can, in prayer, be as the person using an instrument that he cannot play: it just becomes a noise. This prayer was specific. For the word 'prayer' the margin of the King James Version of the Bible states: 'instant and earnest prayer was made.' They saw the need, and flew to prayer. They knew of one who was in prison, and they themselves went into captivity, the captivity of prayer that he might be released. They were held in prayer as much as he was held in a prison cell. Neither would be released until asking became receiving, and wondering became answering. It was the sort of effectual fervent prayer that gets results, when the captive is set free. We need to be free in prayer, as free as the answer is when received. It would not have been enough for Peter to come out with the chains still on his hands and feet. It had to be a complete action that set him free. That intercession of the people was the key to the prison, the 'key of promise' that was used. Prayer will fit into that which locks any person into a situation. When there is no way out or through, then pray, and God will make a way. There was an ability among the people to lean on God when they had nothing else to lean on. They could only get into that cell by praying and staying with that prayer until Peter was released. Desperate people use desperate measures. This sort of prayer passes from one to the other.

As we pray, iron gates will yield

Each petition offered did its own work, in that it was part of the answer, as the prayers were offered together. As they pleaded, the gates yielded as if an invisible hand was pushing them open. They prayed, and in doing so took hold of the Hand that rules the universe. Intercession is to let go and let God. It is to have limited knowledge, and pass that knowledge to the One with all knowledge. Seeking lets God work it out, to let the Lord be the Lord. It lets you know that you are child and He is Father. Others felt the benefit of their prayers. When all is dark, there will always be the consolidation and consolation of intercession. It was this asking that led to taking. It was the coming together that bound them to the one in need. It is prayer that identifies us with each other and the needs and requirements of the human spirit. All prayed but there is only one answer, Peter is set free. The freedom of their speech entered into a life that was set free. The answer seems as if God is testifying to the fact that one prayer is no more important than another. Praying together, we become a great force, even an army. Prison walls, doors and bars with chains cannot stand against us. That is why Jesus said, 'Where two or three are gathered together in My Name, there I am in the midst'[19] —central to all.

As the people came together and would not take 'no' for an answer, they were copying the man they were praying for. As he appeared among them being set free, he was the 'yes' and 'amen' to all that had been uttered to the Lord. They had heard Peter pray; now he was in need, and they would do what they had seen him do. What an example! What an encouragement to pray!

Notes

[1] Acts 9:11.
[2] John 21:3.
[3] John 21:6
[4] Matthew 6:44; 15:38.
[5] Matthew 6.
[6] Ephesians 3:8.
[7] 1 Peter 3:3.
[8] Psalm 46:5 'That 'right early'—'before the dawn'.
[9] Acts 3:6.
[10] Isaiah 26:16.
[11] Romans 8:28.
[12] Job 15:4.
[13] Matthew 4:3.
[14] Ephesians 6:18.
[15] Genesis 32:12.
[16] 1 Kings 17:4, 6.
[17] Genesis 17:4
[18] Ruth 3:15.
[19] Matthew 18:20.

Chapter Ten

THE MAN WHO DID
THE RIGHT THING

Life is made up of choices, and what we choose not only makes us what we are going to be, but tells it own story of what we are. When commitment is made, others read what has been written as we respond to the challenge of living for Christ. Without realising it, we become epistles, read of all men.[1] What we are like is written in a language that all can understand, the language of love, the language of commitment to a cause, as plain as the languages were written above the cross of Jesus Christ.[2] Life is ongoing, but it only goes on as we get involved with all that is around us. No credence is given to spectators, only to participators. Peter never secluded himself in a warm, cosy cove near the beach, to dash in and out when it suited him, he did not live in a bubble. He was real, and reality was part of his reason for living. He was and is a man's man.

Make the right choice at the right time

A man is no fool who can make the right choice at the right time, and the brother of Andrew did just that when he said he must obey God rather than men. (Acts 4:19.) As a man he gave that which he could not keep, to keep that which he could not give. One choice was here and now as seen in the Council before which they stood. Obeying God was better, far better than sacrifice. If we sacrifice without obedience we simply offer a bloodless sacrifice to God. It is not acceptable because it has a torn ear, a blind eye or with a torn hoof, it is not the whole truth and nothing but the truth. The part can never be the whole.

Peter was not prepared to walk away from confrontation. He would not walk round it as Israel had walked around Jericho.[3] If he did, the walls would fall down on the seventh day! The way out for him and for you is not over or under, not down and out, it is straight through. He had faced the salt of the sea, the waves and the worries, and he treated everything the same. Nothing was to be avoided, for he believed, as we do, that, 'all things work together for good to them that love God.'[4] It is in weak moments that we see the true strength of the servant of the Lord being made manifest. *Maturity* is being every part a man. If you were to cut Peter into little pieces, every piece would have been a parcel of strength.

With God, two is a majority

Peter with John had to face real trials, as they stood before the Council. They were going to be rejected as a garment tossed on one side. Cephas had to decide whether to accept the status of rejection. Would he go with popular opinion or stand with John? Then it would be two against many, but his consolation was that with God two is a majority.

Decision leads to description, definition and dedication. The *mature* person will always have these qualities. Even when he feels he is poor, he is very rich. The Council in Jerusalem has long gone. We do not even remember the names of the men who tried the two apostles. The *maturity* of the man remains as ancient landmarks which they had been commanded not to remove.[5] Simon made a momentous decision to obey the Lord, and because of that his *maturity* was developed even further until he grew into the fullness of the stature of Jesus Christ.[6] Life is not all pain; there is room for groaning and growth in God. This experience of being thrown into a dungeon was all part of 'growing up in all things' that Simon wrote about in both of his epistles.[7]

Between the challenge and response Christ will meet with you

The alternatives presented to Peter are the very things that make him appealing to us as we study his life. It wasn't easy, for when he made any allegiance it was as if he was launching a boat into a rough sea, not knowing what the outcome would be. Be assured that, when we have to decide, there is a Christ who will meet with us between the challenge and the response. He will be there as the Arbiter and Daysman* who would judge between one party and another in any conflict. Jesus had told them that if they were hauled before the leaders, not to meditate on what they should say, for the Holy Spirit would be with them as their Advocate.[8] Whilst in prison they heard the whisperings of the Lord in the gloom. He used the darkness as a blackboard on which to write the lessons of life. The Battle of the Ages not only rages in the wide world, but finds a place in the hearts of all who believe and want to 'know' the Lord. We get to know the ways of the Lord by being challenged, by making the right assessment in the way we act.

What we commit ourselves to is so important. If water gets below a certain degree, it becomes ice bound. The glory of Cephas is that he never stayed as he was. Everywhere he went was another crucible, always changing as he moved to the next stage of glory. What has been 'lower' in temptation must become higher in fulfilment and obedience.

Christ is between challenge and response

We define most things by what we see, hear, touch, smell and know. Decisions colour our thinking, praying, witnessing, living and dying. We achieve so little because we make the wrong choices, yet we can achieve so much when we make the right choices. New worlds were discovered by Christopher Columbus because there came a day in his voyaging when he put the maps away, and faced those things that had never been charted by man.

Peter was facing the same affronter who falsely accused him of wrong. If Peter had succumbed then, what was to be a glorious life

---

*'Daysman'. See Job 9:33 [KJV] and my book *In Sickness and in Health*, p45.

could have been empty, just been another pebble on the beach instead of pearl quality. We sometimes make a choice, and it is as if we have planted seed in a field. The harvest of that choice is not seen today or tomorrow but in the distant future; it is revealed in a *mature* man or woman. If we are to be disciples of the Lord and Peter, then we must make choices that make us better, not worse. Part of the word 'choose' is 'choice'. That which you choose makes it choice to you.

Decisions are those rare moments that make us noble, to accomplish great things for God. There doesn't seem to be anything special about the decision, but future and eternity are riding on it. Sometimes we say 'no' when we mean 'yes'. On other occasions we say 'yes' when we meant 'no'! Whatever we meant to say, we have to abide by. Decision is part of discipleship. It tells Whom you are serving, and following, even where you are going, and when you will arrive. It tells who is following and who is leading. It marks out those who know where they are going and those who are just going. The word 'choose' comes from a Latin root equivalent to that suggesting 'to taste'.[9] If we are the 'salt of the earth' we must taste as if we are. Our likes and dislikes must be the shadow of our holiness before the Lord. We have 'tasted of the world to come', and based on that we make our choices. Simon must choose the lesser or the greater; it was a matter of choosing light or darkness.

The voice of the Lord needs to be heard and understood
In Acts 4:19, 20, Peter and John were called before the Council, and given the advice of the religious. Accept that, and become as trapped as the Council were in their ceremonies! This advice was measured to keep them quiet, to stop the move of the Spirit of God. Peter had to make a choice whether to listen to human voices or to be in tune with what the Spirit of God was saying to the Church. If we don't know what the Lord is saying, then the best thing is to wait and see. The man who waits will see, and when the scales fall from his eyes he will have understanding clearer than daylight. Give one ear to the human voice and four ears, the inner and the outer, to what the Lord is saying. In one of the Psalms, when speaking of Jesus it says 'My ear you have digged.'[10] The dirt and the wax need removing so

that we hear clearly and act decisively. We have not heard when the Almighty has spoken because we have not listened. Listening ears become 'tingling ears'[11] —'tingling ears' that quiver as an arrow in flight because they have heard truth, and know they have a target in life. Some people 'tingle' with fear as chattering teeth do when they are cold and fearful.

There needs to be a little bit of Samuel in all of us. His name means 'heard of the Lord'. Even the name Simon, when given to Peter, suggests 'hearing'. That is why Jesus sometimes refers to Peter as Simon when He wants him to give all his attention to what is being said and taught. (John 21:15,16,17.) Jesus said, 'They that have ears should use them.'[12]

The young fisherman knew the will of God and as a *mature* person he made the right decision in Acts 4:19, 20 when he said, 'Whether it be right in the sight of God to hearken unto you more than unto God, you judge. For we cannot but speak the things which we have seen and heard.' It is *maturity* that recognises all we hear and say, or wherever we go, is in the sight of God. Cephas never dealt with the speculative, it was the spectacular. His was not a 'cunningly devised fable,' but a sure word of prophecy, seen and heard.[13]

Your choice must not be a 'stab in the dark'

We must never be as Jonah, who tried to run away thinking that the presence of God was just in one location. That Presence was with the Galilean long after the Council had disbanded. What Cephas was lived on in that Presence, because it was 'God before whom I walk'. 'You God see me' is the theology of Abraham and Peter. Not only had they heard the teachings of Jesus, they had seen that teaching in action, and their decision to follow God's way rather than man's was based on the heart knowledge of what the Lord had caused them to see and hear.

There comes a moment in the affairs of men when we are called to choose. That choice will take us north, south, east or west. Even Judas went to his 'own place' by choice.[14] Cephas chose to do what he considered to be the right thing, but it had also to be the righteous thing. This was not a whistle into the wind, or a guess, he had seen God at work, and he wanted to follow Christ who is the Way all the way from Calvary to Heaven with hell in between, if that was demanded. The fire received at Pentecost in the shape of a tongue must now become their tongue and illuminate their way. God never leaves or leads us into the dark when we make His will our will. This was no easy option; it 'flew in the face' of advice from spineless and spiteful men. They were not only onto a sure thing, they did that which was worthy, true and 'noble' (used to describe an obsolete gold coin).

In doing this the fisherman revealed the *maturity* that had been developed in him, changing him from a fisherman into a rock which could be trusted to remain the same whether the tide was in or out. No more shifting sands, he had a soul and spirit that was determined to follow the Lord.

Tongues of fire and rushing wind is not maturity

The tongues and fire of Acts chapter 2 never suddenly produced *maturity* in Peter. Throughout the Acts of the Apostles the thing he suffered and saw enlarged him in every aspect. There is an element of faithfulness in everything he does. The last orders he received from the Master always received priority over everything else.

When we hear the voice of the Lord and respond, all other voices are a mere blowing of the wind. That which is said or suggested by Satan has no 'part or lot' in the life of the child of God. The right decisions made by Simon would lead to righteousness, not ruin. To decide for right is promotion not demotion. You might be 'put down' but only until you rise above all things and all things are 'under your feet' as they are under Christ's.[15] Make yesterday's failures the carpet you walk on today; let each broken thread be woven into a wonderful pattern of holiness. Let the past be past, and the future beckon you on into greater exploits.

When all becomes stagnant or against you, as it seemed to Simon in a prison cell, God turns again the captivity of Zion, and we flow again like the streams in the south. There was nothing prodigal about the way in which Simon lived. He would never become the twin to doubting Thomas, or brother of Demas who loved this present world more than the voice of God. As that voice spoke to Peter, he was prepared to live as an echo because it was the Lord's voice. He realised that same voice had marshalled trees, flowers, rocks and seas, sand and scenery together when it had sounded in the Beginning.[16] God had been at work in his life arranging it for His pleasure. He became part of every miracle and every moment was sacred because it produced the sacrifice of *maturity*.

You stay with what you believe

To believe is to 'stay with' what you accept. It is the figure of the man walking along the furrow behind the plough pulled by the oxen. This is a true definition of discipleship that brings rare qualities to every quarter. We take what was ours and present it to Him, even as Simon left his fishing boats, tackle and nets. What in a wayward life has been 'pearls before swine' become pearls fit for the Master's use. The son of Jonas became jewel quality. You can take your stand by what you say. 'Here I stand, I can do no other,' said Martin Luther during the Reformation. That love for the Lord will climb every mountain; cross every desert, ford every stream. It will not leave you with clouds forming but with a rainbow as a token of His covenant. Adventure means A.D. venture, after His death A.D., a venture after the resurrection of Jesus. If all Bibles were destroyed, live your life so that men would still enjoy the revelation of God as seen in you. Become a page of the Holy Book. When one missionary went to an unknown tribe and preached Jesus to the people, they said, 'We know the Man you are speaking of, He lives with another tribe.' And they introduced him to another missionary who was working in a different area! Simon was prepared to 'walk the talk' and 'say the sentence' received from the Almighty.

When we do that which is defined as right we are never on trial. It wasn't Peter or John pleading for their lives. They had such a quality of life that no man could take it from them. It will never die, because the quality of it is God's nature, and the quantity of it is Eternal. Pass judgment on it but you can never sentence it to death. Push it deeply into the deepest sea, as where Peter began to sink as he stepped out of the boat,[17] but you will never drown it. Many floods cannot destroy it. That which is in the believer's heart is more than a finger drawing in the sand. They became the interrogators, inviting the Council to judge what had been decided. The Council was left thinking about all that had been said, that would reverberate in their conscience for many days because it had the 'ring of truth'. The authorities knew they were 'untutored and ignorant men,' yet they listened. In his *maturity* Cephas had the inner teachings of the Spirit of God. The fire he had received was burning convictions into his spirit. If you gaze into an open fire you will see a pattern formed among the red hot coals.

It is worth listening to a committed person

With Peter there was a deeper learning and teaching. The Spirit of God had entered where no human voice might go. It was intellectual but is also inspirational and inwrought, a real depth in what had happened to the one in training. Commitment, and what the committed person has to say, is always worth listening to. Their words become a challenge to all. Some can speak words of silk when there is sourness in their soul. That which is born out of experience and not education will count for everything. There was a call by these saints to take up Arms as found in the Gifts of the Holy Spirit.[18] There was a sharp edge as they spoke to the men who had gathered. What the Council said was just gabble; what the disciples said was clear and concise, words on which you could hang eternity.

Peter was not trying to lead anyone 'up the garden path', he was seeking to lead them to the Tree of Life, to the Paradise of God. Cephas did not seek to bring anything to an abrupt halt, he simply made a way to continue these things which had already begun in Acts 1:1. It was part of all that Jesus began to do and to teach. Note 'doing' is placed before 'teaching'. It is what Simon said that put the Lord back into His rightful place. It was as though Simon was saying, 'You have to take notice of what the Eternal has to say.' It has to be listened to and 'worked out with fear and trembling'. It must not be left, but must be taken hold of, because your eternal welfare depends on it. What was said told all those listening whose side these prisoners were on. They stood where they could hear His voice, and see His face. They were true evangelists, true messengers, and each one a 'gospel', sent from the scene of the battle bearing 'good news'. No trumpet blower going before Nero or Caesar had ever heralded more loud or pure notes than these two who were going before the King of kings.

The right thing was the real thing presented by Peter. He could say 'What I do now is a greater thing than I have ever done before.' The Lord will present us also with choices that become opportunities to influence because we are well trained enough to be trusted in all circumstances. It would have been a catastrophe of cataclysmic proportions if Peter had wobbled at the decisive moment. He did not bend or blow in the wind as a leaf loose from a branch. Having done all, he stood, acquitting himself as a man with a future, reaching forward to his destiny. Simon knew the old adage 'When in Rome do as the Romans do.' Being in Jerusalem he did what Christians should do: the right thing, the holy and the only thing, the hallmark for all who will follow Jesus. When you have tried your best and do not know what to do or where to go, simply be the man or woman of God. Let others know what your convictions are. Do not be 'mealy mouthed' or 'loud mouthed' but have a silver tongue when telling of the wonders of your God and King. When you have told all you know, you still will not have touched the edge of infinity.

Manhood must be matured into sainthood
In life, womanhood and manhood has to be changed into sainthood and servanthood. You are what the Lord has created you to be. Every part of creation is dressed in its full glory when it does what it has been created to do, whether that is to fly from branch to branch, as a bird, or as a fly, from wall to wall. The twinkling star is never more glorious than when it twinkles in the night sky. It needs the blackness of night before it is appreciated; even Peter and John required opposition. All these rare qualities were in the son of Jonas as he stood before his persecutors, not as one under authority, but as one who had authority from above.

In the Acts of the Apostles it is recorded eight times that they were 'bold', which originally meant that they stuck out like a piece of rock.[19] They had 'free utterance' of speech. The son of Jonas did not say things simply for effect. What he did say had tremendous depth and conviction. Long after the Sanhedrin had gone, the words of this disciple would haunt them. Here was a man prepared to do what they could never do. They were strong and brave in a crowd. Peter stood with John and faced the onslaught of the enemy. Here is the strength of unity in *maturity* displayed. They were not afraid. They were assured; awake to the opportunities opening before them.

The only 'hellish' thing about truth is the hell it seeks to warn us of

All the Council could say had to come within the power of tradition. They had rigid guidelines. Simon spoke as the Holy Spirit gave inspiration. These men were accused of disturbing the peace. When they stoned Stephen, they saw his face as the face of an angel.[20] You cannot disturb a peace which does not exist; the crowd of oppressors knew nothing of the peace of God. Peter and John were bringing in a new way of life. The synagogue was losing some of its adherents. These men were turning the world upside down, and must be stopped. Threatening will never bind truth. Truth can never be cast into 'outer darkness'. The only 'hellish' thing about truth is the hell it seeks to warn us against. The young fisherman was prepared to stand out and be different.

Sometimes that boldness was in the Holy Ghost, at other times it was when their prayer for boldness was answered. Peter became as bold as a lion because he obeyed the Lord. Obey the Lord and do what you want! God turned the situation to Simon's favour. When they did the right thing the opposition became the lion whose mouth God had shut tight. There is a confidence when we have not only thought or said but also when we have done the right thing. You have proved that the power of God is greater in you than that within the world.[21] What men say will pass away, but what the Almighty has said will last for ever. It is a promise; it is as unchanging as the character of the Lord. 'Heaven and earth may pass away but My word shall endure forever.'

Don't add to or take away from what the Lord is saying

To hear and know what the Eternal has said allows you to walk away from situations, to keep yourself unspotted from the world. He is a happy person that knows what the Lord has said, who stops where the Lord stopped. There is no Revelation chapter 23 for the believer. We sometimes add to the Scriptures or take away from them, using our own words to supplement what we think requires something extra. That which has been added by you can become the fly in the ointment that makes the whole thing smell. We can use the 'bits' and 'pieces', added together they lead us into 'bits and pieces' instead of the whole. Walk in the light, talk in the light, as He is the Light. When the Council had said all they had to say, that was the end. We have a Lord who speaks to us every day, so that in our choices we have words of comfort, command and something to centre our hearts on. He always concludes with amen, meaning that is not the end, just a part of what He has to say. When Holy Writ is rolled up, the Voice of the Master is not silenced. When angry men speak we wait for the end with pleasure. When the Eternal speaks we listen with bated breath for more, because His words are sweet to our taste. The crowd will always have 'itching ears' as they wait for what they want to hear. We say to Jesus, 'Master say on.'[22] When it was reported what the Lord was doing in the Acts of the Apostles, they said, 'If you have any word from the Lord tell us what it is?'[23] All they did before this Council was to repeat the words of Jesus.

When we know what the Eternal has said, we can walk tall. The very first temptation was in the words, 'has God said?'[24] What the Council said to the Galilean seemed a foreign language without an interpreter. The Christian walked away; he was going somewhere while they were going nowhere. What Cephas had in God expressed continually the nature of the Eternal in life.

You hold the key to your situation

There was a conviction about the way Simon son of Jonas lived. He knew that whatever the choices, whatever the temptation, and however loud the voices were clamouring for attention, he had to do the right thing. The men they stood before would not appreciate what he did. These men did not hold the keys to the prison cell. The disciples held all the keys. One such key was the key of life; the Master's key was that *maturity.*

The whole church rejoiced when the disciples returned to tell their story. Added to what they already believed and had received was the ability of the Almighty to contain the religious as well as the heathen. In the Old Testament the accusation had been, 'Your God is a god of the valleys but not of the mountains', thereby limiting the power of God. The Lord was on the move into every segment of society.

Peter might not have seen much happen as he walked away from the Council. It was probably a lonely walk, but it was a walk with God. He walked from the crowd to the Church with his companion. They had something to tell, to share. It was a new thing, a new beginning that the Eternal had done. They reported a miracle of deliverance, and that was worth listening to. These were not old rags and bones thrown together as when some speak, this was the description of the miraculous. What they reported was not 'off the cuff' it was 'out of' their character. Have you every thought how you would describe a miracle to someone who had never seen one? Those gathered as the church were not with John and Peter when they came before the Council, so they needed a full explanation. There were many hallelujahs! Praise the Lord! Amen! As Peter proclaimed what the Sovereign Lord had done. Was there ever a report listened to with such intensity? Were words ever spoken as important as these? Infant words of a new born child as they learned to walk with God.

Peter walked knowing he was doing the right thing. He did not go with the crowd; he dared to stand against the popular vote of the day. While all were saying one thing, in obedience to the Lord he was doing something completely different. The choice had been made, and it was his right choices that made him the man he was. *Maturity* is a matter of choices that distinguish us from others. Peter was no floating log of wood or loose oar from a boat. His choices turned a fisherman into a disciple and a disciple into an apostle, and in it all we see the nature of Christ in the *maturity* of the man.

Decide and dare to do the right thing

It was this decision to do the right thing that created a servant heart in the fisherman. He could say, 'Whose I am and whom I serve.' It is serving God with obedience before we serve others. It is to love the Lord your God with all your heart, and to love your neighbour as yourself. There was something quite selfless in the decision of this young man, as he mirrored the miraculous. As we obey the Lord we obey others. What I am to the Lord I am to the I AM. What you are to the Eternal you are to yourself and others. If you are true to Him you will be true to others and true to yourself. You will never be bigger or greater than when kneeling before God. As you kneel in prayer that is as large as you really are. You are the measure of your prayers. If you want to see how important you are, then add up the answers to your prayers. What is in the parcel is always worth more than the string that binds the contents together. You are more important than your prayers. The stand you take and the witness you offer as the prayers you pray become the 'initial evidence' of *maturity*.

When God sends a test, or places you in a trial, it is a matter of choosing and going further with the Lord. It can mean choosing that which is wrong as Eve did when choosing forbidden fruit; the result was sin and a Fall. Peter could have been the 'hail fellow well met!' Friends with all at the expense of his friendship with the One he served. There was no running with the hounds and the hare. He was never one thing to one, another to another. He knew that the Jehovah of the Old Covenant hated mixtures. If you are going to serve whatever you serve, then serve it well. Whatever you are, don't just be 'good', be 'great'. Whatever your hand finds to do, do it with all your might and mind. Peter did not go on one leg as one injured in a battle, or in some half-hearted manner. He meant what he said and said what he meant. *Maturity* is such wherever we are, whether the sun shines or not it remains the same yesterday, today, tomorrow, just as Jesus portrayed in the Book of Hebrews 13:8.

To hear the voice of God is manna

There is no situation in life or death that we should give credence to more than the revelation given to us by the Lord. We should go on in its power for many days, as Elijah did when he was fed by an angel. To hear and know the voice of God is manna indeed. Those around you must not be allowed to dictate you out of the will of God. Peter would not be 'shouted down' or 'put down'. Prominence comes through perseverance, not popularity. The crowd must not be allowed to become your spokesperson. Nothing must stop your ears as the crowd stopped their ears when Stephen called upon the Lord to receive his spirit.[25] It was obedience before sacrifice. He was going to obey even if he was the sacrifice. The flames get hot when we are called upon to make the supreme sacrifice. As we lay on the altar that which is in our lives, Christ-like we offer to God what Jesus offered on the Cross, which was true likeness to the nature of God.

Peter and John were being commanded not to speak in the Name of Jesus. The Council wanted them to be empty echoes instead of those with authority. This was to be their hour of glory and victory, and should they turn on one side as those wounded in battle? They would never be as their forefather Ephraim who turned back in the day of battle as a warped bow.[26] As these two disciples followed Jesus, they were able to make life changing decisions that led them into future miracles and testimony. This was but the start of the beginning, it was not the end, not even the beginning of the end. They, let loose, were presented with an open door.

Today you can demonstrate your maturity
It might seem as if Peter had been reading Psalm 23 when he answered the authorities, 'He leads me in the paths of righteousness for His Name's sake.' Those are the paths that lead to Heaven, part of the ongoing way. I am going the way of His Name, not the 'way of all flesh'. Whether it is of shame or of being shunned, I must go that way for there is no other way. There will never be a better day than this day to demonstrate your *maturity* as you make known the glory of the Lord. Simon took the right path leading to the right place with the right motives in his heart. If God calls you to walk an uneven path full of rocks and stones, He will provide you with the right shoes. If you come to a swollen river, you will find that you can walk over it, because the footprints of Jesus are there after He had walked on water.

This was not the time for Simon son of Jonas to walk on water. That would not have demonstrated the will of God. It is quite amazing how many are ready to do anything but the right thing. Cephas must walk the path of the just, shining like a light until that Perfect Day. Things are right in your heart and around you when every beat of your heart beats triumphantly, as loud as a drum, when every step is a step in the right direction, because the Lord's directions are always right. If you choose your own way, and there were those in the Acts of the Apostles who did, it will lead you into ever decreasing circles until that circle becomes so small it is simply a full stop. It is by your words that you are condemned, yes, but it is also by your words and works that you are acquitted! Simon was simply demonstrating the teaching of the master: 'That which had been declared to you in secret (even in a prison cell) declare from the housetops' —let it be utterly known and shown from the highest vantage point.

Here was God's man prepared to take a stand on the Word of God. Miraculous men operate in the miraculous. This thing was not done in a quiet corner, it was done before many witnesses. There was nothing 'shy' about the young Galilean. The lovely thing about *the man who did the right thing* is that he has left an example as mentioned in 1Peter 2:21, suggesting the first letters of the alphabet, and we make up the rest of the words. This example – the first line that we copy when learning to write – leads us through the wilderness up the side of mountain, even through the 'Slough of Despond'.[27] When looking for an example, look no further. Open your Bible, turn to these pages, and you will read it written there *the man who did the right thing.* 'Go and do the same!'

Notes
[1] 2 Corinthians 3:1, 2.
[2] John 19:20.
[3] Joshua 6.
[4] Romans 8:28.
[5] Proverbs 22:28.
[6] Ephesians 4:13.
[7] 1 Peter 2:2. 2 Peter 3:18.

8 Luke 21:14.

9 See Chamber's 16th Century dictionary.

10 Psalm 40:6.

11 1 Samuel 3:11. See Dr. James Strong Exhaustive Concordance.

12 Luke 8:8.

13 2 Peter 1:16.

14 Acts 1:16–20.

15 Ephesians 1:22.

16 Genesis 1.

17 Matthew 14:30.

18 1 Corinthians 12 and 14.

19 Acts 9:27,29; 13:46; 14:3; 18:26; 19:8.

20 Acts 6:15.

21 1 John 4:4.

22 Luke 7:40.

23 Acts 13:15.

24 Genesis 3:1.

25 Acts 7:59.

26 Psalm 78:9.

27 Mentioned by John Bunyan in 'Pilgrim's Progress'.

Chapter Eleven

THE MAN AND THE
COMPANY HE KEPT

When Simon Peter the son of Jonas was a child, as all children do, he related to the things around him such as boats, fish, the sea and the call of the birds. These things contained happy memories for him. Fishermen were numbered among his friends. He spent days, months and years with them talking, eating, and sleeping the sea and fishing boats. They possessed what possessed him. The sea with its storms, shoals of fish, boats, nets, sand and shore were his daily companions. Memory Lane to Peter the fisherman was a visit to the open sea.

The natural never meets the needs of the spiritual
One sure thing about life is that whatever organisation we belong to, be it club, pub, or social service, it lacks something. There were times when this young fisherman's heart was as empty as a beached boat, or a shell without a pearl. Just as a glass of cold water from the tap lacks salt, so did his living without Jesus Christ. We also can be a part of many things, but not one of those things can fully satisfy the spiritual longing within.

Being a fisherman, Cephas knew all about empty fishing vessels and empty nets. The waters can be deep but the boat empty. That is why Simon needed something more. Cephas knew the difference between the pebble and the pearl. He found what was missing when he was found by Jesus Christ.[1] Before that moment he was lost. When

Jesus rose from the dead, this young Galilean fisherman entered into fellowship with the 'company' of people he went to on his release from prison. They were the other half of his heart, his heartbeat. In times of need and stress it is good to go to those who will be a physician. Peter's friends did not utter empty words of comfort. He was lost without them, they were lost without him. He had what they needed, and they had what was necessary to him.

The initial twelve followers of Christ were a great company of people. There was Judas with the 'bag'. There was Thomas with no 'belief'. Then, there was Andrew the 'bridge builder'. Then there was Philip the 'bringer to Christ'. There was James and John who wanted to 'burn' people with fire. John was transformed into the 'beloved'. Added to this list was Simon Peter, the 'brusque' fisherman. These became the materials for the Carpenter of Galilee.

The social never meets the need of the spiritual

There is an aspect to life that is more than social, that is the spiritual. There are people who have so much and they possess so little because there is no spiritual aspect in their lives and living. There was a deep longing within Peter for something deeper than a man, and his boat or the sea. Even this scholar of the sea knew that there were different depths to any stretch of water. Was there something more to life? Were there deeper associations that he had never entered into? The answer was yes. Fish and a boat could not reciprocate the desire that was in this young fisherman's heart. Peter could and did mend a net, but that net could not speak to him or become a true partner in life, because it was a tool, an inanimate object. He needed the Church for the deepening of his spiritual life. As the face of a friend is like 'iron sharpening iron'[2] so we need each other. He needed a place to grow where he could be challenged. There was a depth in his heart that the deepest sea could never meet, longings within him that the finest catch of fish could not match. He needed the local congregation and they needed him. When he was on the sea, it was one way sailing, but he needed something that would be two way. We may think that the placid sea is best for a fisherman, but he needs strong waves, storms and currents, the cross-winds the rocks and reefs. It was all one way in Peter and what he could do for the nets in mending them, what he could do for the boat in repairing or painting it. He badly needed something to become part of him, the other half.

The company you keep will declare your convictions

The 'company' that he was part of, under God, would become the very tool that would produce *maturity* in him. There is nothing like friendship to find you out! There were certain things in his life that his mum or dad could never deal with. When we don't let others deal with our faults and failings, the Lord performs His rich renewal rectification. Even brother Andrew lacked when it came to developing Simon in the spiritual realm. All he had passed through had not met the need and produced the man. It was not just one great thing that produced *maturity* in a life, no angel visitation or portent in the sky. It was almost like grains of sand being turned into diamonds and precious things in his life, as imperceptible as the tide going out or coming in little by little. He would never be a 'nine day wonder', but he would be a person produced by the workings of the Spirit, for those workings are given for the profit of all.[3] One of the greatest miracles in the New Testament is the changing of the life of Cephas.

Peter gives hope to everyone desiring to see *maturity* develop in their life. It did not happen suddenly in the Gospels. In Acts 2:2 it states, 'Suddenly' there came a sound from Heaven as of a mighty rushing wind', but it did not mean that Peter was 'suddenly' different! God's 'suddenlys' sometimes take twenty or thirty years. The flimsy and the ephemeral can happen in a moment; *maturity* takes a little longer.

Every church has rainbow colours in characters

Throughout the Gospels and the Acts of the Apostles, if you look carefully you will see a kaleidoscope of happenings in the colours of Peter's life, black, white, red, yellow, pink, a whole rainbow of covenant is being formed. There are exciting moments, and hours of despair. There are prison moments and there are pulpit moments, pain, poverty, purity and passion. All are working together for good, and emerging we see the new man in Cephas. Not Peter the brother of Andrew or Peter the Galilean, but Peter the Christian.

As Simon was drawn to Jesus Christ, he was introduced into a deeper fellowship. That would take him to all un-gauged depths! It would take the 'sea of His forgetfulness' to achieve it. When the disciples first met Jesus, they asked where He dwelt.[4] They followed Him, and spent the day with Him. That was the beginning of the fellowship that would result in Peter being in the church. There was a groaning within that could only be satisfied by the glory of God. That deeper fellowship found in the church was defined as 'walking in the light as He is in the light'.[5] The apostle Paul speaks of 'coming together' when they met as a church,[6] as if different parts of the Body had been in different locations. Simon became part of those working, standing, staying, praying, and suffering together.

Christian fellowship is deeper than human relationship

Simon desired a new depth, deeper than the measure of a man's mind, and he found it in the birth of the church. He began to mix with a Brotherhood deeper than that enjoyed by Andrew and himself, as a brother. They were fond of each other, but in the church this had to be multiplied. The bond in the church can be greater than the bond of flesh and blood. In the New Testament, believers are referred to as brothers and sisters.[7] The association between Andrew and Peter had been built on 'family ties'. This new association was built on love, far more than just a business partnership. For too long Peter had walked along the shore line, then Jesus told him to cast his nets into the deep.[8] When he did so, the nets were so full he required assistance from others. Life had been as a long walk on the beach searching for that pearl of great price. The time had come to begin stepping right into these new depths of experience.

There is so much in the church for us as we *mature* with this man. Make him your brother! Think of the church as he thought of it, defending it, loving it, caring for it, willing to serve it as if it was Christ, and it is Christ! 'Inasmuch as you do this for one of these you do it unto Me.'[9] You will not destroy it as Paul did when he tore it as a wild boar tears trees apart.[10]

You have no need to go to church to be a Christian
There are those who will tell you 'You have no need to 'go' to church to 'be' a Christian. The premise is all wrong. You do not go to church 'to be' a Christian. You go to church because 'you are' a Christian. You take your Christianity with you. You do not find it or leave it in the church. You cannot pick up or put down *maturity* like a song sheet. Peter did not go to this local church to 'get' but to 'give'. He came 'not to be ministered unto but to minister.' It wasn't what he could take out of it but what he could put into it. Whatever a person thinks of the church, always remember that 'Jesus loved the church and gave Himself for it.'[11] With all its spots, wrinkles and wrangles, He loved it, He does love it and He will love it for all eternity. We should love one another as Christ loved the church, and 'gave Himself for it.'

There had to be much shaping and guiding before Simon fitted into this community of believers, some shaping before there could be sharing. When you fit a new piece into machinery, if it has not been fully tested, it will not take the strain but will succumb to the pressures put upon it. The Carpenter of Nazareth had to perform His best work, and reveal the magnificence of His skills, in the life of the growing apostle, even as Bezaleel (shadow of God) did in the Old Testament.[12]

You are the greatest miracle the church will ever see
God performed a great miracle through Simon in Acts chapter 10. The extent of that miracle reached into the heart of the man who saw a vision. The greater miracle was that Cephas saw himself made a lively stone in this Building called the church. When he was released he took his liberty into the church, as recorded in Acts 4:23, 'Being let go they went to their own company.' The Galilean youth set free was as a trapped air bubble rising to the top of the water. It will go to that which attracts it. Like will migrate with like. Parts of the puzzle will fit together.

The church's unity is its strength
Those of the same heart and mind will stand, work, witness and win together. Small fibres are not strong, but when woven together they

will clasp each other as lovers. Nothing will separate them. The Book of Ecclesiastes states that, 'Two are better than one'.[13] The writer of the Ephesian epistle reminds believers that the 'work of the ministry' is for the 'perfecting' of the saints.[14] In the word 'perfecting' we see a joint being put back into place. As a Body we are joint to joint, so that we can have movement and express love. To be part of the church is to be a joint that has been put back where it belongs. It is lower leg and upper leg working together as a person walks to their destiny. They did not look for an excuse to stay away from church; they sought an excuse to be there. A dry single stick is easily broken, but try breaking a bundle of twigs, the bundle will break you! Its strength is in its unity, its oneness in its closeness. Psalm 133:1 says, 'Behold, how good and pleasant it is for brethren to dwell together in 'unity'.' The word 'unity' describes corn blowing back and forth in a strong wind. Bend one stalk and you bend every stalk. They stand or fall together. Each stalk provides a shelter from the strongest impact of the wind.

Become a help, and not an hindrance in the church

Peter and John went from prison to pulpit, from chains to crowns, from the darkness to light. The emptiness and the darkness in the prison did not become part of them. We, like the *maturing* son of Jonas, can walk through a situation of hurt and pain without carrying that pain because we have *matured.* The chains or the stocks were not taken to the church to be moaned over. Peter and John took with them to the church those things that would minister grace to the listeners. The depth they experienced became part of them. Peter was a true 'help', one of the ministry gifts of 1 Corinthians 12:28 describing 'frapping' tied around a ship to strengthen it during a storm. He carried with him healing, not only in miracles but through the words he spoke as he reported to the early church. He took grace with hope from the prison to the people. Let me ask you a question. When you rise to speak, do people listen with great intent, with as much intent as troops listening to final orders before going into a battle? There was nothing negative about their approach. Simon's sayings were music to the soul and healing balm to hearts that had been hurt.

Fellowship can bathe wounds and heal pain

They went where there was a congregation of believers. In the darkness and dreariness of the prison cell, their congregation had been rats, rags, and ruffians for cell mates. They spoke now to Christians who appreciated what was said and readily agreed. This wasn't pouring oil on troubled waters; it was oil coming together with oil under the anointing of the Spirit. They met as those who had been absent for a long time —a prison sentence! What they had lacked in the dungeon they found in each other as they met. Light and flower meet together in the radiance of the sun. Here was light given by every believer who was walking in the light. The bread and water was not sparse, it was found in Jesus the Bread of Life and the flowing, thirst quenching water of the Holy Spirit.

Any bruising and wounds were nullified by the blessings they received. Aches and pains lost the ability to torment as they spoke. There was a word of encouragement; the faint heart received new strength. Those who could not continue, after listening to Simon felt they could go on forever, could reach the other side. Valley, mountain and broad stream became easy to conquer. You can do it when two conquerors are with you. If you listen to a modern mountaineer, you feel that you can climb every mountain, and you practise by climbing small furrows. Inspiration was imparted. It was as if the Red Sea and the River Jordan opened up before them again. What Peter and John had to say was like the stones that Israel took out of the River Jordan when God parted it, as a testimony to help future generations.[15] The weak said they were strong. As they gave so they received. These believers waited as young birds with open beaks ready to be fed, ready to be taken on to the next stage in their development.

Being part of a church makes the church part of you

This was a praying, witnessing, welcoming, Pentecostal company, a company with conviction and a common cause. These were the 'Good Companions'. They spoke with one voice. They prayed as one prayer. They witnessed as one man. These were true 'bricks'. They were so close you could not tell where one commenced and another concluded. The word 'company' can suggest a 'circle'. They were not years or seats apart, but were in each other's heart. They carried the cares and woes of one another with them. Here was the pastoral heart of Peter on full display. Christ was their Head; they were His feet, hands, lips, heart and voice. When they sang, it was with one voice, the voice of God's child crying to the Father. They were as those planted and growing to produce fruit. 'The gathering of the people shall be unto Him.'[16] They gathered as 'one' because they were gathering together to One—Jesus Christ.

The church is a friendship with fellowship, a community, caring, defined as one's own in the word 'company'. Every church should produce a feeling of belonging. What is mine is yours, and what is yours is mine. It is like wedding vows, 'For better for worse until death do us part.' They had all things in 'common'. The English word 'common' has two roots, one meaning 'together,' the other means 'serving,' 'obliging'. Coca Cola the American drinks firm has a mission statement which says they want to be only an 'arms length away from the thirsty'. 'Company' is defined as 'coming together'. Laugh, weep, cry, sing, dance, worship, pray and witness together. All this tells its own story of *maturity*. Peter needed the church as much as he needed Christ. One is the tool of the other.

The gates of hell shall not prevail against the church

Simon Peter did not rob others of their *maturity*. He took with him what he was, and used it to glorify the Lord. He had been promised fish but he received *maturity*. Arriving at the church he had something to give that was worth receiving. He had been in the depths of the sea, and in the depths of a prison. He had something that was worth listening to, because he had been in prison with Jesus. Peter, a prisoner of Jesus Christ. The title of his message could have been: 'How Jesus operates in a prison'. When all self-interest is lost we stand and stay together for ever. There were 'men and brethren' along with the women who met together. Just as the boards in the Old Testament Tabernacle had a gold rod running right through them,[17] these believers had something in their hearts that was common to all of them. It is our common aspects that make us so appealing. It is that Christ-likeness that corresponds to what is in the life of another.

As one stood they all stood. It was to this 'company' that Peter and John reported as those sent into the Promised Land and came back with a 'good' report.

The church produces maturity in its members

The church does not exist for itself but for those outside. As they went home, that was when their mission field opened up before them. Just as Jesus went from the synagogue to heal the mother-in-law of Simon Peter, so we should return in the 'power of the Spirit'.[18] All the teaching had to be lived out in the towns and the villages. The church was the school and learning centre. Worship was not for them, it was meant to glorify God. The church does not exist to give you good feelings, but to convict about sin. Heaven wobbles when it hears deep-dyed sinners coming into a church proclaiming how much they enjoyed being told of their condition. One of the old laws of Wales was that every home should have two pathways, one to the well and the other to the church.

God will put those alongside who are of the same nature and have the same vision. Men and women of supreme quality. They did things 'for' and 'to' each other that were so helpful. They ministered to one another in *maturity* as if that 'other person' was Jesus Christ resurrected from the dead. A good church produces *maturity* in its members.

God 'added' to the church.[19] He laid others 'alongside' to share the burden even as the disciples had shared the miracle of loaves and fishes. Simon Peter was one of those burden bearers. We are *mature* indeed if we have developed enough to share another's burdens. If we have been buried with Him in baptism, we have been laid alongside in the same grave. If we share the same war, the same battle and death, surely we should be willing to share the same life. We 'reign in life with Him.' They were laid alongside as sheaves of corn brought into the barn after a bumper harvest. You do something that enlarges them 'provoking others to love and good works'.

Don't 'under achieve', be more than what you are

The church will only be as big as you are. It says in one scripture that they had John Mark as their servant —under rower.[20] He was one among many rowing the boat in the same direction. The 'under rower' was a trainee. He had to take that position before taking hold of one of the main oars. Peter had been such an 'under rower', now he was expected to use his promotion for the pleasure of others. Promotion to him meant *maturity*. One Roman leader was taken captive by pirates. On the second day he was directing the crew; on the third day he was made captain of the vessel!

God has 'added' to the church, and has put many different people alongside you. Apart we are nothing, together we are everything. This was true when describing the work of the fishing nets made up of small meshes. They were there to help and not to hinder. The Lord will increase the church as faith increases. When we ask the Eternal to 'increase our faith' we hardly realise we are asking that the church should be increased daily. Increase of faith is required, not to believe for miracles, but to have something extra when dealing with fellow believers. Increase me so that I can increase them. The depths of faith I go into, I will also help them into. These were able to help others because they had entered into *maturity*.

The church should be a working model of Jesus Christ

The Church has been defined as a 'place for rescued souls'. We are brought to that area when we have been saved from the sea to give us the breath of life that Elohim breathed into Adam.[21] We are tired and weary, and it is here we receive our 'second wind' as Pentecost visits us again. Tired and as those 'weary and heavy laden', we receive 'times of refreshing from the presence of the Lord'. That 'refreshing' wind blows us back on course. We have been like those in Hebrews 2:1 who had let things 'slip' —drift as a boat not secured. There are times when we all need to 'breathe again'. All these ministries were in the church that Peter was part of, because it was part of him. If every one in the church is your brother, sister, it will be easy to treat them as your twin.

Matthew Henry, when writing about the church, said, 'How lovely is the sanctuary in the eyes of those who are sanctified.' *Maturity* is sanctification in all that we do. It is to act as if we are in the Acts of the Apostles. Peter was an 'act' of an apostle in his *maturity*. There will always be a number of ways to spread the light of your *maturity*. By candle, electric light bulb, through fire or reflected through a mirror. How great is the church if you are great? It will never be any greater than you; it was no greater than Peter. How helpful it is if you are helpful, because it is a reflection of what you are. It was a reflection of Cephas the stone. When you blame the church you are blaming your own inadequacies! In each disturbance you are witnessing your weakness. In those things which are strong or weak you see the weakness or strength of each believer. Each church should be a song of the redeemed, everybody taking their part in the choir, singing this great anthem as in the book of Revelation.[22] The church is so wide when it welcomes those in need. There are no fences; it is like walking into a field. The church was meant to show mankind something of the character of God. When a youngster had the meaning of the church explained to her, and all that it was suppose to do, she said, 'My what a good idea, I wonder where God got it from!'

We must recognise the need of fellowship in relationship

Peter belonged to a church with all its difficulties, as we do, yet it did not stunt his growth into *maturity*. The fish must become a whale, the pond a sea. When Peter and John were threatened, and then released, in Acts 4:23 they went to their own company. In his *maturity* Simon recognised his need of fellowship with others. In those areas where he was weak others were strong, and where he was strong others were weak. The church is so cosmopolitan in its Christ likeness. What he didn't say, someone else said. What he didn't know, someone would know. What he wasn't, someone would always be. The very word he required was given to him by one of these gathering together; they were so desperate for one another and for the fellowship of believers. They needed each other; they needed to report what had happened, 'to bear witness' as John Baptist, who said, 'Look at the Lamb of God.'[23] It eases the pain and the strain when we are able to tell how we feel.

We are companions of the Cross

The church is called a 'company'. It was to that particular grouping of people that Peter came, the 'companions' of the Cross. The word 'companion' defines those who eat from the same basket and share the same bread. This is Communion. To share the same bread from the same basket and drink wine from the same cup. They shared the Bread of Life with each other. Seven times in the Book of the Acts of the Apostles the word 'company' is used.[24] The word 'company' is 'ones own'. It has within its folds the meaning of 'peculiar', that which is 'your own'. The Queen of England has a private church called 'the Royal Peculiar'; she is responsible for its upkeep and ministry. That word 'peculiar' describes fruit that is 'peculiar' to a fruit tree. Apples to an apple tree, pears to the pear tree, grapes to the vine. In the church, which should be the Paradise of God, we need the Tree of Life found in Jesus Christ.

Every member is your brother or sister

It is the *mature* person who sees the church belonging to Christ, and also belonging to them because they are part of it. If it introduces one thing it is that of responsibility to Christ, and then to each other. They didn't only have practical preachers but preachers who practised what they preached. These were Kingdom men and women. 'I am my brother's keeper,' is the answer to Cain who killed Abel, and asked the question, 'Am I my brother's keeper?'[25] 'Keeper' means to 'spy out' for my brother. I must be a 'keeper' of sheep for the great Shepherd. To watch out for another to help them over the broken bits of life. In so doing I become as Moses' father-in-law Jethro was to Israel —eyes. The young man in the making was one of those 'eyes'. If people are looking out for you, then you know where you are going. In England, the 'God Channel', directed by Rory and Wendy Alec, have an opening phrase which states: 'Television that 'watches out' for you.' The church should be and is a reflection of you.

We are part of a company of people

In the Old Testament definition of the word 'company' we have described what a church should be. The word 'company' means 'a traveller'.[26] A different Hebrew word used for 'company' can suggest a 'cord'.[27] We are bound together by the cords of love. Another word translated 'company' is given as a 'troop', referring to an army.[28] In Psalm 68:30 the word 'company' describes that which is 'alive', 'living', 'active'. It is 'strength' and 'force'. In the Song of Solomon 6:13 it describes a 'dance' a 'chorus'. That should find ready acceptance in some churches! In Luke 2:44, 'company' suggests 'journeying together'. It is from the Greek word that we obtain the English for 'synod'. In Luke 9:14, 'companies' mean 'florets', daintily arranged flowers to make up a posy. These small flowers have been made into a garland of friendship, to be hung around the Prodigal's neck when he returns to his father's house. The people sat down in 'companies' as bunches of flowers. In 1 Samuel 19:20 'company' describes those who have been 'called together' which is a true definition of the church called 'out' to be called 'in'. We are a company that has met together by appointment. Peter was part and parcel of the whole. It was here that he could develop into all that he had been called to be.

The church will only be what you make it, not what you make of it

Simon Peter recognised the value of belonging to a group of people who gathered in the Name of the Lord. There is safety in numbers. If you fall, they stand. If you wander, they remain faithful. If you lack faith, they have faith. His heart was their heart, his soul was their soul, his lips their lips; he was truly part of a Body. It takes a certain *maturity* to see it like that. If the apostle Paul's definition of the church as a Body is correct, then we are part of that Body. Cephas naturally went to his own people because 'birds of a feather flock together.' 'Where the carcase is, there the eagles will gather.' Those who know something of the Dove of God will fly together and land together. They will meet with one purpose of witnessing to the goodness of the Lord. They had a focal point of faith and mutual understanding. Only when they met together could such Scriptures as 'they that are strong should bear the infirmities of the weak,'[29] be fulfilled bearing the 'infirmities' of the weak in the 'infinity' of Jehovah.

King David, when referring to his own people, could say that they were 'bone of his bone and flesh of his flesh.'[30] Your own 'company' is your own 'business'. 'Mind your own business!' The Greek word for 'company' used in Acts 4:23 is *idios* from where we obtain the English word 'idiot,' In its original use and meaning, it meant a 'private person', someone who could finance the Grecian Games or other social activities. It meant any person who did not take public office, a person who had an opinion who was usually very rich.

You define what the church is by your life

There are many terms which define the church. It is an 'assembly', it is a 'social gathering', it becomes to you what you want it to be. It is the quality of *maturity* found in Peter that helps you to help the church. We always need to see the 'bigger picture'. The church is bigger than any one person. The oak will always be bigger than the acorn. It is our vision of what the Church is that makes us what we are. You reflect what you feel about this 'company'. You are the church. The world has never seen the inside of a church. You are the church turned inside out. The world has no church but you. You are an ambassador for Christ. Your 'papers of acceptance' are in the fact that you are an epistle, not to the church at Corinth, Thessalonica or Ephesians, but an epistle 'from' the church to the world, and read by all men. The best translation of what you are is Jesus Christ. 'Be like Jesus this my song, in the home and in the throng. In my work and in the world I would be strong.' *Maturity* will be manifest in your weakest and strongest moments. Some are 'self made' others man made, but the world is looking for those whom the Lord has made, and they are His 'liege' people. Free and unfettered. The term 'liege' was given to the German tribes that overturned the Roman Empire. It was further used to mean those who are true to their chief. It defined those who were true and loyal, true to royalty.

Notes

1 John 1:40, 41.
2 Proverbs 27:17.
3 1 Corinthians 12:7.
4 John 1:36-40.
5 1 John 1:7.
6 1 Corinthians 11:20.
7 1 Peter 2:17. Philippians 2:25. Romans 16:1.
8 John 21:6.
9 Matthew 25:40.
10 Acts 9:21.
11 Ephesians 5:25.
12 Exodus 31:2.
13 Ecclesiastes 4:9.
14 Ephesians 4:12.
15 Joshua 4:5.
16 Genesis 49:10.
17 Exodus 36:33.
18 Mark 1:30.
19 Acts 2:41, 47.
20 Acts 12:25; 13:5.
21 Genesis 2:7.
22 Revelation 5:9.
23 John 1:36.
24 Acts 4:23; 6:7; 10:28; 13:13; 15:22; 17:5; 21:8.
25 Genesis 4:9.
26 Genesis 37:25.
27 1 Samuel 10:5, 10.
28 1 Samuel 30:15, 15; 30:23.
29 Romans 15:1.
30 2 Samuel 5:1.

Chapter Twelve

THE MAN WHO COULD NOT BE BOUGHT

'Every man has his price' is a worldly phrase, although some men are above price. What they are worth can't be calculated, measured or weighed. How can you evaluate *maturity* and all that is associated with it? Show me the highest point of the heavens or the lowest depth of the sea, tell me how much all the treasure in the world is worth, and I will tell you the full extent of those who have been enlarged by God. Value is personal to an individual. The *maturity* and quality of character is seen in what we are rather than in what we do or say. If some people's worth had to be weighed on the scales of truth, you would see the writing on the wall: 'you are weighed in the balances and found 'wanting' —'too light'. (Daniel 5:27.) To be weighed and 'found wanting', to be assessed and found deficient, is to be as a candle without a light.

The closer you get to some, the holier they are
The closer you get to Peter and to all those who 'can't be bought' because they are *mature*, the holier they appear. They do not 'talk down' to others, but talk 'up' into another realm. Meeting them is like stepping up onto another rung of the ladder. These are the people who will give a push at the steepest part of the incline. It is *maturity* which has weathered many a storm, has gone through all the seasons,[1] and becomes part of the truth, the whole truth and nothing but the

truth. You cannot place a value on that which is above value. The value of some precious metals and stones is determined by weight and measure, and not by the appearance. We move into another realm and language and refer to their intrinsic value as 'carat'. In the past, precious things were weighed using a seed or a bean to determine the worth.[2] Hence the saying, 'That man is not worth a bean!' True worth for Peter was found in the words of Jesus when He said, 'Unless a seed falls into the ground it abides alone.'[3] The secret is in the burying of the old life, and the resurgence of the new.

Peter was a man who could not be bought

As we read Acts 8:9–24, it declares the character of Peter as a man who could not be bought. He was above rubies or silver and gold. 'What shall a man give for his own soul?'[4] What value shall we put on that which has been developed into holiness? When he said to the man at the Gate Beautiful, 'I haven't got any silver or gold but such as I do have I will give to you,'[5] revealed the emptiness of his pockets and the fullness of his heart. When we allow the Lord to develop us, we have that which is beyond the realm of age or coinage. Simon had a full heart when it came to relationship and holiness. He stood out and was different, as different as a soldier in uniform is to a civilian. What price shall we put on truth and *maturity*? It is something that cannot be bought or taught, but must be developed within the human heart. All the circumstances around this young disciple became the sides of a melting pot.

The gifts given by God have to be developed

The theology of Simon the sorcerer, whose heart is money-centred, is that the gifts on display belong to the man who uses them. What he believes will not allow him to look higher and see God as the Giver of every perfect gift.[6] Many times the Lord will give you a gift, but it is small and has to be allowed to grow. He might only give a handle, and you need to take the metal from life in order to see the blade develop into a sharp cutting edge. God may grant you a smile but you have to turn it into laughter. Simon the sorcerer never realised that the gift, the hammer, saw, chisel of the Carpenter might be borrowed. This gift that he wanted to buy was God! All you have in God is on loan to you. Money is merciless and mercenary when it is part of the make-up of a man. This man Simon the Sorcerer had money to spend, but he wanted to spend it on the wrong things. If only he had money to give! The materialistic can never take the place of the evangelistic. What we buy and sell is never as rich or as full as what we receive as a gift. Gifts are given, not begged or bought.

Peter would not be bribed

The 'magic worker' wanted to offer the disciple a 'bribe'. The word 'bribe' comes from a root meaning 'loaf' or 'bread'.[7] Peter would not accept crumbs when he had the Bread of Life, the full loaf in Jesus Christ. The trickster offered stale bread with mould around the edges. The hunger in Peter's heart was not for money but men, not for riches but the riches of His grace. This young Galilean ate, slept, breathed, lived and loved the Kingdom of God. The word 'bribe' a 'loaf' came to mean a 'crumb', and we are more than sparrows requiring crumbs. The crumb can never take the place of the loaf, nor can money take the place of a life of supreme quality. The Kingdom of God is the whole loaf. If Simon the fisherman had accepted the offer, he would have accepted that which was as small as a crumb when compared with the largeness of God. What Peter had was not 'pie in the sky when you die' nor 'meat on the plate while you wait'. It was 'bread in the bin when you come in'. He would not use money to reach his objectives. He was so full of the Holy Spirit whom he ministered; there was no room for such things as the money that was offered. He would not take the money and be 'taken in' by it. He would trust God, and that might bring money. Jesus had said, 'Seek ye first the kingdom of God, and all these things shall be added unto you.'[8] The man who tried to bribe Peter 'put the cart before the horse' when he first offered reward without success.

You can never out-give the Lord

Simon the Sorcerer could never out-give God or Peter. How much is 'success' worth? Certainly more than a 'crumb' for it suggests to 'come up on top'. What is it worth in human terms to be a minister of the gospel? What price peace, health, joy, longsuffering, patience, holiness and devotion, all of which are part of the Spirit of God? When you have given all, there is still so much more in the Lord. His hands, as His pockets, are never empty, for He opens His hand and satisfies the desire of every living thing. Peter 'put his money where his mouth was'. Tainted money finds no throne in truth. You can't put finance into a man whose pockets have been sewn up, or are so full that they cannot receive any more. 'A purse is doubly empty when it is full of borrowed money.' Trying to buy a miracle is like trying to obtain part of the moon!

Simon son of Jonas was offered 'money'. 'Money' comes from the word *mint* where it was made. *Mint* is from the Latin *moneta* (the warning one), a surname of Juno, in whose temple at Rome money was coined —meaning *moneo*, 'to remind'.[9] The Bible gives many a warning about its power, but it had no power over Peter and John. That offer was about as acceptable as a glass eye to a man with a good eye. It should remind us that money is transient, a good servant but a poor master. He would not become a servant of money; it would make him a slave to it. Many a person has accepted a gift for something which was God-given and God-owned, and it has bound them hands and feet, seen them cast out into the outer darkness of the deepest dark —the darkness of hell! Hell is the farthest point from Heaven. It could never be said of this believer and his money: 'whose I am and whom I serve.' Peter didn't do as Judas did after accepting the bribe to betray Jesus and threw the money on the temple floor.[10] Simon the son of Jonas strangled it at birth! It never touched his hand or his heart. The 'taint', the dye from the money, was not allowed to spread as a plague. His heart was too full to make room for that which had been offered to buy him, so that the sorcerer would own him body and soul. The cell that some are imprisoned in has doors and bars that are coin shaped. Ask any embezzler who knows something of the power, dominion and worship of coins. Coins make no crowns for Christ. A mountain of money is not worth a penny when compared with mercy and forgiveness and all that the Holy Spirit means to the believer.

Money will always find its own level

Simon the disciple of Christ said, 'Let your money perish with you!' He was sending the money to the same level as the man who offered it. If Peter had accepted it, then it would have resulted in him being as out of place, as out of circulation, as a coin lost in a drain.[11] Money will perish, but the plan of God continues developing. That man is so blessed who can move through piles of money with his hands in his pocket because he cannot be bought. The hands that were laid on others to receive the Holy Spirit were never lifted or offered to receive a gift as an offertory box.

Simon son of Jonas had decisions to make. Our decisions today will make us what we are tomorrow. What you are today is the result of decisions made in the past. Decide for right today, and tomorrow is taken care of. If you deal righteously with the present, Jehovah will take care of the past and the future. There might have been the temptation in Acts chapter 8 to emulate the sin of Ananias and Sapphira as in Acts chapter 5. The man who is strong is strong in all things. Love is *maturity* in all things. It is being 'all things to all men', in that it never compromises its principles. This is only one aspect of the enlargement of Cephas, and through Holy Writ we are called upon to witness every scene, hear every word, and see every action. This *maturity* is not found in an art gallery or in a line of statues, it is in living, breathing, deciding, following, Peter.

There must be sincerity in the heart

There was no 'guardian angel' leading or teaching the man who could not be bought. In Acts chapter 8 we see this young man without strings to hold him back. The world and its love of money were not coiled around his heart. We know what he is like in the home and on the street, but what is he like at work, not simply when he is operating the word of the Master? What you are in private you will become in public. What the potter deals with in the Potter's House is brought into the open for public inspection. We get the word 'sincerity' from the fact that broken pieces of clay, such as a finger, nose or ear falling off a statue would then be stuck back on with wax or honey. If they were placed in the heat, everything that was not genuine fell off. A certificate was given with every article purchased which said 'sincere', 'without wax'. The road that has too much sun can melt and become a sticky mess of tar. This leader of men was not like that. He could be trusted, tried and was triumphant, able to turn temptation into triumph. He was able to kill that which would kill him.

You will be offered many 'get rich quick' opportunities

It was during his normal ministry that an offer was made for him to avoid doing the right thing. There will be numerous opportunities to get rich quick, even if it means digging your own grave, and being buried by your desire. There may be a thousand suggestions but none of them are real. They lead you 'up the garden path', and in that garden there is no money tree. Here was a 'get rich quick' opportunity if ever you saw one. The words of Simon the Sorcerer were 'Give me this power,' after he had offered money. He thought the power was in the money. He believed that 'money talks', but forgot to think that it also silences when it is offered to keep a key witness quiet. What speaks to men is dumb before a holy God. The currency of the Kingdom is never related to the currency of the realm, there is no relationship or family bond between the two. Faith never did have coin features. What Cephas was involved in had the image and superscription of God stamped upon it, not the figure of a human king.[12] Two realms were at work in the life of the man who could not be bought, the world of commerce and the world of character. Here was a 'tug of war', each side pulling in the opposite direction. Jesus standing with Peter meant there was no competition!

Real riches cannot be bought, they can only be given

Real riches are truth within. The tenacity of truth is worth more than mountains of millions! What price would you pay for an easy conscience that allows you to look God in the face without feeling ashamed or condemned? These are the treasures in earthen vessels. This disposition of the apostle was not as a crown of gold on his head, but a circle of glory that became the circumference of his life. Here we have the mode and the model of *maturity* witnessed in refusing to accept the unacceptable.

The man who can't be bought has a deep source within himself that has no financial attachment; it cannot be reckoned up or worked out by mathematical calculation. Peter was independent. He could further the Kingdom better by not bowing the knee in reverence to what was on offer. He wouldn't be a fish to be caught with a hook and bait. In John 1:47 we read of an 'Israelite in whom there was no 'guile', no 'bait'. If he had taken what had been offered, it would have been bribery, a mockery; that Kingdom he was building on would have become a kingdom of silver and gold, and moth and rust would have corrupted it. If Peter is going to take the part of the Samaritan in the Parable of the Good Samaritan, and leave two pence to pay for the man's rest and recovery, the Lord would provide that finance and not the wheels or weasels of industry.[13]

Satan desires to sift you as wheat
Simon the disciple of Christ took his stand and would not accept a payment for the Holy Spirit. He 'stood his ground' —ground that you can build on, just like the wise man who built his house on a rock. Peter became the rock Jesus had predicted that he would be. He stood resolute. Do you remember what Jesus had said to him on one occasion? 'Satan has desired to sift you as wheat but I have prayed for you.[14] When you are strengthened, strengthen your brethren.' He does this each time we read Acts chapter 8. He is a fine example of all that is Christian.

Simon Cephas was making a choice between the 'here' and the 'now'. Would he 'feather his own nest' or build something so permanent that time could not reach or touch it? What Peter was is still with us, because it was what the Holy Ghost had produced in him, making him into a *mature* man. It was that 'holy thing within you' that helped him to make his choice. He wasn't into 'nest building' but Kingdom building. Here, now, he could have received his wages in what was offered. He decided that his reward was in the future rather than in what was on offer. He could not take anything from the open hand of Simon, because he was a son of Abraham. Abraham had refused to take even the latchet of a shoe, and it could never be said that anyone, apart from the Lord, had made him rich.[15] True faith is speaking for itself, as he replied to the sorcerer.

You are richer than a millionaire

The man of God was already richer than a millionaire. You cannot assess or count spirituality and godly choices. You measure the growth of a tree in a season not by its leaves or trunk but by its fruit. It was this choice not to fall under the spell or into the worship of money that led him into his next phase of ministry and revelation. Peter could not accept anything from the 'hand of magic', there was no horoscope reading for him. His future was written on the palm of His hand. He that is full cannot be made more full by adding a few pence to what he is. Riches have wings and will fly away,[16] but those who trust God will fly with the wings of the Dove of God. They shall mount up as eagles, running and not being weary.[17]

Don't let an unnecessary weight be put on your shoulders

Can you imagine how this millstone would have become such a burden to Peter in the future? It would have always been on his conscience, biting deeply into his heart and life. Everything he saw and did would have the shadow of money over it. 'Ill gotten gains' will make you ill. A whole bag of drachmas could not have produced one dream! Love of money can be the form of 'many kinds of evil'. It is not the money that is wrong, it is the love of it. The man who was offered money for the Holy Spirit had already made his choice. It was not offered as a sacrifice but as a payment. We do not give to God in order to pay Him for anything. How can you pay the Lord for sunshine, stars and the sweet zephyr of the morning?

Peter didn't want to be a mixture of many things

The sorcerer saw this as another investment. He had probably bought everything in life that he had. You can have lands, houses, clothes and all material goods, but there are some things out of reach of the grasping hand. It is not what you possess but what possesses you that become the false god. The sorcerer viewed the moving of the Holy Spirit and His manifestations as another way to enlarge his business. He could have justified what he did by giving some of it away to the purposes of the Lord. The 'means never justifies the end'. Simon's pockets were bulging with his ill gotten gains, but they were not full enough to meet the longing and the zeal in the heart of Peter. If it had been accepted then the son of Jonas would have become a different mixture, and the Lord hates mixtures. Cephas would have had the voice of Judas, who sold the Lord for 30 pieces of silver, ringing in his ears for all eternity.

Maturity in the Holy Spirit cannot be bought, but it can be given and it can be received. If you are a slave to money, then you are a slave to all things. Many a man has put his 'shirt on a horse' and spent the rest of his life naked in character. Money has brought bondage to so many. You are God's money box, His treasure in jars of clay. The life of the Spirit is invested in you.

You cannot sell what you don't own

There are principles involved in buying and selling. The man offering the money thought he was in the market where everything in the auction goes to the highest bidder. You cannot sell what you don't own. 'Buy the truth and sell it not',[18] means it will cost you to know the truth and be true to your convictions. Conscience can make cowards of us all. The fisherman was not his own, he had sold himself to Jesus. He was a 'love slave' of Jesus Christ.[19] Don't accept all that is offered. Remember there are no pockets in a shroud! What will you do when the money is spent? 'My Father has bread enough and to spare.'[20]

Whatever the amount offered was, we do not know. You can't give to the man who has everything. The finance offered would soon disappear. That which is born of the Spirit of God will outlast the shine of a coin or the picture on a note. There is always the choice of what we can see, taste and handle here and now. The choice took the Galilean miles apart from the man who made the offer. It might be one decision the size of a coin, but what a wide gap it produces at the end! That which was paper thin can be turned into miles at the end of life if the wrong decision is made. One had coinage, the other had character. One had money, the other had *maturity*. In every choice there is a voice which says where we are, what we are, and where we are going. Peter was investing in the Kingdom, not in himself. He was not the source of interest. The man handling precious gifts of the Holy Spirit has no time for the bribery. Many a person has let the chink of the coin sound louder than the voice of God. They have felt the shape of the coin, and in caressing it have lost the love of God. Don't spend time with the 'money changers', spend time with Him who changes life.

Money can be a passport to everywhere but not to Heaven!

Money talks, but its vocabulary is limited. It might present you with a compact disc of its successors, but it will never mention its failures, those it has left in ruin, tormented forever in the black of night. Money can be a passport to anywhere but Heaven. It is no door into the family of God. It can buy an orchard of trees but it can't create one. It can buy an apple, pear, lemon, banana, but it can't create one.

We will always sow to the future, the present or the past. 'What a man sows, that will he reap.' Peter revealed where his heart was and in which direction his head was turned. 'Money talks', but is quite speechless before the Almighty. God knows what a person has given, but He also knows what a person has held back.

Money has purchasing power, but that power diminishes when it is compared with the work and worth of Christ on the Cross. There is no limit to the power of the Lord, but there are limits to whatever money can buy. It cannot buy the Baptism in the Holy Spirit. As you have freely been given, give to others pressed down, shaken together and running over. Be careful how you handle money because money would handle you. It starts with a small coin, and grows into something bigger, something which originally you had control over, but which now controls you. There is no pleasure in being controlled by something as remote as that which can be scattered into the wind, to be blown over the hill and far away.

That which is given is better than that which is bought

The best financial reward in the world is in Ephesians 4:8 where it states that He has 'taken captivity captive and obtained gifts for men'. In the giving of the gifts there is the picture of the Roman General returning from a successful campaign, moving progressively up the Apian Way into the city of Rome. His soldiers accompany him with sheathed swords, bringing with them the spoils of war, garments, cattle, jewellery and slaves. As they travel, the soldiers begin to throw the coinage, taken from the country they have captured, to the crowd. Jesus has conquered, and has given gifts to men, gifts of the Holy Spirit, promised and given as He ascended on high.

The things that money cannot buy

What money can and cannot buy: It can buy a Bible but not a blessing. It can buy a pew, but not purity. It can buy you a pulpit, but not a sermon from the heart, a church building but not a church. It can buy interesting things but not interest or inspiration. It can buy a prayer-room but not a prayer. It can buy medicine but not healing. It can buy many things in life, but it cannot buy life. It can buy a surplice but not sainthood, a cassock but not a character. It can buy a crown, but not a kingdom or a throne. These things have to be fought for and captured. It can buy you a 'lift', but not love, the crowning grace of life. Peter could not be bought because he was not for sale. There was no price tag on his life. His was no cheque book Christianity. Jesus had taken away the price tag when he purchased Peter with the price of His blood. As Peter thought about the majesty and the glory, the bystander was thinking in terms of money. God had poured out His Spirit, and the magician saw it in terms of magic and logic which could be bought. The Holy Spirit abiding in Peter could not be found at the end of a magician's trick-stick, but at the end of another piece of wood, the Cross. One was thinking faith, the other finance. Your money perishes with you if you only see coins in characters. If you can be assessed in human terms by commerce, you are not worth much. Sheep were seen as money in olden times. A man's wealth was seen in the number of sheep he possessed. He had to be careful that the sheep did not possess him. Buy a farm, buy a house, buy a boat, possess them but don't let them possess you. Jesus told a parable in Luke 9:57–62, where one bought a field, another cattle, and would not follow Him because of these excuses. They had not realised the worth of following Christ.

Finance can be a substitute for faith

Many a person has been bought with money. Unlike Naboth, they have been willing to sell their vineyard and the inheritance of the family.[21] Money can't buy the real you. There was something richer and rarer than gold, which the hand could not take from this son of God. Wealth will always be in well being and not in the whims of the day. Sell out to the Kingdom, but do not sell the Kingdom and become as that profane person Esau, who sold his birthright for a bowl of soup.[22]

I Timothy 6:7–10 warns against believing that you can purchase anything with money. The warning is displayed as a notice in a field, telling of the bull that waits to charge if you trespass. Verse 9, 'They that crave to be rich fall into temptation's 'snare', a metaphor taken from the picture of a wild beast that springs to take the bait, but does not see the deep pit below the bait or the spike that it is impaled upon as it springs to take it. Money is not wrong, but it is when we think we can use it to purchase what is good and godly.

Don't be guilty of 'simony' when losing your testimony

From this incident in Acts 8:9–24 we have coined the word 'simony' —the buying and selling of religious things unlawfully. It is to buy and sell those things that do not belong to you, under the cover of an ecclesiastical cloth. To steal is to break a commandment. It involves the sin of covetousness, as most gambling and raffles do. Simon the son of Jonas did not seek to take from the church, he sought to put something into it. He realised that those things of an eternal nature could never be bought, for they are as rare in quality and quantity as the sun, moon and stars. They can be looked upon and admired but cannot be purchased. The word 'purchase' means what it suggests, to 'chase' something until we catch it. The sorcerer was chasing his own tail like a dog, the circles were ever decreasing.

There are gifts in the Kingdom of more value than the gold of Ophir.[23] There is a way set out in the Scripture how we might obtain them. Peter had been preaching such things. There is no place for the robber who 'climbs in some other way and seeks to break through and steal.'[24] God will not give His glory unto another.

Peter belongs to a list of stalwarts

Peter belongs to a long list of 'stalwarts' —men of eminent worth, who would not surrender what God had surrendered to them. This includes the Scottish Covenanters who gave their life for what they believed. Simon belonged to the list of martyrs, who were burned at the stake, and others had their bodies placed in the sea off the coast of Suffolk, England, and as the tide came in they were drowned.[25] He belongs to the list of David's greater men. He stands out more than he did in Acts chapter 2, when he stood up and was bold. Peter is part of 1 Corinthians 13:3, one of those who, with love in their heart, had offered their body to be burned. That choice will make choice. May God make you fit to live or die, and to keep true while you live, as Peter was. If you do, each succeeding generation will rise up and call you blessed. There will be no bony finger of the skeleton of Simon the Sorcerer coming up from the grave and saying, 'You were only in it for the money!' The clouds will never part, and a form of a 'Christmas Carol' past come to accuse you as in 'Christmas Carol' written by Charles Dickens. You will have an easier conscience, filled with such a peace that money can't buy, but which God can give. With the apostle Paul, Peter could write and say, 'I have coveted no man's silver or gold'; [26] 'there is no Achan in my character. I have followed the charter given to the church by Jesus Christ.' You might be 'made of money', but there are some things that money cannot 'make'. A man can 'make' money; the money does not 'make' the man. As long as time endures and the clocks tick, this man will not be remembered for the size of his church, his great sermons, his abilities or his power of prayer, but because he was *the man who could not be bought*. He will be remembered as one set free by a ransom paid by a King. Love will always be more than pounds and pence.

Notes

[1] Matthew 16:26.

[2] Silver, gold, precious gems were weighed by using a seed or a bean. See Chamber's Dictionary of the Etymology of Words.

[3] John 12:24.

4 Matthew 16:26.

5 Acts 3:6.

6 James 1:17.

7 See Chambers dictionary of Etymology of Words.

8 Matthew 6:33.

9 See Chambers dictionary of Etymology of Words.

10 Matthew 27:5.

11 The word 'perish' in John 3:16 means to 'be out of circulation'.

12 Mark 12:16.

13 Luke 10:35.

14 Luke 22:31.

15 Genesis 14: 23, 24.

16 Proverbs 23:5.

17 Isaiah 40:31.

18 Proverbs 23:23.

19 Romans 1:1.

20 Luke 15:17.

21 1 Kings 21.

22 Hebrews 12:16.

23 1 Kings 10:11.

24 John 10:1.

25 Read 'Foxes Book of Martyrs'.

26 Acts 20:33.

Chapter Thirteen

THE MAN WHO LET GOD WORK THROUGH HIS HANDS

Many Christians look for a special anointing before attempting anything for God. Many look for 'tongues of fire' when in fact they have been given 'hands of help', convinced that unless a 'spiritual utterance' is given they have not been used by God. Others look for what they feel has been lost when it is still is in the hands that God has given to them. Some will to be used as a carpenter like Jesus, others as a goldsmith, silversmith, lapidary, mechanic, builder, fabricator or ploughman. All work with their hands. Peter the son of Simon was prepared to let the Lord work through his hands. One definition of the 'hand' in Exodus 9:8 according to Dr. James Strong[1] is 'two fists full'. Many weak minded people think that in order to be used by God they have to see letters of silver and gold in the sky at night. They are looking for something they will never find. They never equate their hands with the workings of the Holy Spirit as Peter the apostle did. Some churches never move forward because they are waiting for revival, and while they wait they decrease, because they do not use what they already possess. Every church should have 'bread enough and to spare'[2] in the gospel they preach, but that bread needs distributing to the poor. All who would be *mature* need look no further than to their own body to see the glorious gifts that God has given.

Your two hands are talents

The finest musical instrument you will ever have is your two hands! As we use them to clap we are using a talent given by the Lord. Hands as the hands of Simon are tools, and need to be used. Most of what Peter was involved in was associated with his hands and his body. Two of your best talents are sometimes buried under the work that you do. 'Familiarity breeds contempt' when it actually should breed 'contentment' knowing that what you have is being fully used by the Lord of glory. God wants to fill your hands with substance, ministry and the means of being a blessing.

When you meet someone, the first thing you do is to give them your hand. You are offering your hand to help them in whatever way you can. Your hand is added to their hand, and two are better than one, while four are better than two. The giving of the hand is the symbol that you are one with them. Many of us first came to Christ by raising a hand in an evangelical meeting. You give your hand, and then give your heart as that association deepens into friendship.

Talents traded lead to more responsibility, and responsibility expects *maturity*. There is a text in the Message Bible in the Book of Hosea, chapter 8:4–10 which says, 'Wheat with no head produces no flour.' The writer is suggesting that we need character if we are going to produce the real thing. Your best talents are always with you, but they should not be left hanging by your side. Let the Lord perform the miraculous through the means that you have. Don't let it go to waste because you have no conviction or require a revelation of all the good things that the Lord has given to you. Jesus entered Heaven with marked hands, bruised hands, blood stained hands, hands that had been used to help the world.

Use your hands to bind up the broken hearted

Like Peter you also have two hands to use, yet even when used to bind up the broken hearted or to bless with all spiritual blessing, we rarely recognise it. Your hands and the work they produce can be a source of recognition or inspiration. We are looking for others to be used in the Kingdom, when the Kingdom should be used in us. If you only gaze at cows and sheep you will not have milk or wool! It is not always through spiritual gifts that the Lord works. If the hand is involved we think that Heaven is excluded when in fact it is included. There are things to be accomplished that can only be completed by you. Some deeds are the shape of your hand. Simon the fisherman fitted into situations as the hand will fit into a glove. What is happening, has happened, might not seem miraculous to you, but it will certainly be a 'sign and a wonder' to the recipient.

What you do sanctifies your hands

Hands are necessary to worship. Lifting hands in praise turns them into holy hands. Something as mundane as hands can be so blessed and consecrated. In the hand you have that which 'seizes,'[3] and with your hands you can 'seize the day!' They can unravel all that is in knots and tangled, the very things sent by God to sort out a life. Where the tongue fails, the hand prevails. You will influence far more people by what you 'do' rather than what you 'say'. They will count your words as pence and your deeds as pounds. If every character was as well constructed as the hand, we would be great in every aspect. They say that the plan of life is in the palm of the hand. I prefer mine to be written on the palm of His hand —the crucified hand. Hands are used to serve, bless, wave goodbye, say thank you, lift and shove, carry or stroke, hold another's hand —all are part of your handiwork! Where would Peter Simon be without his hands? Where would you be? The using of the hands is not in question, it is the recognition of what we do by using them as a talent, and part of our ministry, ministry that we have confined to the back of our minds.

God spoke to a king through a hand

When God wanted to speak to a king, He used someone's hand to write a message on the palace wall. It had something to write, and it told a story, Daniel 5:5. It was a hand of judgement but it can be a hand of blessing. One finger, the fourth, wrote the message. If God can do this with one finger, how much more can He do when we give our hands to Him? If you give your talent, then as God found a wall for the finger to write on, so He will find an area for you to be successful in, where you can express all that you are. Some mighty portent would have been the choice of the theologian, or an angel, but God chose a hand. That hand did not cease writing until the message was complete. It is quite useless commencing something that we never complete. What is in your hand, within your own capability, needs setting free in order to set others free. That hand can untie the knot and loosen those things that bind and limit. Even when Jesus had performed many miracles, and Cephas witnessed them, there were always those standing on the sideline waiting to use their hands to remove the plaster, the bandage or the patch. It is within your hand (within your power) to exercise what has been given. The hand that is full cannot receive any more until what is inside of it is let go. The Lord will send something new to the empty space. When Peter poured out, the Lord poured in.

Jesus used His hand to convey a message of forgiveness

When a group of leaders began to condemn a woman taken in the very act of adultery, the Lord Jesus Christ wanted to teach them a lesson they would never forget, and, as His messenger and chastening rod, He used His hand, to write on the ground.[4] From those fingers came words written in the sand that all might understand. The power of the hand worked, for, 'they went out one by one.' When this same Lord wanted to teach a lesson on giving, and how important it is to see and know what we have really given, what did He do? He sent a widow woman with two mites in her hand, to put into the offertory.[5] In the story of the feeding of the five thousand it was a little lad's hand, and the mouths in the crowd that were fed, the lad's hand and God's mouth, because what the Lord Jesus did spoke to the people. The lad with five loaves and two fish clutched them in his hand, until they were needed. In the life of Abraham, God revealed Himself as Jehovah Jireh, 'the Lord will provide'.[6] It was God's hand and Abraham's mouth. Every field is given a rich harvest because the hand of the farmer had been waved across as seeds were thrown across the freshly turned earth.

The apostle Paul let the Lord use his hands

Paul's epistles contain some of the deepest theology in the New Testament. It is estimated that he wrote thirteen epistles. Where did they all come from? Where did these miraculous words of faith, hope and charity come from? Many came from a prison cell, from the hand of the apostle as he began to write. Watch out when pen and hand get together', for the 'pen is mightier than the sword!' Without the hand there would have been no writing. We accept that what he wrote was God-inspired, but what we can't understand is how those things you do with your hands can produce the wonderful works of God. All the New Testament epistles were the work of the pen in the hand. We think that to see such wonderful works we have to go down into the sea during a storm.[7] They are there for our taking if we will take off our mundane spectacles and accept new vision in the far-seeing faith of Abraham, who saw the Day of Christ afar off and rejoiced.[8]

God used the hand of Moses

When God needed a leader for the nation of Israel, He commenced His training of Moses, saying, 'What is that in your hand?'[9] Moses had something in his hand that God wanted to use. You have the same contents, but you must stretch out your hands as Jesus did on the Cross, and loose the contents, such as ambition, greed and jealousy. If you do, the Lord who dealt with Peter and produced *maturity* in that one life will do the same for you. When Moses released what was in his hand, it became part of miraculous power, the source and sort of deliverance that a people required.

In America they speak of 'hiring hands'; in marriage we speak of 'giving the hand'; in Christianity we speak of 'filling the hand'. The showing of the hand in an evangelical appeal is a token of complete surrender. In the days of George Whitefield and John Wesley, to acknowledge their decision and commitment, people would write their name and details on a piece of paper, and send it to the front of the church, thereby committing their hand.

Each finger on the hand represents a ministry

Acts 9:8, speaking of the 'hand', suggests to 'lead by the hand' as a cheer leader, while Acts 13:11 means 'one who leads by the hand'. It is always good to lead by example. There are those in darkness who need you to lead them, as the Galilean fisherman sought to express the character of Christ through his hand. The lovely thing about the hand is each finger can represent something. Held together in prayer they can shape a church steeple. One finger for pointing, one for beckoning, one for strength, another for comfort, and another for a firm grip. One is stronger than the other, one finger needs the other. Divided they fall while united they can help another to stand. It is the hand that enhances your reach, makes it that little bit longer. The hand is used in embracing, marrying, cleaning, and ironing, weaving, stitching and mending. Dorcas in Acts had done so many good works with her hands, and it was the Lord who sent the hands of Peter into that death room to help when other hands had ceased.[10] When Peter's hand took on the task, new life and light with a smile from a resurrected person appeared.

Hands were used to untie the knot of death

These were fisherman's hands, used to tying and untying knots, but they had never before untied the knot of death. They had crafted a vessel and handled silvery fish, but now they had been called into a new role, that of crafting a life, as Simon laid his hands on Dorcas. They found a new direction and dedication when they were surrendered to Jesus Christ. He 'gave her his hand',[11] and in that one act he was providing what she required. All that is needed, sometimes, is a human hand to lean on or to catch the tears of another. It is into a human hand that some would like to cast their sorrows. When we go into His hand, it is with bruises and hurt. When that Hand opens, we are not crushed, we are a new creation. One translation of Romans 12:1 says, 'Present 'all' your faculties' to God. This includes your hands when others cannot reach the top shelf and you bring to them that which has been out of reach.

Your hands are what you were born with

Acts 27:19 suggests that which should be done with your 'own' hand rather than somebody else doing it for you. As they cast out the tackling of the ship, so it was for Peter to lighten the load, and that same work is for you to do also so that others, as seagoing vessels, might be free to sail to their destination rather than suffer shipwreck. 'Many hands make light work.' They make gospel light work and help it to shine. When the fisherman lost the oars, or the boats had been beached, he still had his hands.

Your hands are what you were born with, your gift from the womb. When you have a spiritual birth as in John 3:7, you have hands that are given to a different Body —the church of Jesus. He that has ears should use them, so too, he that has hands. They are not for decoration but for multiplication as you perform acts of faith.

The keys of the kingdom have been committed into your hands

Peter had feet to walk, a voice to preach, eyes to see, lips to speak and legs to run. Within his own personality there was an Aladdin's cave of precious things. Our emphasis at this point is on the hands of Cephas. Into those hands Jesus had committed the keys of the Kingdom, and they had to be used.[12] It takes every finger to work together for good before a key can be turned in a lock. 'Lock, stock and barrel'. If you get the key into the lock, you will get the stock and the barrel. The key in the hand is an introduction to greater things. Don't look for the key to the problem, use the key, and stop using the problem. Remember, 'some have entertained angels unaware.' Yes, but angels have entertained some unawares also. I prefer the 'hand ministry' rather than the 'mouth ministry'.

For Simon to use the keys he had to be convinced that they had been put into his hands. The old hymn said, 'Nothing in my hand I bring....' When we come with empty hands we receive Kingdom keys. Simon Peter had to find the locks for the keys. The locks were the difficult situations he came upon. In a crisis, he simply took a key, turned it, and the whole dilemma was altered as the key turned. Cross keys are part of the arms of the Archbishop of York, England. The 'House of Keys' refers to one of the three estates in the Isle of

Man. The church must be a house of keys, every member of the family carrying a key ensuring they are never locked out in the cold dark night.

These keys were not symbolic, as many of our keys are today. Some houses have a master key that will open every door, but it still needs a hand to be put into. The freedom of the city is given to some, and they are handed a symbolic key which allows them to go anywhere in that city. Some are wooden keys. We are interested in a key formed from the wood of the Cross of Christ that meets every need. Peter's hands contained the keys, even when it appeared that those hands were empty. We still have the 'Key of Promise'[13] even if we lose everything else.

'Consecration' means to 'fill the hands'

It is not enough to know that what you are and what you have is in Jesus, it is acceptable and necessary to take it with both hands in consecration and use it fully. The very term 'consecration' in the Old Testament means 'to fill the hands'[14] symbolic of the priests holding out their hands for a piece of the sacrificed animal. To have a 'full hand' means we are consecrated to the Lord.

The devil will never be frightened by music that sounds more like rattling keys and chains than worship! No battles are won by 'sabre rattling' or firing guns into the air. They are won as we step forward from the shadows and touch people with bleeding souls and wrenched hearts. Ointment is in your hands. Simon Peter did not have to be clever, he only had to believe. There were places he preached at, as in Acts 10:44 the house of Cornelius the centurion, where the Holy Spirit fell upon those who listened. It happened without Peter really knowing that within his heart and cloistered in the words he spoke was the key to the situation. He gave the key a large turn, and the Gentiles on the outside were brought inside, the locked door opened. They would be no longer as dogs under the table eating the crumbs.[15] God does not want you to live on 'crumbs of comfort'.

In your enlargement, see that as a key for the situation. Not a literal thing, but something that has been put into your hands as a handy weapon. Who ever heard of any General winning a war with a key! God's weapons are foolish in order to challenge the wise. His methods are your hands. There must be the key of conviction in your conscience, a key of commitment to the cause. The man with a key fears no doors. There is no door so closed that it cannot be opened, and no door open that cannot be closed and locked with a key. Keys do not only open doors, they keep them shut.

God puts the key into your hand

The key without the hand, as the man without the help of Jesus Christ, is quite useless. You will find the keys for your hands hanging on the nail of the Cross. You have to get close to Christ to see where they are. If you do not have enough faith, then watch how Jesus and Peter were *mature* enough to take what was theirs in God. Which part of your body do you want God to work through? Let it be your hands as they are surrendered to surmount.

The prayer of the infant church was that Jehovah would 'stretch forth His hand to heal' (Acts 4:30). His hands became their hands but they had to be sensible enough and spiritual enough to realise that His hands were their hands, and His feet their feet. He has no mouth but your mouth, no feet but your feet, no hands but your hands. As the Master commits things to the slave's hands, so the Lord has committed His goods to us. The steward of the house, as Jesus is called in the Book of Ephesians – the 'Steward of the Ages' – always carried the key.[16] The key opened or locked the door to his master's goods.

Your hand can be a well-worn tool

Hands are marked by the works they have performed. Some are blistered, have callouses upon them or skin missing from the palm. They are like a well-worn tool. Some are aged, others are furrowed. These marks are as medals received for hard work. It is as if nature attests to the work these hands have performed, stamping on them all the evidences of where they have been and the things in both the natural and spiritual that they have accomplished. We need the marks of Jesus Christ on our hands, speaking of our achievements in Him, as the apostle Paul had the *stigmata* of Christ in his body.[17]

In Acts 3:7 it was Peter at the Beautiful Gate who took the man by the right hand, the hand of authority. God had used him in performing a miracle, and now the hand of Peter was taken to help the man onto his feet. Blessed are those hands that are able to help people onto their feet. It was partly because of the hand of Simon that the man went into the temple walking, leaping and praising God. The hand gave him the final push. Your ministry can do the same. As the hand is a ministry of the human body, so your hands can be expressions of your ministry to the Body of Christ, it can be a bridge over troubled waters. The power of the Almighty went from the hand of Peter (God requires a platform to commence with) right down to the ankle bones. Strength went from the hands to the feet of the man. Your hands in humility can make a deep impression on another person. When you have no feet like this crippled man, God has many hands to work on your behalf. Waving fingers can result in dancing feet. Heart and hand ministry releases human misery. Hand service can result in heart service.

The Lord determines what His and your hands are going to do
Acts 4:28 their prayer was that God would perform through His hands whatever He had determined. In Acts 4:30 the prayer was that the hand would be stretched forth to heal. He did it by answering prayer as they prayed for people. They went forth as working, helping, healing hands. (Acts 5:12) 'By the hands of the apostles were many signs and wonders wrought.' Simon the son of Galilee was one of those mentioned. When it says 'signs and wonders' were 'wrought', the word 'wrought' suggests an animal skin, stretched and dried, cut to shape, finally finding its place in the whole scheme of things. It was 'wrought' by the working together of hands. The word 'wrought' can apply to the tilling of the field. 'Wrought' is the past plural tense of 'work'. It is that which is produced by energy and conscious constant effort. These hands found in Cephas and others were in the working of the Holy Spirit as people were healed.

The power of the whole body is in the hand. It is an extension of the body. As believers we have to be an extension of the Body of believers. The church should be full of hands holding keys. Very often we do not recognise times when there has been a key in our hands, yet we have used it to the glory of God. We need to be *mature* enough, having our inner eyes opened to realise what has happened. Keys of the kingdom held in the hand of a willing worker are not always key-shaped, that is why we do not recognise them or their power.

Peter used his hand to lift up Tabitha
In Acts 9:41 the Galilean gave Tabitha his hand, and lifted her up. This was after a marvellous miracle had been performed. You are *mature* when you realise that by using your hands you can lift people up, not only in a physical, but also in a spiritual way, as you allow the Lord to strengthen your hand and use it to strengthen others. Many a hand has passed on a lovely bunch of flowers, and the very act, along with the perfume from the flowers, has been a remedy. When you are dispensing blessing, pray for hands like shovels! When you are doling out criticism pray for hands the size of a fly's wing! Your hand and all you say can be a sublime source of strength. Ministry of all types can be in the 'lifting up' of those whose spirits have died within them. This sort of hand brings hope where there is no hope. Don't just lift people up, stay with them to keep them up. Peter lifted Tabitha up as one would rescue a body from the sea. To him she was a real gem, and in lifting her he saved her from being left down and out permanently. Simon was prepared to lift from somewhere to something, to lift those who were below him to where he was! *Maturity* teaches you to gather together what has been scattered and to lift it up. Let the Lord give you leverage power in all that you do. Leave people standing on their own feet rather than in a 'fainting fit'.

Hands must have no chains on them
In Acts 12:7 the prison doors opened and the chains fell off his hands. Simon had been bound by chains. Hands bound by chains operate no keys. The very thing that limited his ministry was released by a miracle. God was giving hands back to the Body. Hands that had been delivered would deliver, and by the power of God Simon would remove chains from others. The key that removed your chains and unlocked doors for you must be taken and used. Your hands must not

be left in prison. There must be nothing to restrict your ministry for the Master. The hands that God had helped could now help others. Chains had held them together to limit freedom and movement, but once set free they could worship, build, bless, coax and care.

Let Christ take the old key from your hand

There is an old French custom involving a key being thrown from the hand. When a man died, if his wife had not the resources to pay his debts, she took all the keys of the house, and threw them into the grave of the dead man, signifying that no one could enter the premises and take goods away, because the keys had been removed. When you came to Christ, the key to your old life was taken and thrown into the pit. Jesus took it into the grave with Him. It means there is no way back into the old life style and nature. The key has been thrown into the sea of His forgetfulness. There is no key that can enter what has been locked and secured. The best way to keep free in God is not to have any locks. Do not provide the devil with opportunities of entering into your life again. You have been forgiven forever for debts you could not pay. Get another key that will enable you to enter into a new life. The keys to the old nature and lifestyle were buried when your old life was buried in Baptism.

Hands not only mend nets and boats, they can also mend lives

Simon son of Jonas could dress himself and see to the needs of others only when his hands had been set free to be what the Lord had created them to be. God, through angelic ministry, gave Simon hands that could tie up or set free, hands that could loose and let go. They could and did mend nets, but they also mended lives. The same hands that took the grave clothes from the body of Lazarus can be your hands with God working through them. In the thought of 'perfection' we have the idea that a thing is functioning, performing what it was created to perform, to be what it was created to be. A chair is a chair, a door a door, a flower is a flower, and a star is a star, but what are you? When you reach your full potential and begin to operate in the sphere you were created for, as a bird in the air or a swan on a lake, then you will be described as *mature*.

The hand is a symbol of life

Acts 12:17 Cephas used his hands to still the crowd. His testimony followed the hand that was raised, as if it had been lifted from the dead. The hand he presented to the believers gathered together had been set free as any soul delivered from sin. There were no chains; he was free to move his hands in any direction or to send a message. If anyone waves a hand, it becomes a symbol of life. Here was the epitaph to Peter's imprisonment, a hand free to be held up on high as a testimony, like a flag, to the deliverance of the Lord. The Lord God had given him back his hands, and with those hands came the freedom to do and to be. He could now give to others what they required. He could open his hand and satisfy those around him. He must not 'sit on his hands'.

Simon Peter had a full hand

When Peter began to testify what Jehovah had done for him, it came out of a full hand. God had put something into that hand worth sharing. The hand was put up to stop the crowd, to get them to listen. What gracious words poured from his lips once the hand had been used? The hand raised can mean stop or go. It meant both as Peter went before the believers. The hand is the mediator of the body, it is an ambassador. Each finger can carry a message, from the wagging finger to the beckoning one. A mute person appreciates the power of the hand at work using sign language to convey the language of love. There is an advert in 'Yellow Pages' in Britain which says: 'Let your fingers do the walking.' It suggests that as you use your hand you are able to find what you need.

Peter's hands were not simply an addition added to his body, they were an integral part of the man. As the Lord God used him, he would use others. In the recognition of what he had and what we have there is inspiration to take us further, deeper and wider until we take hold of those who have been defined as straying sheep, people who have gone beyond the boundaries need rescuing. Some need help in many other ways, and it is your hand that can be used to meet the need. Before your hand can reach out as a talent to be used, it has to be raised up in surrender to the Lord. In the Old Dispensation whenever they wanted to confirm a promise they raised their hand, as if calling upon God to witness that they would be true to their side of the bargain.

Throughout the Acts of the Apostles, Peter was a 'handy man' in the sense that he let the Lord take the hands that were offered to be used in helping, caring and nurturing others. When he began to write his epistles, he did so using a pen in his hand.

Notes

[1] See Dr James Strong Exhaustive Concordance, published by Baker House. See Dr. Young's Concordance to the Scriptures, published by Lutterworth Press, Cambridge.

[2] This was said by the Prodigal Son when returning home to his father in Luke 15:17.

[3] See Chambers Etymological Dictionary published 1940.

[4] John 8:6.

[5] Luke 21:2.

[6] Genesis 22:8, 14.

[7] Psalm 107:23.

[8] John 8:56.

[9] Exodus 4:2.

[10] Acts 9:36–40.

[11] Acts 9:36–40.

[12] Matthew 16:19.

[13] The 'key of Promise' was used by Pilgrim when held captive by Giant Despair in Doubting Castle. It was this key which opened the door to freedom.

[14] Exodus 29:9, 29, 33, 35; 32:29.

[15] Mark 7:27, 28.

[16] Ephesians 1:10.

[17] Galatians 6:17.

Chapter Fourteen

THE MAN AND HIS SHADOW

'They brought forth the sick into the streets, and laid them on beds and couches, that at least the shadow of Peter passing by might overshadow some of them' (Acts 5:15.) Sometimes secondary principles are more important than first causes. The shadow of Peter became like the ministry and influence of the man. Here in this verse, God turned one man into two, for He not only used the man but also used his image as it was thrown along the ground like a cloak to rest over sick bodies. When the shadow passed on, it left sunshine behind in the form of healing. There is no part of a holy man that the Lord will not use. *Thinking of the man and his shadow* you might say that there is nothing in a shadow! Precisely! And that is why the Eternal used it. Free and empty of other substances, the Lord could take it and use as a bridge to health. That which had been empty filled with such fullness.

God uses that which is associated with you

People had such faith in Simon the fisherman that they believed even his influence at the extremities would be thoughtful and helpful. There comes a place in *maturity* that everything we say or do is made to count for Christ and His kingdom. Even representation which is not substance, and might even be seen as having no power at all, is made powerful by the Lord. Everything associated with you, the

One you serve takes up and puts on, this becomes like an apron worn for service.

There are times in life when even the most casual thing, such as a shadow, reaps tremendous benefits. Every part of Peter was surrendered to Christ, and from that surrender we see the surrender of others. He surrendered, and sickness surrendered its hold on a body. What others lacked the reflection gave, presenting them with something outside of themselves. You can give hope, and although it is only a shadow and cannot be grasped hold of, the Master uses it to bring sunshine to a life. What was on the outside of the Galilean was able to meet their needs. Dark shadows in fears and sicknesses had entered into lives. God took what was causing fear and sickness, another shadow, and used it to help in time of need. It seems so strange that 'He who knew no sin was made sin that we might be made the righteousness of God in Him' (2 Corinthians 5:21).

People can take refuge in what you are
The Lord took a shadow in order to chase away the shadows and nightfall in the life of others. People can take refuge in what you are and what you have from the Lord. *Maturity* is as diverse as it is dutiful. There are many sources of healing in *maturity*. There were different sicknesses but that which came from the body of Peter met with them all, and chased them away into the darkness of the night. The shadow will always operate in the brightest of life. Unaware of the fact, your shadow and your influence falls across the sick bed of others. What you are in your heart you will be at your extremities. These who were touched did not live in the shade; they were made alive because of a shadow. The miracle was that a shadow, a thing without substance, could have substance, could take hold of a man or woman and raise them to their feet. This had never been seen before; it might never be seen again. A part of a person that others can see through can be taken and used. Sincerity and simplicity are like that, without a fold.

A reflection is not much to cling on to. Taking hold of it is like trying to grasp the invisible, but when it comes from a *mature* person it is able to help others with a real need. God is able to make something extraordinary from something we would consider to be flimsy. That dependent on the midday sun was taken and used because the hour had come for the Lord to work. The shadow became the 'image' of the invisible God.'

Hezekiah's healing was found in God turning the sun back ten degrees. (2 Kings 20:9, 10, 11.) In this story it was the shadow of a man used to enlarge the Kingdom of grace. The healing went deeper and further than any silhouette.

Your influence is part of you

A shadow wears no clothes and contains little colour. It is simply a reflection, but a reflection of all that you have allowed the Lord to do in your life. It is the contour of your Christianity and Christlikeness. Its centre is in you, and its circumference is in those who are touched with an unseen hand as large as a shadow.

Your shadow is your friend; it tells others all about you. It is an ambassador of what you are. Through your influences men come to know what to expect. You send the shadow of your substance to the right, or to the left, in front or behind, depending on where you are standing. Like the first bud of spring, it tells others what to expect, even as the first bird of the long awaited summer sings that warmer days are on the way. Peter had much to offer, and so have you. Let your weakest image in a shadow become your strongest point. Let it contain healing, helping, touching and caring properties. Prayer was answered without being uttered. God will work through prayer, and even if you don't pray He will still perform His best acts. When you are not at your best, let the Best be seen in your all-round influence. If you remain in the shade you will have no shadow moving in the sunlight. Step into the brightness and the best as you walk in the light as Simon Cephas walked in the light.

The Lord makes important what you think is insignificant

When Jesus said to Cephas 'Follow me and I will make you a fisher of men,'[1] Peter could never have imagined that Jesus would use a small piece of shade in order to help another. What might have been a dark, shapeless blob was given hands, feet and a mouth to serve the

Eternal. God makes important those things we feel are unimportant. This shadow should have conformed to all that Peter did, but it stepped outside of natural laws when it produced healing and hope. It is faith that connects us to the power of God, and it is sometimes faith in the most menial thing, such as a sparrow, that brings teaching and deliverance.

Sir Walter Raleigh put his cloak over a black, muddy hole as the Queen of England stepped out of her carriage. She simply trod on the coat. Love covers a multitude of sins.[2] You can have something which, as a coat, covers the pit of hell, and stops those who are going towards it with the legs of a centipede. Peter had become another Bezaleel, meaning 'the shadow of God'.[3] If you can't be there in person, then do what this apostle did, send the very best of yourself in a letter, or word of consolation, or in a figure of representation. These in need will take what you have offered, even from afar.

You are responsible for your ministry

You are responsible for your ministry! Totally responsible for what comes into your life and what goes out of it. Where you stand, it stands; where you sit, your influence is always with you. Create a large enough shadow to reach and influence far and wide, near and dear. Be as the English car 'Rolls Royce' which is the best of all that is British. One model has the name 'Silver Shadow'. The only silver Simon possessed was in his shadow. Let your outer circle of influence be as Elijah's mantle that parted the waters of the River Jordan to enable another to cross over. (2 Kings 2:13, 14.) Let your shadow be to you as the cloak which the apostle Paul left at Troas with Carpus (2 Timothy 4:13), full of memories. He had gone through storm, wind, shipwreck, and yet the cloak remained 'ship-shape'. Stained with brine from the Adriatic Sea, it remained as a true warm friend. It was the same through rain or shine, it was part of him filled with precious memories. What the shadow of this fisherman brought to sick folk, the coat that Paul desired in a dark, deep prison cell brought him warmth and memories. As he wrapped it around himself, so he wrapped himself in those memories.

There comes a moment for God to act

The Lord didn't choose to use the shadow all the time, but this was the right moment, the right time and the right vehicle of expression, and Jehovah took it and released those who were bound by disease. There was as much healing virtue in it as there was in the garment worn by Jesus, when the woman with the issue of blood touched it, and her flow was staunched.[4] This shadow became hope and joy. It takes great faith to believe that there is something in you, like a silhouette, here for a moment and then gone, because it depends on the circumstances being right. There are talents, gifts and useful commodities in all that we have. The power of God goes through the personality, and even reaches into the shadow of a man. You can cast that which is a shadow over lives without ever being conscious of what is happening. You influence others, and by doing so they become part of all they have ever met, and that includes you. Each *mature* person forms many shadows. Each day a shadow will appear in the sunshine, and each day it is different, because it has risen that day with the sun. There is something in every life that is reaching beyond that life, as a missionary reaches into the misery of others. Jesus had promised to make Peter an influence, i.e. 'fisher of men' but Simon never thought it would be so far reaching.

When we naturally think of the shadow of a man, we think in terms of the man not being as great as he was. The shadow reduces the size, and usually the influence of a person, but here it is different. God takes the lesser to create the greater and the larger. God turned this idea, that we have to be great and in the zenith of manhood in order to be used, on its head when He allowed the shadow of Peter to pass by, and rest on a person just long enough for the shadow to fulfil its calling, before moving on as the sun sets at the end of another golden day. That shadow was temporal but it left something behind permanent.

We all have limited opportunities

The shadow appeared perhaps for a day or even an hour, and each time span had limited opportunities. Our time is a limited time, and we need to let the Master use every part of day and night, so that when the shadow decreases, when our influence passes on, there might be substance left behind in people raised from sickness, and made happy in Jesus. 'The night comes when no man may work' (John 9:4). These people were so sick that they couldn't even stand to their feet to raise a shadow. They came where the influence in the form of a shadow could reach them.

When the Master uses a shadow, it means there is nothing of substance to resist Him and what He wants to do. From that shadow God formed healing properties, and all people had to do was to wait until the shadow passed by them, in order to receive their healing. In this reflection there was enough influence to set men and women free. In the smallest ministry, weakest influence, in that which you would not count as being you, the Lord will take it and use. Oh, to be as faithful as a shadow is to the man! The Eternal is looking for that quality of faithfulness, which becomes the shadow of *maturity*. The praise did not go to Peter but to God —God, who was working in the shadows and behind the shadow through this simple thing, achieved a great end. From that which had no substance came real substance. That which had no memory left a memory.

The Lord heals through the everyday happenings in life
From each person's life there are hands at work in healing, springing from the ordinary and everyday happenings in the life of a believer. Each 'good work' is a replica of what you are. This shade was just what some of these wilting people required. Some parts of a garden need the sun; others require the stony ground, while others need the shade. Some plants do well in thick, clay soil; others require no depth at all, just like a shadow. It is in the shade that some reach their full potential even as those who were sick did as they were healed.

It was no loud voice that helped, no pulpit manner or well-groomed appearance; it was a shadow that stole the show. How gentle, full and fulfilling was the ministry of the *mature*! It was a shelter thrown across their path, altering the way they thought, lived and acted in the future. We begin life with 'substance,' we are born with a substance, with a substantial body. God commences with a shadow. This is not easy to accept. It is not normal conventional thinking. It is that same principle which believes that wind can pass right through a tree or a wall. When God begins to move, He looks to see what is on the altar, and uses whatever is offered. He is never pleased when He demands sacrifice and we only offer a shadow. In Simon the son of Jonas both the man and his shadow were offered and accepted. If God finds nothing to meet His requirements, He will take that which is on the outside to meet the needs inside another.

Your ministry is you; it does not belong to another

All shadows depend on the object from which they are reflected. One shape becomes another in shadow. Your ministry is you; it does not belong to another. It will take your shape. If there is zeal, love, burning passion in you, then that will also be in the service you offer to others. That cup of cold water given in His Name will not be half empty, nor will we be found striking others into obedience with an empty chalice, saying, 'Believe or a worse thing will descend on you!'

There is such a thing as a conscious ministry, even as there is such a thing as an unconscious influence. You are at your best, performing your best healing acts of mercy, when you don't know they are taking place. Peter did not have to organise this happening, it was spontaneous. It is the *mature* man who believes that every part of his life, the sunshine or shade, can be made to count for his Lord. Sometimes in the shade under the influence of the shadow we are able to see things more clearly. What this disciple offered to others was a place of refuge and rest. Those who were over-heated could and did find a cooling influence in a man who simply walked from one end of the street to the other. It does not take fifty years to influence others! When you walk into a life, bring an influence! The shadow will only run if you run. Have something worth having and leaving that will restore another. As we live for the Lord we cast shadows everywhere.

The influence of Simon was more than casting a pearl before swine. It was not just an umbrella for pain or a shelter from rain, it accosted and accomplished! What is softer than a shadow or more flimsy? This dark reflection became a 'waiting room' for those who

221

had missed the last train! It came from the heart of a need, and met the need of a heart. There was enough given to cover all sickness. What had happened to this follower of Christ was passed on. What we do in our *maturity* must minister life and hope to others.

That which seems unreal can be made a messenger of the real
People do not normally follow a shadow for it is not a real thing. The people could not follow it; it followed them until it fell across them. That which appears to be unreal can be made real by the Lord. When God is at work even the flimsy can have substance added. According to the Book of Hebrews the Old Testament had types and shadows to lead us to Christ. Let your shadow become your substance; let your substance become your shadow. God places you into something quite empty, which on first examination might appear to be nothing at all. It is these small unaccounted things in life that lead you on to *maturity*, an enlarging that sees hope for the hopeless and help for the helpless.

Your influence does not remain where it is. You are greater than what you can measure or think. Let your influences be anchored in you. 'It has not yet entered into your heart the things that God has prepared for them that love Him' (1 Corinthians 2:9). There are certain qualities about you that you are not aware of. Others are, and as you pass by something of what you are passes over their lives like a shadow. You introduce healing and help without being conscious of what you have done. Everything you have passed through has added to your shadow. You enter a room, and there is a charisma about you, even though you may not realise it.

We look at our own capabilities through a glass eye
We sometimes look at our capabilities through a glass darkly, through a glass eye. We don't see what and who we are in the Eternal. We think our talents are all in the big thing, when in fact they are released into that which can be quite small and narrow. You might see your talents as rare as hen's teeth, but with God our nothings can be His everything.

This shadow falling as a Godly influence helped them to walk the very street they were laid on, giving them a new hope and a new pathway. Can you dedicate your life to God, so that this can happen? Can you pray that the Lord will make every breath coming from your redeemed body as part of a Ministry Team? Shadows usually end with shadows, but not this flung hand of hope coming from Peter. You can influence those across the sea and across the street by letting the Master enlarge you even if it is only in the measure of a thin dark strip. You can step through a dark reflection into the light.

As these who were healed had to wait for the shadow to come to them, so you must await God's time. When He comes it might only be in a shadow, a very small thing, but believe that this has been sent from God. The feather from an angel's wing is as good as an angel! God doesn't begin with the large or the confident, but with that which is lacking substance and quality. The quality *maturity* from the Lord comes from some strange areas of life. Life is full of shadows, some strange or hurtful, yet each one can be the hand of God reaching out to touch and help you. You might be so depressed that it seems as if a shadow has fallen, and has deepened your darkness. You haven't seen or heard what the Almighty is wanting. He shades you with a shadow before sending you out into the burning rays of the sun to be a witness for Him. Everything on target must spend time hidden in a shadow before being made useful. Under the shadow it is matured. Have faith in God, and that shaft of darkness shall yet be turned into sunshine. There are certain flimsy reflections that, if you walked upon them would let you fall into the sea. Allow God with His many ministering angels to come and strengthen what you have so that just like the shadow of the Almighty, you will be made strong enough to walk and lean upon.

Each thing done and said can be a shadow of mercy

If you cannot get to the person who needs you as they couldn't get to Peter, try getting to the shadow by accepting the lesser thing. If you can't reach out and touch God, turn to His word. It is the lesser opportunity that sometimes leads us to fullness. There are many in the world whom you will never meet, but they can meet your shadow in the prayers you offer for them, or the gifts you give to forward the work of the Lord in their hands. Each amount of money given produces its own shadow of success. You can be healed if you will accept that God moves in a mysterious way.

When Namaan wanted to be healed from his leprosy, he was angry because the prophet of God did not come and wave his hand over the place were he was sick. (2 Kings 5:11.) The prophet sent his shadow in a word. If that word was obeyed the healing would take place. Namaan did obey and was healed. When the Centurion asked for healing for his daughter, he had real faith. He said, 'Speak the word only,'[5] just send Your shadow and that will be enough, and it was enough. The emptiness of God is more full than the fullest thing provided by men.

Others can be influenced in your absence

Those things written in the Gospels and epistles became the shadow of the man. The congregations might never meet with the writers to shake them by the hand, but their writings brought shadows into their lives, a place of true refuge during a time of storm. Your image can be in every corner even when you are not present. How you have arranged your home, organised your furniture, where this picture hangs, where you have placed flowers, are all shadows, which can help others in a time of crisis. You are what you are, and the Eternal will be what He is as He works through these things associated with you. I have heard students preaching who have all the mannerisms of their lecturers, and these shadows have lived on in the students. A shadow is an associate member of you, even when you are absent.

As Peter walked, his shadow fell across them, but he was there in person to back it up by substance. If you promise one thing and do another, your influence will mean nothing. Empty barrels do not weigh as much as full ones! When those who were healed needed lifting up, or showing the way home, he was at hand to follow his shadow with substance. This one occasion proves that the Lord will not always use a mere shadow, or even that because He uses something about you once He will use the same thing every time. When the Lord can't send you, or where you won't even go, He will send your shadow. He expects you as body, soul and spirit to be there and be involved. Only God can turn shadow into substance. At the Resurrection of Jesus Christ, people thought He was a ghost, a shadow, but He proved that He was substance by eating a piece of broiled fish. (Luke 24:42.) Jesus is no figment of the imagination; He is a fact of faith.

You will influence the most when you are the least

There are those who need releasing from that which makes them small. The only way we can help is by becoming a shadow, unnoticed with no great show or shower of words. The shadow can't give much but it can give itself. It has no pockets to empty on the altar because it is empty already. We will influence the most when we are the least. Your greatest moments will be when you feel that you are only a shadow. It is that humbleness of spirit that the God of Jacob will take and use to help another. In olden days when boats had to be rowed, it was the oar which took the boat to its destination when the wind failed to propel it forward. When the sails failed in the harbour straights, it was then that the thin oar came into its glory.

Where there are shadows and darkness it usually means the sun is going down. God reversed the order because from this moment the sun would rise, and all other shadows were chased away by the reflection of Simon. What had been a torment and hurtful was removed by a greater shadow. As the Galilean stood in the presence of Christ, so the shadow of Christ was reflected through Simon. You will reflect that in your heart held dear.

Maturity does not cling to shadows forever

Although they were healed from their sicknesses in the shade, God expected them to come out into the open sunshine. *Maturity* does not cling to shadows forever. There comes a moment as with Mary in the garden of Gethsemane that you must take Christ by the feet to find His hands.[6] When God wanted to rescue the world, He sent a Man in the form of human flesh, to rescue all who were simply sitting in the shadow of death where no sunshine would come. For there to be any shadow, the clouds must be parted. One of the meanings of doubt is to have the mind filled with clouds of all shapes and sizes.

The clouds and the mixed multitude of many things must be blown away so that your usefulness can be seen and heard. God will even use the darkness to provide a light for you, the light of the glorious gospel of Jesus Christ.

Ask the Lord of glory to give you such a shadow, to make you such an influence that those on the other side of the street will be influenced by you. If you can't go to the other side of the world, try the other side of the street! Try travelling as long or as short as your shadow. May the Eternal God give you a shadow so large and yet so light that it can go to where they are and heal them. Every time you post a letter with a word of thanks in it, or a gift for some needy cause, you are letting your shadow do its work. All this was happening to Cephas, the one who had denied his Lord. Even his shadow became greater in his *maturity* than all his influence in his younger days.

God can fill your emptiness in order that you can fill others
These waiting on the streets were in a position where it seemed as if they had nothing to hold on to. You cannot cling to a shadow! God puts something into emptiness that helps you to help another. An artist will cover a canvas with a black cloth —until the time of manifestation, when he removes the cloth, you see sights so beautiful they make you cry. The water he has painted is so real, you look for a cup to dip into it and take a drink. The song birds are so lovely you can hear them singing from the shadow of the bough and leaf.

This was a healing shadow: in verse 16 it says, 'and every one was healed.' Whatever it touched, whoever it lay across, whatever their need or shape the shadow was successful, not simply because Peter was now a *mature* man but because he believed the Lord would take his shadow, and use his influence as a potter might take a piece of clay. God loves a challenge like that! While others came to straighten the sick bed, the shadow of Simon came to straighten out the life. When you ask the Lord to take something that you do not think is of much substance and use it, He does it time and time again. You need to let your shadow pass by, so that as you move on you can see the healing in lives that have been affected by you and your ministry, whether consciously or unconscious! The shadow has no mouth or ears, no feet or hands, but it did the work of God.

Learn to move on after completing your work

The shadow moves on after it has completed its work. Refreshed in the night it appears with the sun, ready to serve another day. A shadow is free; you can't lock it up or capture it in your hand. It goes where the substance goes, and here that substance was the Saviour. Pray that you will do the same as Peter. For the shape to move, you must keep moving. What you do, your shadow will do the same. Normally Peter would lay hands on the sick, and they would be healed. The extraordinary is only given for a time until our task is complete. May you and I be as faithful as this shadow that did not set with the sun but moved on with God, Who provided its power and healing qualities. There came a moment for this shadow to cease and to appear in another form as Jesus did on the Emmaus Road.[7] A time even for the miraculous to appear in a different way. May you be ready for the change of ministry in your life. It can't be all shadow that heals; there must be other things in God that with Peter as a *mature* man we must learn. Only God is forever. Don't remain in the shadows; let the Almighty give you substance as you follow Peter further in Jesus until you become *mature*.

Notes
[1] Matthew 4:19.
[2] 1 Peter 4:8.
[3] Exodus 31:2.
[4] Luke 8:44.
[5] Matthew 8:8.
[6] John 20:17.
[7] Mark 16 :12.

Chapter Fifteen

THE MAN WHO BROUGHT CONVICTION THROUGH PASSION

As years pass and as experiences mark us with an unseen hand, we have something worth saying, and we utter with conviction because it is personal. It is part of human thinking, learning, teaching and knowing. What you say is worth listening to and obeying, because evidence shows that it has worked in your life, making you a fully rounded person. Whenever you read about Simon Peter in the Acts of the Apostles, what he says has an effect. His words and his worth are translated into deeds. Peter did not simply accumulate knowledge, he was learning and in training until he left the 'starting blocks' to enter into the Race of Life.

You can become a reference to spirituality

As you *mature*, your words become words of reference, quote and note, an epistle read of all men —an epistle that has to be filled with all manner of things, both rare and common. Everything Peter says in the Acts of the Apostles is an echo from the past, for he had sat at the feet of the Master Teacher. He had seen crumbs turned into loaves. He had witnessed when Jesus glowed, white as clean snow falling on the Mount of Transfiguration. Often he had seen the Great Shepherd of the Sheep gathering lambs into the fold, leading them in and out into new pasture. All these things were registered indelibly in his heart which nothing could erase. He had seen ships seemingly disappear under the waves, the name of the ship on its prow, but each time it came up through that salty bath, the name remained on the vessel. The teachings of Jesus had been like that in his own life. He was the pebble turned into a rock, and when he spoke it was from a rock-like conviction.

Let there be a ring of truth about what you say

Peter never said anything for effect, everything he said bore the 'ring of truth'. In the Old Testament, God said everyone who heard what He had to say would have 'tingling ears'. (1 Samuel 3:11.) When 'itching ears'[1] were converted, those ears would 'tingle,' would 'vibrate' as a leaf vibrating in the wind, because of what the Almighty had to say. Peter said things that people wanted to hear and also what they didn't want to hear. His voice was loud and clear, yet soft and sweet when necessary.

Ears 'tingling' also can suggest that when they were 'rattled' their ears would also be 'rattled'. The word 'tingling' is applied to lips that 'quiver' with fear. When you speak, it can result in a new direction for someone; mean the difference between life and death. His voice became as the voice of a well beloved when believers required teaching and helping. We need to speak, and when we speak others need listen to what we have to say. The passion in you will put a crown of flame on every word you speak.

Never leave people as you find them

The beautiful thing about the record in the Acts of the Apostles is that we are able to consider the end of Peter's conversation (*Greek*, conduct), and weigh all what he had to say in the balances. Peter always left his hearers with something to do, he left them with conviction. Simon not only faced friends on a sunny Sunday afternoon, he faced many hostile crowds. He had to speak to great and small who would readily discern if this man really believed what he was saying. The former manager of Liverpool Football Club, England, Bill Shankley, was asked if 'football was his life,' he replied, 'It is more than that!' If others are going to take 'note' of what you say there has to be the 'cut of the crystal' about your character, charter and challenge. We never want to be as a 'voice crying in the wilderness' with no message and no direction. John Baptist not only spoke he did so with the deepest conviction, as deep as the waters he baptised converts in, what he said was such a challenge that people flew from the wrath to come.[2]

Peter's conviction was hotter than hell

Peter's conviction had to be deeper and hotter than hell because it was hell that some of them were rescued from! There will be times when you will have to wet your message with your own tears. The desire you have must be moulded into what you say and are. The agony presented in repentance will be the agony and pain of your own heart. What the artist presents in painting is what you preach. You paint pictures. Let it always be a masterpiece of Jesus Christ. Leave no one in doubt, asking: what does this mean? Let your detail be precise and passionate. What is baptised in the listener will first be baptised in you. What we say must be recognised as having salt and being seasoned with grace, as it was in the fisherman.

Simon Peter did not ramble as if going along a country lane or ploughing a field. He knew what he wanted to say and he said it. He never went around in circles except when describing the love of God as a circle that has no beginning or ending. He knew with a passion and conviction where he was going. Some aim at nothing in communicating, and strike nothing every time! Simon Peter aimed straight and true. There was an Everest in his throat each time Cephas spoke, because of his denial of the Lord. Failure in the past did not jeopardise future enterprise.

Let your words be an echo of Christ's words

Every word must become an echo of the Lord. As Peter preached and prayed for the sick, he quoted the words of Jesus, and enacted all that Jesus did. This as his life was a continuation of all that Jesus 'began to do and to teach'. (Acts 1:1.) When we say things, we are not conscious of how we affect others, yet according to the Holy Book the power of life and death are in the tongue. What a weapon is your tongue! It can be a healer to those who are in severe pain, or feel let down by life. It can be a leader as we lead by example from the front. It is recorded in the book of Job, 'by my words men have stood on their feet.'[3] There is a ministry expressed through the mouth. There is a ministry of conviction as we express the perfections of Jesus in holiness. Each word can be a trumpet call to attention, or a sweet musical note feeding the spirit of the dejected. The wise man said, 'I would rather all men think me a fool, than open my mouth and remove all doubt.' I would prefer to rather say nothing and mean something, rather than say something and mean nothing. God spoke with conviction in Genesis 1 and worlds were hung on words. We are judged by our words as much as by our deeds. What you say is an echo of your heart, proceeding as an army of words either to rescue or to defeat. The moment you decide to say something, the letters of the English alphabet come to your aid as an army.

Words can be common, cheap and without depth
The words we speak are common and can be so cheap. 'Cheap as chips', cost nothing, and meaning nothing. 'Let the words of my mouth and the meditation of my heart be acceptable in Thy sight O, Lord my Redeemer.'[4] From these lips came the 'good news' of the Gospels as Peter spoke of the way, truth and life.

We have all heard of the 'politician's promise'. When Peter spoke, it affected the listeners. Throughout the Book of Acts, whenever Peter said anything, it caused a stir, and people were never the same again. In some lives all the ingredients are there, but they need stirring together to make a completely different flavour. What Simon said fitted into lives as if the life had been previously prepared to receive all that was spoken. There are parts of a human spirit that are God-shaped, and which are filled as God is shared with others. His words were attested by his actions. He not only 'looked before he leaped,' but he also thought before he spoke. How different is the *mature* man! What was said came from his heart, and was mantled in sincerity. Warmed in his heart, it melted the hearers. Before the Day of Pentecost and the inception of the Acts of the Apostles, Peter's tongue never seemed to be in gear with his brain. Then, a transformation took place, every word he said was a brick on which to build. His heart was 'inditing a good matter, as he spoke of things touching the King,' (Psalm 45:1). His words gave time, space and patience, and because of that his life influenced men.

Life is an examination and an explanation

It seems as if Simon was always 'on target' when he preached the word of God. The very term 'examination' comes from a Latin word that suggests the 'needle on a balance,' to 'watch it', to regulate the sights of the gun or other instrument of war, then to examine it to see if it is true.[5] You will know if you are true by the conviction of those who listen. Peter had been unbalanced, but when the Lord took him through those tough discipleship courses with many hurdles and tumbles, he was not found wanting. He knew, as a fisherman, how important it was to get the ballast right on a ship. If it was out by one degree the ship might sink. He had been trained by truth for this moment. Peter did not say what entered his head, but what entered his heart by the Holy Spirit. Each word had been through a process of time, truth and hurt. What you say can be a rod to beat people with. When you speak in the Holy Ghost, that 'rod' becomes a 'staff' on which they can lean, and through it the weary find a new source of strength. Sheep were rescued from deep water through the staff of the shepherd.[6]

The first time this *mature* man had to speak was in Acts 1:15. Peter stood up; the words that 'made people sit up and stand up' began to flow from his mouth. If you post a notice in black and white, very few might bother to read it. If you underlined every word in red it would shout out to those who noticed it. The red flag was the Roman signal for entering into battle. The tongues of red fire had sat upon each one of them in Acts 2:4. Everything Cephas said was underlined by the cross and the redemptive work of Jesus. Each time he preached was a 'red letter day'[7] because it emphasised the red blood of Jesus Christ.

The words of the wise are as nails

To use an 'Americanism', Peter never 'talked his noise'. His service was not as an empty valley or an echo on a misty morning. The words of the wise are as 'nails in a sure place'.[8] You can trust them, and hang on to them. Each nail has a sharp point for penetration. Like the promises of God they do not bend, break or fail.

When the young Galilean had to preach at Pentecost, none of his words were wasted. Scriptures record of Samuel the prophet, 'The Lord let none of his words fall to the ground' (1 Samuel 3:19). They were not as crumbs falling from the hand to be eaten by ants and spiders. They were not wasted, they were as seeds scattered, taking deep root, and many were convicted. Under the conviction of Peter's preaching they had said, 'Men and brethren what shall we do?' (Acts 2:37). He certainly made his listeners 'sit up and take notice'. 'They were pricked in their heart' (Acts 2:37). His words did not fall as leaves to the floor to be trodden on, and later rotted away by wind, rain and ice. They entered the hearts of the listeners. Each word was 'barbed', for it had many corners. They were like wartime sea mines with their many protruding shafts that caused an explosion on impact. What he said did not settle easy on their conscience. Every word was a 'blast from the past' and a call into a new future.

What you say can convict and convince others

The word 'prick' means to be 'stung' like a bee 'stings', words meant to produce honey in the believer. Each word had a promise of the Land of Milk and Honey'. The word 'prick' can mean to be stunned as an animal waiting to be slaughtered. It is to be 'stung to the quick'. It is hard to kick against these sorts of 'pricks'. It was not just a 'sting in the tail' but a 'bite from the jaw' that they received. Some speakers lack conviction, and you return home feeling as if you have been ravaged by a dead sheep! This was not the showing of a rasping tongue but the echo of eternity coming into time. It was not the manner in which Simon spoke, but the power the words communicated that made them want to listen. This man said something and each word was cloaked with zeal. The silver tongued orator could speak well, but he couldn't persuade the heart of the people. What Simon said became a dot, a point, a prickle in the heart. Listening to other speakers, they could take or leave what was said. Here, they had no choice but to take it, for it clung to them as a burr will cling to cloth.

In Acts 3:4, the words of Peter were 'look on us'; it was the man's obedience to that first command and initial word, which caused him to take notice. What Peter said was not a summons to appear before a court of law, to be found guilty as charged, it was an invitation to enter the temple, but it could only be fulfilled through healing. It was a challenge to take the first step into the banqueting hall, for a time of non stop music and rejoicing where the music and that challenge not only caused the man to sit up, he also stood, walked, leaped and praised God. What Cephas said was believable, and the man gave heed, in expectation. When you have preached or witnessed, you must deliver. Promises riddled with holes are useless!

Your words can be as silver and your deeds as gold
The man at the Gate was obviously expecting silver or gold, but the very silver and gold were in the words spoken by the disciple. The difference between what others said and what the Galilean said was the difference between darkness and light. The words of a *mature* person are beyond estimation. Many rubies cannot buy them, and much study cannot add conviction to them. They are as silver and gold, and by our belief will help us get to where we want to go. To the person in poverty of spirit they are as good as ready money. When Peter took the man by the right hand, words had developed into works. The two go together, like Peter and John. Words became as 'walking sticks' to the man, the spoken word became the word received, and the word received became the power of a new life.

In Acts 5:33 what Simon son of Jonas had to say was not as acceptable as that previously which had been said. It became as a broken tooth or vile poison in the same mouth. What was intended to make men 'sit up' and take notice became a stumbling block, and chased them away. They were 'cut to the heart', with grinding teeth. Instead of chewing, they spewed out what might have been a medicine to them. They took the medicine without reading the instructions on the label. They were steeped in religion, and when Peter had finished speaking they were sinking fast in that same religion. The phrase 'cut to the heart' means 'bursting with anger'. Maybe his words only reached the outside of their heart? Something had to come out if anything was to go in. This was only part of the anger, jealousy and pride that crowned the heart.

The word of God can cut the heart

They were left in no doubt after receiving blows from the word of God. That which is spoken by the *mature* person will either drive you further out to sea or bring you nearer the land, into a safe haven. It says they were 'cut' to heart. They were as 'cut' as the man on the Jericho Road, left bleeding and dying, sorely wounded.[9] It was the 'cut' of the Great Physician, as He tried to heal them.

That 'cut' was meant to set free from the ropes that bound them. Only God can slice through the human spirit, and touch a heart where it hurts the most. That is where pain has its authority and dominion. The words spoken were meant to free them from religious bondage. But the opposite happened. They were bound hand, foot, eyes and ears in their spirit, they needed an invisible hand to reach inside of them to set free. Who knows the spirit of man like the Spirit of God? They felt they were not being set free; they had chains added to their ropes in the words of the young fisherman. The only freedom they saw in what Simon said was the open door into the abattoir to be slaughtered. They could see no freedom in that which was intended to make them 'sit up'. They were 'cut' very deeply, suggesting that they were 'sawn' in two like a log of wood. If you act 'wooden' then expect to be 'sawn asunder'. The word 'cut' means to 'divide', as you would cleave a piece of wood using an axe. It implies to 'fall apart', because Peter removed the very 'nuts and bolts' of their existence, their religion, and because it was 'man made' a man could and did remove it.

People might hate you but God loves you

The same word 'cut' was used in the Septuagint Version of the Scriptures in 1 Chronicles 20:3, describing people being sawn in two. Here was a divided devotion. One part wanted to listen while the other half became stone dead. The same word 'cut' describes the deep feeling of hatred for Stephen when he preached in Acts 7:54. They knew when Peter had preached that he had borrowed a tool from the Carpenter of Nazareth, and used it as a saw. He saw them as wood to be worked upon by the Carpenter. All they did was to 'sit up', stand up and rebel against what was being said to them. However deep the teaching, they went beyond its reach and voice. One of the symbols of Peter, in Christian art, is a sword. Simon, the Canaanite's symbol, was a saw. Each disciple among the twelve had some tool as his emblem.

The people were agitated by the strong emotion of rebellion. Standing to resist the power and words of the *mature* man. It is amazing how many have much stronger convictions than those received by the Spirit of God, when choosing to go their own way! The way of the Lord continues, the way of the wicked comes to a dead end. The Way Peter presented went from earth to Heaven. This Way became a manner of life and living. They lived the Way, the Truth and the Life.

Speak through anointed lips
In Acts chapter 10, as Peter preached, his preaching was authenticated as the listeners were baptised in the Holy Ghost. These men were soldiers, and what they heard through the lips of the anointed fisherman caused them to stand and be ready to fight. The soldiers were well equipped, they carried the Arms of Rome, emblazoned upon every shield was the glory of Rome. They lacked those weapons that come through the Holy Ghost that would change them into soldiers of the Cross. We can have so much and yet possess so little when we consider all that has been provided for us. Each soldier always carried a little salt. There was salt in Peter's seasoned sermon, and they reached out with open hands in worship; God placed the sword of the Spirit in each hand and heart. These men were well equipped.

(Acts 10:34) 'Peter opened his mouth', and gracious words, words of love, hope and acceptance, came from his lips. His 'one tongue' with a Galilean accent was turned into many tongues as the Holy

Spirit rested on each person present. Peter magnified God with one tongue, and these did the same with many tongues. What was 'one' became many as conviction came, as it had come to the heart of Peter. These were warm words, warmed by a heart that was devoted to Jesus Christ. They didn't have to ask what they should do. The Lord simply did it, because they believed what was said. They took it to use it, and it used them. They as the *mature* will cause people to magnify God in many different languages. There are tongues known and unknown, tongues of men and of angels, these were the tongues of men dipped in fire.

The Holy Spirit can appear as a garment

Peter preached about the anointing of Jesus (Acts 10:38) and as he unfolded what had happened, that same anointing fell on them. In Acts 1:8 the metaphor of the Holy Spirit coming upon them is as a cloak falling onto shoulders, or to be dressed in a certain garment. There will always be an enlarging of the heart to receive more of God when we speak from experience. These other tongues were God's amen, the Lord confirming all that had been said. God was stamping something on them as a seal invades the territory of the wax.[10] What had been in Simon's life as granules of grace became pounds of passion as he preached. The branding iron had been taken from the fire and applied, marking out every believer as belonging to the Lord, sheep of His pasture.

What Peter said on each occasion cannot be faulted. He was not so much a theologian as a man with a burning conviction, as much as the burning bush that attracted Moses.[11] He was no Mount Sinai belching fire and smoke. What he said was well directed, forcefully and faithfully expounded. Each time those who had 'fallen' away, to the right or the left were made to 'sit up', 'stand up' and 'grow up'. Even in deep waters they were handed a lifeline, enabling them to be rescued and brought to safety. There is safety in numbers, but there is also safety in one, if that one is this young fisherman. When he preaches, he is lowering his net to take a catch. There has to be in the *mature* man the ability to help people to grow in the grace and knowledge of our Lord Jesus Christ. What you say is not for your sake but for the sake of the listeners, so that they might move on to become believers.

People with the power of God will be recognised

Simon Peter said, 'Tabitha arise.' She opened her eyes: and when she saw Peter she sat up.' When she looked at Cephas, she saw more than a fisherman or a man, she recognised a man who had power with God. While she was dead he was speaking to a lifeless corpse. It was as if he was preaching to the unconverted. Men who are *mature* will always provide something new to look at. He was still there at the introduction of new life to help her. Peter had been taught through his fishing experience that you stay with a thing until you get results. He had the patience both of a fisherman and a saint. If you are going to make people 'sit up', they will to do it because through good or ill you have stayed with them. Faith became faithfulness in the man of God.

Yet in the sleep of death she could do no 'good works', yet Simon was performing a 'good work' in a miracle. Dorcas 'sat up' while Peter lifted her up. He had a lovely bedside manner, but the *mature* ministry does not stop at the start or end at the ending. It never sees its work finished. There is no ending of the day in the work of the Lord, only the beginning of some new thing. There are always additional human touches required before you can see people delivered. What was death became life through the words of the Christian worker. This was part of the: 'greater things shall you do, because I go to the Father.'[12] Here was proof that He was with the Father. God, through the Galilean, was taking care of His children.

It doesn't matter how far you have drifted

It was the words spoken by the apostle that made her 'sit up'. It did not matter how far she had drifted away, in whatever sphere she found herself, it was his words that led her to sit up. There is a voice for us that will travel to the highest heights and the deepest depths in order for us to hear and respond. Sheep are never lost on the Mount of Forgetfulness where the Eternal cannot hear their sorry bleating. Passion producing conviction must help people to change their position from being dead to being made alive. That woman could see nothing, hear nothing and do nothing. It was the spoken word, thrown as a lifeline that brought her back from the deep dead. The church will always require those who can speak life into people and change their relationship to God. Cephas found her lying flat and dead. The gracious words he spoke saw her sitting up and in her own mind. How different to the words of the funeral undertaker as he lowers the body into the ground. This was not ashes to ashes, dust to dust, but from death to life. The woman had not heard a word, but she somehow realised that Peter was the substance to follow rather than just the sound of words. People don't simply want to listen to a voice but they need virtue to follow.

We all need someone to follow and something to obey

Sometimes people will not hear a word you utter. Peter was prepared to stay where she was until she was made whole enough to go where he was. It was not what Peter said on this occasion but what he was, what Tabitha saw that made her 'sit up'. In the church today we need a prophetical voice that will disturb the slumbering Woman identified as the church in the Book of Revelation, and bring her back from the dead.[13] The woman lived on in the echo of Simon's voice, and the happiness of his smile.

When Dorcas 'sat up' it was the beginning of that which had been produced by the words of Peter. The words spoken were made flesh. A word is enough to see a person resurrected, there must be more words of encouragement. Sit with those who are in pain until you feel their pain. Stay with them until their eyes are open and they are fully awake to God. It is useless getting them to 'sit up' if you do not get them to stand and walk forward into new life. There is only one letter at the beginning of the English alphabet, the letter 'A', but there are many more to follow. None of them mean much until they come together in unity and march as an army to make people 'sit up' and take notice. These words were spoken to encourage all those who have been hurt or have died, to get up and go on. These expressions of your innermost being need to be thought and said. As the words without the man are nothing but thoughts, so we without

Christ Who is the Word of God are nothing. Choose your words so that they become choice words. Choose your words and what you are going to say as you chose Jesus Christ.

What was a burden was given legs to walk

Peter had come to the house, and was going to lead Tabitha out along the same path that he had trodden. Peter went into that death chamber alone. One set of footprints went in, but two came out. Resurrection power will cause you to use what you have. One went in and two came out because there was something in Simon that made people 'take notice' and 'sit up'. You can say and do as much as you can, but others have to learn to 'sit up'. It is the first step to walking and talking. She learned this because of what Peter had said, 'Young maid I say to you arise.' Based on those few words from the *mature* one she 'sat up'. To Simon Peter this was part of a new creation, something the Lord had done as he spoke the word. He had in the back of his mind the words he heard when fellowshipping in the flesh with Jesus, 'Speak the word only, and my servant shall live.'[14] Peter was simply copying the Master. He wasn't simply a servant of the Master; he was a master servant, a living echo of what Jesus had taught. Peter became a word of triumph in the battle for a life.

We see the *maturity* of the young man in that he copied what he had seen Jesus Christ do. We are called to be imitators of Jesus. Peter became the carbon copy of his Master's deeds. Jesus asked the people to leave before He prayed for one, and so did Simon. (Matthew 9:25, Luke 8:51.) There is a pattern to follow if people are to 'sit up'. Jesus said, 'Take up your cross and 'follow' Me.'[15] Walk the same way and plough the same furrow.

Peter went a step further when he offered Tabitha his hand. He was saying, 'I will be as a hand to you.' When people are made to 'sit up' they see new ministries in mercy extended to them. It was through his prayer that she found another position, not laid down in death surrounded by the garments she had been making, but in life.

Others will never rise above your station

If by your testimony and preaching you do not get others to 'sit up' then they will never rise above the station in life where you found them. This woman was in a room with closed doors, and darkness prevailed as it did over the world in Genesis 1:1–3. Peter was involved in a creative act when she was raised from the dead. God creates from nothing; Peter created out of existing materials when he spoke the word.

There is nothing like somebody being raised from the dead to get the attention of others. God used a burning bush to attract Moses,[16] Peter used words of command. He took power over death. As her eyes were opened she saw one man, Peter. Let it be that when your eyes are opened the Lord will let you see Jesus. If you do, you will 'sit up' and take notice of the plan He has for your life. He that shapes a star to shine has plans for your life. He does not throw things together, and say, 'This is what I threw in and this came out.'[17] What Peter was doing when he offered her his hand was saying, 'there is more to follow, there is more if you will follow.' Tabitha saw life as she entered back into life through the apostles' prayer. 'Go on to know the Lord', and learn to follow a *mature* example, it will lead you into a fuller, newer life in Christ. Follow in your *maturity* that speaks Christ, lives Christ, imitates Christ and echoes Christ. If you do then as Tabitha you will not only 'sit up' you will make others 'sit up'. How high you sit they will sit. What depth you have will be created in others. Your fellowship with Christ will become their fellowship.

Discipline can die as you deny life its action

(Acts 9:36) Dorcas is called a 'disciple', from which we obtain the English word 'mathematics'. Disciplined numbers produce correct answers. Disciplined lives produce discipleship. In spite of her good works she died. The heart and soul went out of discipleship. The 'ship' had gone from the word 'disciple-ship' and she was left with something that meant nothing in the word disciple! There is no such thing as a dead disciple or a disciple without the heartbeat of Jesus in them. She died in her discipleship. It had come to an end. Her training and learning, because this is what 'discipleship suggests, had come to an abrupt end. The lesson taught had slid off the open page. Peter was there to reveal that there was a future for her. All the garments of love, grace, righteousness and faith had not been completed. Her work was unfinished, incomplete with strands hanging loosely. She would still weave a web on the trestle of time. God had more cloth to offer to her ability, but for now she had run out of the cloth of life. You may run out of the materials of life, your needle may have a blunt point, and you are finding life so difficult. Peter gave her new materials to work on. Her life's work did not finish with death. She found what Rahab the harlot discovered when she hung up a scarlet thread as she was threatened by death.[18] That cloth gave Rahab hope, and when Peter prayed he brought the same help to Dorcas. God had more materials for her to use.

Faith takes you into a higher realm than fate
The 'three fates' the Romans believed in had appeared, Clotho held the stick (Falstaff) on which the flax was placed before spinning, Lachesis spun the thread of life, and Atrophos cut that thread when life had ended. Faith takes fate into a higher realm. Jesus stepped in through the words that His disciple spoke, and the silver thread was united and lengthened. You do such a thing every time you encourage somebody. What is dying and will die, you encourage to continue. As you do, you lengthen hope and faith.

A small fishing vessel is called a 'smack' because it can dart among the rocks and reach fish that a larger vessel could never find. We need to be as this vessel, going and coming, finding and seeking. Add some 'smack' to your ministry through *maturity*. On English television there is an advert for a fruit drink called 'Tango'. When you drink from the bottle, a man steps from the shadows and sharply slaps your face! We need those who will testify, and as they do, people are challenged.

Tabitha found a new womanhood
What Peter did filled those garments with a body, and restored the woman's role as a disciple of Jesus Christ. It meant that through Cephas God was extending the woman's cloth of life. More material

would be transformed by her when she had been transformed by the power of Christ. Many have 'caved in', and your role in life is to be *mature* enough to minister to them so that their work can continue. You have made them 'sit up'. Let your words be few and far between. When you speak as those representatives of the Lord, your words will have power and healing in them, because of your passion that produces conviction in others. They will find it easy to get up and go on in the power of what has been said. As Peter said on another fishing expedition, 'We have toiled all night, but at Your word, I will let down the nets.'[19] The nets were thrown over the side of the boat, and they found new depths and fish that were plentiful. There is no scarcity in the Lord.

A wooden rocking horse will take you nowhere, When your religion becomes like that, it lacks the kick of the mule, and wins no races. We need the kick of a horse so that, when we speak, others not only realise what has been said, but it remains with them as a bruise in the heart. Have the real thing, be the real thing, do the real thing, and when it is counted you will be accounted as *mature*.

Notes

[1] 2 Timothy 4:3.

[2] Matthew 3:7.

[3] Job 34:2.

[4] Psalm 19:14.

[5] See Brewster's dictionary of 'Fact and Fable'.

[6] See author's book 'Paths of Righteousness in Psalm 23'.

[7] The feast days and the first day of the month was marked in red on early calendars.

[8] Ecclesiastes 12:11.

[9] Luke 10.

[10] Mark 16:20.

[11] Exodus 3:2.

[12] John 14:12. Greater in volume and number.

[13] Revelation 12:1–17.

[14] Matthew 8:8.

[15] Mark 8:34.
[16] Exodus 3:2.
[17] Exodus 32:24.
[18] Joshua 2:18, 21.
[19] Luke 5:5.

Chapter Sixteen

THE MAN WITH A VISION

It could have been just another normal day when Simon Peter went to pray on the housetop at the home of Simon the Tanner in Acts 10:9. I don't think he had any idea at the moment of the things that God had prepared for those who love Him. The Almighty likes a challenge like that! Things would happen that day that would change Simon's life forever. True vision will always do that. It wasn't just a 'dream' that engulfed his heart. It is called a 'trance' in Acts 10:10, then a 'vision' in verse 17. He had to receive what the Lord was waiting to give him. We extend and enlarge our heart's capacity when we pray.

Heaven is open when earth is closed
It was a real, tangible vision. The heavens open when earth is closed; even as they did for Elijah during a drought.[1] It is in the opening of the heavens that earth situations for which we seem to have no answers will open up. The puzzle can be great with pieces missing, but the Creator has the missing piece, He is that which is missing. The sheet might have been folded flat or even have many folds until the Master filled it with good things. In the 'many folds' of that sheet, the 'manifold' (many folds) grace of God[2] would be revealed. The Eternal was communicating that He had a place for the outcast and the outsider as both birds and beasts were. The Eternal had it

all wrapped up and ready for delivery even before the fisherman prayed. Vision does not differentiate between one party and another, one thing and another. As the sheet, it is the whole of the vision for the whole of mankind. If you have lost your vision then take another look at Jesus Christ.

The invisible can become the invincible

Cephas went to pray, he fell into a trance, where the invisible became the invincible, the unseen greater than that which is seen. While he was praying – meditating (as a cow chewing the cud) – God was working. Meditating is learning from that which is being turned over and over in the mind. True vision will always be received through prayer. What the praying man saw was something which included everyone, for it was 'full of all manner of four footed beasts, creeping things and birds.' Many lives are as an empty sheet still waiting for the Lord to fill. Those who are immature still ask the Lord to give what He has already given!

Notice how large an affair it is when the Eternal gives, it takes a sheet, not a hand or a thumb nail, to contain it. This was no copy of a previous happening in Jerusalem. What Peter received was not a satellite of another church. This vision was virgin territory. If doors are not opened to take us further into Christianity then there is no vision at all, only a 'strong delusion'. It fitted into the need, containing a picture message from the Supreme. Simon saw what was happening even though he seemed to be in a state of stupor. In a vision, some people see far more with their eyes closed than they do with them open. The *mature* person sees more when on their knees than the philosopher sees when on his tiptoe. Others say far more with their mouth tightly shut than the person who speaks 'parrot fashion'. Doing nothing, he received and saw everything in minute detail.

What does seeing a vision mean?

When we speak of a vision, what do we really mean? It will take all your *maturity* to give a correct answer. The answer is found in the *mature man*, Simon the fisherman. The word 'vision' means 'a sight' that is 'seen'. The Greek word *horama* is translated 'sight' once in the Gospels, and 'vision' eleven times in the Acts of the Apostles.[3] It is that which is capable of being 'seen' and 'stared' at, brought so close that you can't miss it. The faculty for receiving this was the Holy Ghost. Seeing a vision means you are able to see the things of heaven on earth. The vision is in the heart, while for the visionary it is simply in his mind. It is seeing the invisible and knowing the unknowable. It is that which comes from a Divine source into the human heart and mind.

The Old Testament, 'Seer' was a man who 'saw' things. Abraham saw them afar off.[4] 'Slight not what is near through aiming at what is far.' There has to be the unlocking of the supernatural world. It contains more than your capacity can receive. A vision will always be tomorrow seen today. Simon saw it before it happened. He 'looked' and 'saw' before he leaped. There are many aspects to this revelation. A vision seen in the past will always bring you sunshine on dark and dreary days. Vision is taking a look at things through God's eyes. It is seeing the future in the present, a revelation given to move a man forward.

The hand of the Lord was controlling the affairs of men

The problem was not to see or hear something from God as the sheet was lifted and lowered, it was, and always will be, how to interpret what we see, and what to do with what is revealed. God used a number of things to confirm what He said, such as doing something three times, then sending men to knock on a door just as the Spirit had said, 'Three men will come to you.' A vision is given so that you might divide it among those who need it. It wasn't meant to be gathered into twelve baskets and left. There are no hopeless situations, only people who are hope less. It is not dark clouds that obliterate the vision, only what we allow to come between us and our God. Too many people have their eyes on the tail lights instead of the headlights. There are people looking back to where they have been rather than concentrating on where they are going. If you see with the inner eyes of the heart, then your natural eyes will see it come to pass. What commences small can grow as large as the Heaven it came from. What Simon saw made him what he was going to be.

His future days and plans were in what was revealed. It was part of a process leading into *maturity*.

What we pray and what the Lord sends dovetails together

While Simon Peter was dreaming the dream and seeing the vision (Acts 10:9–20), God was sending messengers from another area, and these two acts of God would dovetail together as Peter stepped down from the house top, led by the Spirit. When the Lord grants a spiritual happening and awakening, you might receive it in a stupor, but you need to be wide awake to see it implemented. A dream must not remain between the bedclothes; it must be developed in future days. That which is seen in birds and beasts must become men and woman who need setting free, and this Peter was the one to execute that ministry. It went beyond his imagination, and seems to have been contrary to his convictions. 'I have never eaten anything common or unclean.' Note, the Lord took a scripture and something from sacrifice and offering, and used it to convey this message. It was this 'seen' that changed the hunger of Peter into reality as he went in obedience.

You become your vision

The visions we see are a reflection of our spiritual hunger. If there is a longing in the heart, God will enlarge that hunger until we are ready to be shown what to do; it is then that we accomplish what has been revealed. The revelations of God are not flowers to adorn a garden or jewels to adorn your fingers. Things we 'see' must become things we 'do'. What we 'know' must become what we 'are' to determine where we 'go'. God takes what might seem to be broken sticks, and they bud, blossom and bear fruit as we readily respond to what the Almighty is saying.[5] (Acts 10: 19.) The direction of the Spirit followed the revelation, and Cephas was led word by word and step by step. He heard the Spirit's voice louder even than his own.

Plans are revealed in visions

Peter went to the housetop to pray of his own volition, but as he came down he was led by the Spirit as a son of God. He ascended without an answer to prayer. He descended with the answer firmly pressed into his heart. He came down with a plan that was revealed in a vision. He did not return from prayer empty.

The sheet was 'knit' at the four 'corners' (verse 11). J. A. Alexander commenting in the 'Geneva Commentaries' says about the word 'knit', 'It was a 'sheet sail'. 'This was something used by the Lord that Simon would be familiar with, and it suggested to him that he was going on a journey, he was going to sail a boat.' He knew the thrill of the fishing trip. This awaiting him would bring a greater challenge than walking on water during a stormy sea. 'Knit', literally 'tied,' 'bound,' and 'fastened.' 'Corners', literally 'beginnings', but in the Greek word it can also denote extremities or ends'.[6] This was the day and the hour of new 'beginnings' for this *mature* man. A new day had dawned. The sun had set on the old dispensation. There was only one way to go when he left this house and it was the pathway suggested by what he had seen. It was the commencement and, with God, would have a glorious fulfilment. As for the out-workings of that vision, Peter could say, as Christ said from the cross, 'It is finished',[7] when he heard the Gentiles speak in other tongues, as they received the Holy Spirit.

Vision is God fulfilling what He has promised

If the Lord is holding the vision, as He was holding the sheet, then all will be well. Nothing will fall from it. Nothing will be lost, nothing fly away, nothing creep away, and nothing run away. Here were birds and beasts. Birds mean that you can 'fly' with what has been revealed, beasts that you can 'run' with the revelation. If the Eternal commands then you can creep with it, seeing Him fulfil what He has said little by little, sometimes at a snail pace.

It is a 'full' sheet, and there will always be completeness about that which is shown by the Lord. In it He reveals what can out-fly and out-run us in birds and beast. Nothing on earth or in Heaven can out-manoeuvre Jehovah who leads us. Revival is captured and captivated by God. It brings the fierce and the gentle together. That which would run or fly away comes to stay. What God takes in His net is used to convey His will. The vision came to Cephas; he had no need to seek something to see, say or do.

Doing the will of God satisfies your hunger

That which had been received was so good, it was like eating a meal. Simon had said grace before the natural meal he was expecting to receive as a guest. The Lord is saying as in John 21:12, 'Come and dine.' 'Rise, Peter kill and eat.' This vision might have reminded Peter of that occasion recorded in John 21:9. If we are given to a great appetite, that very desire will be taken and used to convey a message. Jesus said, 'I have meat to eat that you don't know anything about.'[8] Peter was told to rise and kill and to eat what had been killed. There has to be a death before there can be a manifestation of life. That within the sheet must be killed before we can experience new life. Here we have a copy of what happened to Abraham in Genesis 22:2 when Jehovah told him to offer Isaac as an offering. Before he could kill the lad, Jehovah Jireh provided an offering.

Vision makes you do those things you have never done before

In everything received from on high we have our part to play. God has no empty chess boards, the players must be in place and ready to be 'pawns' as the Master begins to move the pieces in His direction. The man who was a fisherman by trade was asked to be a cook, to cook a meal out of what he had seen. He could never eat any animal with the blood still remaining in it. Revelation will bring to the fore any hidden talents. We want the revelation without the challenge that comes with it. We must be prepared to be something else, to be somebody else. God's callings are His enabling. We must become 'all things' to all men. It might mean a change of occupation. The Galilean fisherman had to eat what he prepared. That would enhance many cooks —if they had to eat what they had cooked! There is the suggestion here of responsibility for what we do.

The vision must be worked through before it becomes acceptable to others. Men are looking for others to do what the Lord has told them to do. Don't expect others to rise and kill if you are not prepared to sacrifice things to God. The Eternal provided the sacrifice. Peter provided nothing but his prayer pattern. Go to pray with a large heart because you never know how large the answer might be. The son of Jonas had to play his part in this whole venture. You will have a great hunger rise in your soul before you look at what is seen by God. Here Simon had to do some neck wringing in the killing of the birds. That would be messy! There would be feathers to pluck before the birds were offered. God was suggesting that Peter should kill that which was alive, in order that something dead in the Gentile race could live. The old principle was being applied, dying is living. God asked Simon to prove his willingness and obedience. If you are looking to the Lord for a vision, it will not come to make life easy; instead it will be difficult, very difficult. Cephas had to go against all he had been taught since he was a child when he was commanded to rise, eat and kill.

Vision produces abiding fullness

After that vision from God, everything else would have seemed empty, an empty sheet with no birds or four footed beasts. He had left empty nets and boats when Jesus called him. The son of Jonas was called into something that was full, but not full of fish caught, by himself. Peter did not fill the sheet, hold the sheet or decide what would be its content. The Lord decided all that. Things at this point were taken out of the hands of Peter and placed into the hands of God. If a bird or an animal should fall out of the sheet, then the Lord would catch it, before it fell to the ground. He that looks after the sparrows so that not one lands or takes off without His care, can look after the content of any venture.[9] An immature man might have tried to fill what he saw with his own desires and expectation. Here was material to build those three booths that Cephas had suggested building in the Mount of Transfiguration.[10] This man had grown up since those far off days.

Visions given by God are not always acceptable; they seem to be contrary to human thinking. We want the acceptable, and that which will bless us. If it is self centred then it is not of the Lord. If you are saying 'what can I get out of this' then it is not revelation but a ghostly nightmare. The man whose name suggests a rock had to put something into it. One thing was missing from the sheet full of birds and beasts, and that was Peter. If Peter had been immature, and not obeyed swiftly, then the only house ever to be built would have been the one in which he stayed at Joppa. God was seeking to build another house, another temple that included the Gentiles. It was a house where prejudice could not hold sway that went beyond the acceptable or the bounds of human thinking. In the vision, the Almighty was illustrating that He could bring things of a different nature together —as Jew and Gentile, seen in beasts, birds and creeping things.

The vision continues even when you disappear

The Gentiles gave the Jews the 'creeps', hence 'creeping things'. When God reveals the cost, the pain and hurt that the vision will involve you in, He sends the sheet so that when it is empty you can wipe your eyes dry, bathe your wounds, and wipe away the blood. Use it to wipe away the sweat, to keep your feet clean as you travel. Peter was left with this cloth, and in future days, he would use it in memory of what the Lord had accomplished through him. On a cold night, when the shadows of doubt began to appear, he could wrap it around himself. At any meal table he could take part of the cloth and wipe his hands clean knowing he had done the will of God. It would serve as a good servant's apron, or could be torn into cloths placed on people to bring healing.

If the content of what was revealed had been left to Peter, he would have put things into it of his choice. Legalism would have had a coronation day! It would never have introduced the Gentiles to Jesus. If it had been left in the dreamer's hands, it would not have been long enough or strong enough to lower from Heaven to earth right to where Peter was. When we come to the end of our measure and stretch, it is then we must allow another to take over Who can reach so far, and yet be so near. If you are at the end of your 'tether', take hold of this white sheet. As it fulfilled its ministry in containing the birds and the beasts, then do what has been asked of you. Be as devoted as the sheet was to the birds that it held for the future.

Vision united high and low, rich and poor

The Lord used the natural appetite of a man, hunger, when appealing for Peter to do something new. This which was introduced was not only foreign to the nature of Peter, it was a new thing. He had sailed boats, caught fish, weathered storms and even taken a fish out of water with money in its mouth.[11] He had never seen a white sheet filled with fullness, never been told to empty it. Once it was empty the Infinity would put something new into it. The fulfilling of any vision is to see it through to the end, until every bird and beast has been released. It is within your power to do this. The only way out is through. In our human nature we want something new before we have used what has already been provided.

What the praying man saw and received was only part of the whole. There was much more sheet to be revealed. The Eternal will only give you the measure that you are able to deal with. If you had the sheet and all that He has for you, you might trip over the material and enter an early grave. There were many other four footed beasts and birds to be included. Sovereignty is merciful, God only reveals a little at a time. If Peter had seen everything at once, it would have bowled him over. Presented with a 'facts' sheet before he commenced, he would have hidden his face in the sheet even as Elijah hid his face in his mantle. The sheet would have suffocated him. The birds would have pecked him to death, the beasts would have torn him to pieces, and the creeping things would have crawled all over him. He would have felt that he was sinking below the waves of the sea again. The sheet was 'lowered' from heaven like a flag of surrender as if the Lord was saying 'all that is mine I am surrendering to you. All that I have is yours if you will surrender to me.' It can seem as if we are being asked to do things contrary to nature. If we go through life like a train following the tracks then we will not reach or touch that which is defined as glorious. We can never stick rigidly to what has happened in the past. Faith sees normal procedures suspended for a time. How often do we hear the words, 'We have never done it this way before!'

The Lord will test your obedience in small things

If you are *mature* it doesn't guarantee you a revelation, but it does grant you the opportunity to do something new for your Master. Peter's *maturity* was seen in his response. He did not agree at first, but then he saw common sense and did the only thing which was the

God thing. God will notice how you deal with sheets before He will ask you to make beds. How do you handle bandages? How do you care for those in need? These are part of the training for receiving something special from the Lord. He grants one sheet to see how you will serve in that realm before introducing you to something else. If Simon had tied himself up in the sheet, or tied the sheet in knots, that would have been the end of the matter. The vision was not intended to see him bound hand and foot. Its mission was to see him set free in order that he might set others free. It became the starter's tape and the finishing line of what he had to accomplish. If you know where to start, you will know where to finish. If the start and the finish get mixed up, disaster will follow. You will think you have arrived when you have only just begun, or you will think you have only just begun when you have finished!

This was a new way of doing things. Tailors, dressmakers and fashion designers commence with cloth. This disciple must commence with the essential principles of that which was revealed. It might have been better understood if it had been revealed as a new net with fish, or a bucket of water with fish in. He would have understood that better because that had been his way of life. He was not familiar with birds and beasts, but to help him a sheet (a fishing sail) was used.

This vision brought something new
The priest always killed the animal. The priest was there to make an offering. Now it was not the old way that the Lord was spicing up, it was a totally different approach. It was the end for four footed beasts and unclean birds. The sacrifice had been offered in Jesus. The hand that let the sheet down is the same hand that will take it up again. When you have had enough of the vision, or you are too tired to complete it, then Jehovah will lift it again, to return it when you are refreshed. This sheet was not the starting tape to the big race. It wasn't the finishing tape either. It could be moved one way or another. Unlike some, Peter did not take the sheet, frighten the birds and beasts away, and use the sheet to keep himself warm. Vision is not given so that you might be well clad, and have all the fineries of life around you.

If Cephas had an allergy to birds, then he must have the faith to overcome that allergy. Faith becomes daring, and it is not squeamish. It believes and therefore it does extraordinary things. It can run further than four footed beasts, and fly higher, lower, wider and deeper than any feathered bird. If necessary it can be as wild as a beast, fly like a bird, but also move at creeping pace when required.

You must learn to trust what has been revealed
As those birds trusted the hand of God as they folded their wings, so must you. Those creatures never used their feet or claws to arrive where Peter was. Vision can take the claw and the snarl out of a situation, turning lions and tigers into lambs. Pigs and pheasants are brought together in God. If it was left to the Lord then He would use something different after the first principles of faith had been thoroughly used. The birds and beasts had to rest in that comfortable sheet, and forget that they could run, crawl or fly. If God holds the sheet then I need fear no evil.

See how the *mature* Peter handled the situation. He put two and two together and made four! This white sheet filled with flying and creeping things was the plan of God. The will of God was delivered to his door as a postman delivers a parcel; the words written on it said 'Special Delivery!' The revelation commenced right where Peter was, not in some far off country. It might develop into something that can be used elsewhere, but we must commence where the Giver commences.

That which is revealed will be completed
That which is seen and received was as large as Simon's heart. God cuts the cloth to the measure. He was not asked to let the birds fly or the beasts run, and then spend the next fifty years trying to catch them. The fulfilment of the vision commenced with a death. Something had to die as Peter was told to 'rise and kill.' True greatness begins when you are out of the way. It was when Adam slept that Elohim created the greatest vision ever in a woman.[12] Men have been looking at that vision ever since, but for the wrong reason and with the wrong application!

It seems to suggest in this event that when we are at our lowest ebb, when we are going to sleep, when we feel we are inadequate, it is at that time we receive new direction. We think we must be successful before anything is revealed, but revelation from God makes us capable. God knew the talents of Simon. Within the realm of that human life there were certain abilities. There might be buried talents, but Peter is told what to do. He had to take and use what he 'has' to receive what the Lord 'has'. The son of Jonas did not enter into the sheet to fight or wrestle with it. Accept as a *mature* person what the Almighty is saying to you.

God reveals the future in the present as if it was the past

The Infinite will go to extremes to get you to see something for the future. Three times the sheet was lowered and raised, as if to emphasise to Peter that the God who lets down can also lift up. If you don't respond the first time, He believes that you will respond on the third invitation. It was not a different sheet, it was the same sheet, the same birds the same beasts, the same opportunity granted at a different time. If God knocks three times we must be as willing to go as if three doors have opened before us. What happened was speaking volumes to this disciple. It was so important it had to be repeated three times.

God lowering and lifting the sheet reminds us of the vision of Jacob who saw angels ascending and descending on a stairway that went all the way up to heaven.[13] The revelation is safe if it is left in the hands of Elohim. Sadly men take it from the hand of God, take hold of the four corners and use it for their own splendour. It was not three different visions, it was one. There were no changes everyday. You will meet people who hear something different from God for each hour of the day! God did not change His mind; He changed only the order of the revelation. Sometimes it seemed higher, and at other times it seemed lower. How low the Lord will stoop to whisper into deaf ears! You would be forgiven as it came lower to the earth if you thought it was the end of the matter. No, the Lord was saying, I am going to lift it up again and again. He does this as an encouragement by telling us that the things we have difficulty with present no difficulty to Him. The Infinite and Peter stayed with what was given and revealed until it was fulfilled. Peter put his fisherman's sandals on and followed the men who had been sent to help him to fulfil what the Eternal had revealed.

The vision received might be for a different area

God can show you something that is not for the area where you are, but is for a future venture in another place. If Peter had sought to implement what the Lord had revealed in the house of Simon at Joppa, it would have resulted in failure, because there were no Gentiles gathered together in that house. Time and place fit into the revelation. When the thing is repeated often it means the time is now.

The sheet knitted at the four corners so that it wouldn't fray, and what it contained wouldn't become too heavy. Eternal balances are perfect! The burden is measured to the strength of heart and capabilities. God puts just enough into that which you require, no more and no less. He knows what you can handle. If you cannot handle the full sheet the first time, God is so gracious in that He will lower it again and again, giving many opportunities to do what He has shown to be His will. The sheet being lowered and taken back into heaven, gave Peter enough time to let prayer develop him into a stronger man, so that he could handle what was being thrust upon him.

The vision and the voice of God go together

When the Master has shown a vision for a venture, do not be afraid to ask Him, and expect Him to speak. What was revealed was followed by a voice of command, and in the obeying took that vision a step further. If you can't handle all you have been shown at once, then the Lord expects you to take a little bird and a little beast and make that sort of sacrifice. If you commence with one item you can deal with two, and on to something larger. Try using bird feathers to begin with, and later try killing the birds. Can you be trusted to hold the sheet? If you can't then you will not be worthy of dealing with the contents. The vision will return sometimes in youth, then in mid-life, or into old age. You have still some more birds and animals to sacrifice as you seek to do the will of the Master.

For those things to be included in the vision and in the white sheet, they had to be caught. What the Lord had done historically in bringing the animals to the open door of the ark[14] He did when presenting this vision to the *mature* man. If it is of the Lord, stop striving, and rest. The Eternal will make things run into place even as the beasts came into the ark. He can make things fly into place as the birds flew into the sheet. If it is a slow process, then creeping things will creep in at the precise time and occupy that which has been provided for them.

Notes

[1] James 5:17, 18.

[2] 1 Peter 4:10.

[3] Acts 9:10, 12; 10:3, 17, 19; 11:5; 12:9; 16:9, 10; 18:9.

[4] John 8:56.

[5] Numbers 17:8.

[6] J.A.Alexander in the Geneva Commentaries.

[7] John 19:30.

[8] John 4:32.

[9] Matthew 10:29, 30.

[10] Mark 9:5.

[11] Matthew 17:27.

[12] Genesis 2:21.

[13] Genesis 28:12.

[14] Genesis 6:18–22.

Chapter Seventeen

THE MAN WHO SAW IRON GATES YIELD

When the iron gates were closed it might seem as if the Book of Life for Peter the fisherman was also closed. It could have been sealed with seven seals, but Jesus Christ kept it as an open diary of the miraculous in the *mature*. God had not finished with the future apostle. We may think we are reaching the end, then another beginning is found in the word Alpha.[1] This was not the end of what the Almighty would do; it was the writing of another chapter which would include *'iron gates yielding'*. God adds so much to every life, and we have to remain open, even in a prison, for Him to complete the good work that He has begun in us.

We are often restricted for our own good
The fisherman from Galilee had often been fishing. If he caught nothing, then he simply tried again, he had freedom as a fisherman to work where he chose. This was not so when he was cast into prison in Acts 12:1–11. There must have been the torment of hell in that spirit of the man who was used to the freedom of the sea, wind and water. In prison he was like a caged bird unable to wander, to come and go as he pleased. A feeling of being in something he could not get out of must have flooded his mind and heart. When he had tried to walk on water, he began to sink.[2] The prison was one of water, but Jesus was at hand to help.

Was this the end of the plan of the Lord for a life? Must that discipleship and *maturity* finish so abruptly? The person who is imprisoned within the arms of Christ need fear no cell, chains or bars. There are designs of God that are not seen clearly in the daylight. To understand fully we must enter into the deepness of darkness. Many a person has found a light switch when stepping into a dark room. The Almighty on the outside of the prison performed miracles rich and rare, could He do the same on the inside? Sometimes the doors have to be closed to shut us in with God. It is sometimes the Almighty's way of training wild nature —the nature that was in Peter. It is in the darkness that the diamond finds its prisms. In difficult experiences things are added to us that could never be received as we listen to the plaudits of men.

It is in captivity that we find a new freedom
What Peter had given to the Lord in a life surrendered was now being held captive by a foreign power, fast bound by chains, soldiers and a steel door. There were thoughts of death and evil against the one who had been ordained to life. It seemed as if the Galilean was being placed into chains never to be set free again, yet it was in that captivity he found a new depth in God. As we are bound, and difficulties become so dark, the words of a hymn can come to us: 'Imprison me within Your arms and I shall conqueror be.'[3] It is as we are bound that we find true freedom. It is when we enter our darkest moment that we find true light, trusting which is unseen rather than the seen, not those around you but that which is within you.

When one plan crumbles in your hand and runs through your fingers as the desert sands, the Lord has another far more glorious plan, for both Peter and yourself. *Maturity* is always being added to. It never comes to an end. It is not an end in itself; it exists so others can be helped. If Peter could come through, so could every believer.

As they were locking the doors shut, the Lord was opening other doors. Doors that men close, and lock tight, present challenges and opportunities for the Master to reveal that He is Sovereign even in a Roman prison. He not only holds the keys, He holds every link of the chain in His hands, and turns links of rusty chains into crowns of gold.

If the attitude of the heart is right, then even the clanging of chains can become sweet music to the soul. That which is developed into *maturity* no outside influence can touch. Thoughts and happenings that would bind you in chains cannot touch or arrest *maturity*. It cannot be washed or rubbed away, or be concealed in the darkness of a cell. Paul and Silas when in prison sang praises to God. This whole story is the song of a soul set free.

Opportunities to pray are provided

What happened to Cephas and to the church presented them with an opportunity to pray. When darkness falls and you feel bound hand and foot, then pray. There is no need to be cast into outer darkness, where there is wailing and gnashing of teeth.[4] It was not a matter of reading a prayer or repeating parrot fashion something written down. They read and spoke what was in their hearts, expressing their hopes and fears with deepest longing. Prayer is stronger than locks and chains, and prison doors that are shut. If Peter did not get out, then he would go through that darkness as a shining light. You cannot be in total darkness if the Light of the World is with you. Their prayers were 'tight' and 'held fast,'[5] as if they were gripping a rope to keep a vessel near the shore. They would not let Cephas drift.

The Eternal has many means of driving us to prayer. When they prayed it was 'instant and earnest prayer'.[6] It reached 'boiling point'. To pray that the will of God will be done is a sure light in a dark place. There was nothing cold or formalistic. It breathed passion and desire. Some remembered what had happened to James, and to John Baptist. It was the sort of prayer that does not bend bars or snap chains, but it does see doors open, chains falling from the wrist, and is so wonderful that Peter can hardly believe it is true. Confirmation that prayer works is when it is answered? If that is your belief then think again. The *mature* person knows that God answers prayer even when there seems to be no assurance of the answer.

Simon would take consolation, would feed on his memories of what Providence had done in the past, and it became a rainbow for the future. He was left in prison just long enough to learn something else about the Lord. When we think we have learned it all and know it all, then it is into a dark environment that we must go. What was 'black night' contained the glow of a miracle.

The praying heart never lacks a praying place
The praying heart never lacks a praying place. What happened did not shut the mouth of Peter as the lions mouths were shut for Daniel.[7] He would not let the pain and the sores keep him from praying. The worse it became then the more he prayed. He prayed from the worst place on earth until God sent him the best thing from heaven, an angel. I would rather pray and have angels for companions than rough, tough soldiers. As these Roman soldiers remained true soldiers in that prison cell, so Simon remained a true spirited soldier of Christ, revealing his discipline and *maturity* through his prayers, prayers that were not bound by walls or cells, but marched right out into the presence of God, and as his prayers had gone out of the prison, so this man followed them.

God has a thousand ways to answer every prayer
God does not answer the prayers of Peter or the cry of church in the same way. There was one way into prison, the cell door. When God answers, it gives a million opportunities. What was one becomes many as the Lord freely reveals His love in an answer. In this same chapter 12, James had been killed with the sword. This could have deepened the darkness into midnight blackness, but it was not allowed to do so. When the apostle Paul went to prison there was no release, yet it gave him a great opportunity. Although he was handcuffed, he was not handicapped! His deepest theology came from a prison cell. His prayers are out of this world because they touched another world. Peter was released from prison, but it is not the will of God to follow the same pattern on every occasion. He delivers some with bread from Heaven. He delivers another using ravens' wings; those greedy birds, those scavengers, gave up their food that they fight and squabble over.[8] To another He sends a napkin that is prayed over, and one is healed.[9] We are dealing with a God of adversity and diversity.

The fragrance of your life can affect others

The *maturity* of Simon is seen in that he accepted the cell as if it was a palace. Wherever he went it was turned into a palace of prayer. It became his headquarters, and despatches were sent to heaven from this battlefield in a dungeon. The rats and the filth were lessened at the mention of the Name of Jesus, for that is as a fragrance poured forth.[10] When Simon went into prison he was like a breath of fresh air. We are a sweet smelling savour unto God.[11] There is fragrance in a *mature* life. He had learned to be content in 'whatever state' he found himself, not with the state or the circumstances but with Christ who is the same in all situations. Jesus Christ is the same yesterday, today and forever.[12] Yesterday, where you have been during your history. Today, where you are at this moment, even in a prison. Forever, for whatever might happen in the future. Peter became a living prison epistle. When he entered, he was marked by the cruel grip of the soldiers. As he left, he had the marks of the making of the *mature* man.

Green leaves turn to brown, the yellows and pinks of summer fade into a November day, but not Jesus Christ. He is stronger than chains or steel doors. As they warp and melt, He remains true to Himself and true to you. The years will fail, but You change not. Other things are folded up as a garment, but He remains.[13] The warder could keep others out, but the proof of Simon's deliverance is that they could not keep God out. You can close the door but you cannot close it to the Creator. The lock and the chain might restrain the hand of the thief, but not the hand of God. It provided the Eternal with an opportunity to reveal Who ruled in the affairs of men. The mishaps of the *mature* become the miracles of the Master in a moment, in the twinkling of an eye.

Challenges bring change

It was a challenge that brought about a change. If Peter would give himself as much to God as the key to the lock, then he would be free. He did not know what awaited him at the end of his prison sentence. He knew who would wait for him in the Person of Christ Jesus. When he came out of prison he did not come out of Christ. He came out with Christ. He was as manacled to Christ as any prisoner bound by chains. He did not have to push or shove, shout or rave; he only had to believe that the Lord who had let him in would bring him out. No darkness is forever. You have to be like flowers which take their colour from the bulb planted in black soil. Many a flower has not been seen in the night, but in the morning has shown its colourful head to the world. They bring something with them out of the dark pit. Some floral displays are so arranged that petals open at every hour of the day. Certain watches do not need winding or batteries, they keep going by the light of day. There is a church that displays the sign of the cross on a wall when the light comes in through a certain window at a certain time. It happened for Peter; when the angel entered the cell, a light shone.

Deep darkness cannot keep out the light

Between links of the chains that bound him, he found freedom. He could breathe a prayer and, in answer to the breath, God the Holy Spirit sent a strong wind to blow the doors open. When all things seemed to work against him, suddenly everything worked together for good because he loved God.[14] No matter how dark the cell it could not keep out the Light of Life. No matter how tightly locked the iron doors were they could not keep Him on the outside. He had said 'None shall pluck you from My hand.'[15] When they chained Peter they were chaining Christ. When they closed and locked the door on the servant, they were doing the same to the Master. God works behind closed doors. His best miracles are seen in the darkest moments and corners of our heart. When all seems to be metal around the *mature* person, that metal is lined with grace as soft as silk.

Peter could have prayed for deliverance. He still wanted to help the infant church which had hardly learned to walk by itself. The way in which he was unceremoniously thrown into prison, with doors slammed and locked, is evident. He went into prison that way, but what a way he came out! He went in as a son and came out as a son. Arrested by soldiers, he walked out with an angel by his side. He went into the cell as a prisoner, and came out as a preacher of truth. The darkness did something to him. That darkness, restriction, became his teachers. He learned to trust God more in the dark. He had faith that the Lord would open the doors, and yet even if He didn't he believed that the Almighty would give him strength, like Samson, to bend the bars and batter open the doors. Maybe he could lift the city gates as Samson was enabled to do through the anointing and strengthening of the Spirit?[16] God has different methods of answering prayer, but His real methods are men and angels. What a difference prayer can make in any situation!

Everything the Lord does points to the future
Acts 12:7 says the angel 'smote' him on his side. The Greek is very strong; it suggests that the angel gave him a real blow to the side, strong enough to wake up any resurrection life that was inside him. The blow revived him, and caused him to stand on his feet. Soldiers were left to sleep the sleep of death. The very directives of angelic ministry pointed him to his future. He had to put on his sandals and his inner garment, and throw a cloak around him as one going into service. None of his belongings were left in that prison. He did not leave a complaining or a wrong spirit. When God delivers, He delivers man, garments and shoes. There was more service awaiting the servant of the Lord. Peter was not delivered for his own sake; it was for the sake of the church and those who were praying. As he came out of prison prayer had been answered, and that bound was set free to be restored to the church.

The devil can only suggest, he cannot command
When Cephas went into the prison, the devil was telling him it would be his last port of call. 'Fill your mind with memories of life at sea and long to fish again because it will never happen.' Instead of weeping and longing for the past, Simon prayed for a future to appear in the present, and it did. This was not a time to let the darkness of the situation enter his heart. The chains were chaffing him, and he felt sore, but no complaint came from his lips, instead they were given to prayer. We sometimes pray for the answer, when in fact we are the answer, as Cephas was. The man inside prison received something from the outside in the form of an angel.

The *mature* always turns to prayer. Prayer takes the hand that turns the key that turns the lock. Peter knew that the 'key' to the situation was to tell the Lord about it. In every situation a way of escape is provided. Sometimes we are not set free because we do not accept what the Eternal has provided. We look for bars to bend, the prison guards to crumble or the head prison keeper to hand over the keys, as he handed them to Joseph. Sometimes it does not happen. Our plans are so far removed from the mind of the Eternal, as far as the prodigal son was from his father's house in the far country.

Don't let your circumstances enter into you

How long did Simon Cephas stay in prison? I am not quite sure, although I am sure that those cleverer than me could work it out. How long did the prison stay in him? He stayed long enough to offer a prayer and long enough to get the answer. If it is in prison or in difficulties that answers are provided, then may the Eternal give you many things you can question so that He can provide an answer. God is the answer. What is your question? He only stayed as long as it took him to believe the Lord. The sentence he was given had not been fully decided. They would recommend death, but God had better ideas.

You might lock up and shut the door, but if it is Omnipotence you will not stop it. You will not put a light out by taking it into the dark. It was created for this, and here was an opportunity for Cephas to shine in dark places. God left him in prison just long enough to work out a plan of escape. How would He do it? What methods would He use? One method was trust, the next faith, the third surrender, the fourth hope, the fifth obedience, the sixth prayer, and the seventh knowing that He will accomplish what He has set out to do! This army of soldiers were surrounding Peter for his deliverance. If these things be in you, there will be a time when the dove is set free to fly in its native sky.

There is a deeper fellowship to be discovered

Shut off from men, he found the Lord to be very near. Thrust into loneliness and deprived of fellowship, he discovered the deeper fellowship of Omniscience. Peter understood in his *maturity* that when Jesus on the cross was engulfed in darkness[17] He did not cease to be Light or the Son of God. The darkness is not meant to diminish you but to establish all that is Christian. Being alone, he moved towards the throne. If you looked closer you would see a third Person in the Son of God, between himself and his enemies when he was bound in chains. Peter enjoyed his prayers but the soldiers endured them! As a birthright some could appeal to Rome, but it always is the right of the prisoner to appeal to God. The hand that places you there will feed you, and at a given time will set you free.

Attacked and falsely accused, Simon Peter retired, not to abdicate his responsibility, not hurt but happy because he knew that God was not only the best and knew the best, but that He would do the best. Everything seemed to have gone wrong, yet here were materials for a miracle, and a place to deposit the glory of God. The best possible thing for this fisherman was to be set free to visit his brethren, to share the experience of deliverance. This miracle lived on in the delivered. He was part and parcel of that Heavenly visitation.

Peter was a man on a mission

This was a man on a mission, and sometimes missions take you through dark tunnels with no end in sight. We must not look for the light at the other end; we must walk in the light that is with us even in a dark, desperate situation. In his *maturity* Providence had provided for him for just such an hour. This chapter of the life of Peter was not hastily written, it was there all the time. Before time began you could read this chapter in the life of Peter. God holds the book of life, and He turns the pages. It might appear as a blank page but there is an unseen hand writing the story of the saint. The Master introduced Simon to the cell. Far above, below and beyond all the workings of Rome or its soldiers was the unseen hand of the Lord. The things around you, your circumstances, are God's way with your soul. What is iron and chain disposition to you is straw and grass to the Lord.

The doors opened of their own accord

'They came to the iron gate that leads unto the city; which opened to them of its own 'accord',' (Acts 12:10). It opened 'automatically' The Greek word is *automatos* —'self moved'. God had practised this when He rolled away the stone from the tomb of Jesus! The iron gates opened of their own 'accord'. ('The moving of itself'– Dr Robert Young.) 'The gates of hell shall not prevail' against the church. The word *automatos* is used just twice in the New Testament, in Acts 12:10, and in Mark 4:28, where it describes the earth as 'bringing forth' fruit of itself. The earth does this when corn is produced little by little, first the blade, then the ear, after that the full corn in the ear. In prison the Lord brought all the seasons together, marshalling them as an army, so swiftly that Peter thought he was dreaming or had been in a trance. In Job 24:24 the word 'accord' is used in the Septuagint Version of the Scriptures to describe an ear of corn falling from the stem, as if it does it by itself. The gates moved by their 'own' impulse. God took something that was dead, inanimate and heavy, and caused it to move with an impulse. I don't think the Lord was pushing the gates. Heavy metal suddenly had a will of its own! He stood before them and they opened as a token of bowing in worship, to let the King of Glory come in and go out.

God acts independently and automatically when we pray

Every word in our modern society that suggests 'automatic' comes from this Greek word *automatos*. Automatic washing machine, dishwasher, doors, stairs, all find their root meaning in this one Greek word. The words authority, author, authentic, autobiography, autocratic and autograph are all part of the family of this word *automatos*. The doors were opened when the Lord arranged all that steel and all that force to move as one heart, mind and soul. The iron gates opened of their 'own accord'—not at the instigation of another. 'All things 'work together' for good' —symphonise, as every instrument plays its part to produce sweet music for those who love God.[18] God arranges things for us so that our lives which were nowhere and everywhere are brought together as part of an orchestra, each instrument playing its part until the whole becomes a well written and played symphony. That which is discordant, and in prison, can through prayer become the 'food of love' which is music. Things happen in our lives, as they did in Peter's, without instigation or impulse of another. There was a Power working from the outside, meeting the need on the inside. That is how we were 'born again' according to John 1:13, not by the desire of human flesh or by command, but by the Spirit of God.

The answer to prayer is God's final decision

Apart from the prayers offered, the Eternal had decided that His son/servant was not staying in that prison cell. What Providence decides is stronger than any steel door; it will fit into any lock to open up the way before you. It is so reassuring when we realise that as we pray the Lord has decided already what shall happen. Before they called, God was answering, and an angel was speeding towards that prison cell. The steel doors opened as swiftly as the angel sped from the presence of the Lord. 'The angels of the Lord encamp around those who fear Him.'[19] One word and one act can open many doors. The Roman soldiers opened the door with one word of command from their leader, as Peter was thrown inside. They had a metal key, but the Key for Peter was the Almighty. The doors opened to let him out, without a word being spoken, shouted or whispered. The command for the doors to open came as the Spirit of God blew as a fresh breeze into the locks and into that stagnant cell.

Let go and let God

The son of Jonas revealed his true *maturity* in this cell because he never uttered a word of complaint. When your source is Christ, your serenity and security is Christ. He simply let go and let God. He was the model prayer and the model prisoner. When God opens doors, men must walk through. The son of Jonas carried no half broken chains with him. In fact when it says that the chains fell from his hands, there is the suggestion that they were not holding him captive, he was holding them! God ensures we do not go through an open door empty, unaccompanied. An angel went with Peter as far as was necessary. What goes into deep darkness comes out if we trust in the living God. Something of the metal doors and bars had entered into his spirit. It says that when they imprisoned Joseph, they put 'iron into his soul'.[20] There is metal for the *mature* in moments of frustration and faith. They are tools used by the Lord, one in His right hand the other in His left.

Notes

[1] Alpha, meaning the Beginning as Omega means the ending.

[2] Matthew 14:28–30.

[3] An old hymn written by George Matheson the blind song writer.

[4] Matthew 13:42.

[5] See J.A.Alexander in the Geneva Commentaries.

[6] See margin of the King James Version.

[7] Daniel 6:22.

[8] 1 Kings 17:4, 6.

[9] Acts 9:11, 12.

[10] Song of Solomon 1:3.

[11] 2 Corinthians 2:14–16.

[12] Hebrews 13:8.

[13] Hebrews 1:11.

[14] Romans 8:28.

[15] John 10:28, 29.

[16] Judges 16;3.

[17] Mark 15:33.

[18] Romans 8:28.

[19] Psalm 34:7.

[20] Psalm 105:18. The margin of the King James says 'they put iron into his soul.'

Chapter Eighteen

THE MAN WHO CONTINUED WHEN ANGELS DISAPPEARED

The time that Peter had spent in prison had been a time of reinforcement. He emerged as one in a dream, because his Heavenly Father had been doing 'dreamy' things for him. Now, as the fresh morning air touched his face, the moment of awakening had come. (Acts 12:10–12.) The grace of God, which had brought him through his prison experience, had become all things to this one man. Whatever size or shape the conflict, grace is designed to cover everything.

God will always be bigger than experience
Cephas might have had the tendency to cling to the angel in the dark night. *Maturity* manifests itself in many ways, one of which is that we do not make the dark happening greater than the One who granted it. There must be no Old Testament activity as when an angel visited people sacrifices were made to them.[1] The past is past, the future must be future. The angel, and all that has happened or been discovered in prison darkness, must be let go in the light of day. When we are in need, God will grant angels to minister and to bring us on our way. The hour of need is given the need of the hour in the shape of an angel.

The Epistle to the Colossians was written to those who worshipped angels. It states that Jesus Christ is far above angels, principalities or powers in this world or the world to come, as the Creator of all things. (Colossians 1:15–18.) The book of Hebrews takes on the same challenge, 'To which of the angels did He say you are my Son?' (Hebrews 1:5). Hebrews chapter 1 shows the superiority of Jesus to Moses, Aaron, creation, angels and Abraham. All these are folded up like a garment or closed like a book (Hebrews 1:11, 12), while Jesus Christ remains, '...the same yesterday, today and forever' (Hebrews 13:8). The enlargement of your heart and how it is done must not be worshipped, it must be let go when it has completed its dispensation. Miracles are only for the moment. You must make no fetish of an experience. Peter was as equally able to accept an angel as to walk away from one. There came a moment when the two must part. Peter went on with God. The angel went back to God.

Take control of that which is controlling you

We all enter phases which pass away. The phase must not see you falter or fumble. It took *maturity* in the heart of Peter to walk into the next phase of faith, when the angel had been there not only to strengthen him, but to set him free in a moment of need. We must not make the page the book, it must be turned. This angel had been a light in the darkness. But Simon Jonas walked in a more permanent light. If we cling long enough to that which has been a blessing, then that very blessing can become a curse, even as the flower of Paradise turns into a snake and causes us to stumble when we require more help to be *mature*.

Angels are answers to prayer, but each answer need not go from faith to a fetish. The angelic must become evangelical in the heart of the *mature*. Angels' wings might cool in the heat of the day, but they are not allowed to put out the fire of devotion, only fan it into a flame. Each messenger carries a message, to the mess created by men. We require that which is bold and strong to take control of those things which control us. Doors will open if first you open the door of your heart. Every chain will be snapped if you see the power of the Almighty stronger than any binding influence. The words spoken by this visitor (and as far as we know it was the only visitor Simon had) meant nothing until Peter began to walk in its shadow. When God cannot come He will send the next best thing, the only thing and the real thing that will help you. Whatever it is, if it brings freedom, release from shut gates, it will be an angel. Deliverance by any other name is an angel!

Learn to follow without question

Those who follow what the Lord has sent, to fulfilment, will have more sent in a time of need. In his *maturity* Simon had learned to follow without question. There was something of an angel in the obedience of Peter. When angels come, they bring Christ qualities to lives. They are 'ministering spirits' sent to minister to those who are the heirs of salvation. (Hebrews 1:14.) Here was an heir in Peter, a King's son in need. One minute all was as dark and empty as night, the next the angel was smiting him to arouse. Life is like that, one moment such a mountainous need, the next the need is met with abundance, pressed down, shaken together and running over, because of prayer. God sends angels to our devilish moments. Those who are weak, in the darkness, with no hope of escape, are sent that which is strong, brave and powerful. The Almighty sends to all at the moment of need what is required and to make them into what He desires them to be. This angel was a tool of truth and it served its Master well.

The finger of God will point the way

There comes a moment and a movement when the finger from the crucified hand beckons, and we go further and deeper into something new. Even angels can become boring if they are doing the same old thing in the same old way. We must travel the way the finger of God is pointing, not the way the wind is blowing. 'If any man be in Christ, new things keep breaking out all over' (2 Corinthians 5:18). There must be something 'new' in the 'new' wine given. The Eternal is full of diversity, adversity and opportunity. We were saved by the 'news', the 'good news' of the gospel. That 'news' continues to be news and will not become history while we are still imprisoned.

Today contains tomorrow in its folds

Learn with the *mature* man that what happens is not forever. It will pass. As the years go by, so the yearning of the soul and spirit increase. You can't measure the immeasurable, faith will always outlast fashion. The Bible often records 'and it came to pass'. Today contains tomorrow in its folds. The ministering spirit sent to help in a prison experience, in the tumble of life, must not be wedded to us forever. We must have new enrichment in the Lord to continue. It does not mean that we are fickle, moving quickly to and fro like a tennis ball being bashed by a racquet.

Peter went on to another street. (Acts 12:10.) There were other places his feet had not trodden. The pathways are plenty when we proceed. One door opens to another as one path leads to another. The Codex Bezae[2] adds, 'He went down seven steps.' He went down a step at a time until he reached the street which was Straight. There were other lives he could influence, and what had happened to him must be passed on. Having had chains on his hands, he had a grip like steel to hold others, some of the steel of the dungeon darkness having entered into his soul. Revival is not a continuation of the same method; it is the renewal of all that is right.

If you think you are indispensable, then go into the sea, and come out, and see what impression or evidence you have left in the water to show where you have been. Breathe into the air; see what there is left of you to be seen. That is about as important as you are.

Don't worship miraculous moments

We will not worship the 'burning bush' or the 'rod that budded'. We will not worship or make a fetish of the 'brazen serpent' or the pen that the apostle Peter used to write his epistles. We will worship the God of all these things. You might be led into a miraculous moment, but then it must come to an end. Israel could not live on the miraculous manna forever. It says 'that same day they ate the corn of the land' (Joshua 5:11). The manna days had gone forever, they had to have other means. You have to be *mature* enough to take out a handkerchief and wave goodbye to all things. What things have meant to you, when they have been your bedside companions, your watchmen in the night, must still be let go, and you must reach for something else. You must be to others what the Lord's blessings have been to you.

When we are in difficulties, the Almighty develops our hands so that we can reach for bigger things. The future is always larger than the past or the present. It is bigger because you are bigger. When Mark Twain was seventeen, he said of his father, 'He is a foolish old man.' When he was twenty one, he said, 'What a wise old man my father is, these last few years he has grown up so much!' You must continue to expect great things from God. The hand that gives is large and contains so much more than what has already been given. We have been happy with crumbs when God gives us this day our daily bread! Do not worship the bread, worship the Lord of the harvest.

It is human nature to cling to things

Human nature makes us cling to things. As babies we cling to rattles and toys. Take a baby to a paediatrician, and they will test its ability to hold onto things. As we grow, we cling to briefcases and suitcases. Part of the grasping hand of Jacob is with us all. We do not want to let go of our history, to see it turned into news. We like to be 'old shoe' and 'old hat'.

There is a need in every heart to leave some things behind, no matter how special they are. Not wanting to forget some things, we take them out again and again. How fond we are of memories! We treat familiar things like family heirlooms; ornaments are strategically placed so they can be seen at every turn. Whether good or bad things, they must become a distant memory. Human nature is amazing in that it will forget the good things, the moments of blessing, yet it will build a permanent altar to those horrid, wicked things that have happened. Simon, in his moment of *maturity*, had to move away from the prison and the deliverer. He must not take a feather from the angel's wings —if they have feathers, or wings? He must write his epistles with a pen of iron, not a pen made from a feather from the visitor's wings. Whatever leaves you, there will always be that investment within your heart of enrichment in the Lord.

By clinging to the past you can be robbed of a future

The angel is only part of the creation of God. The sun, moon, trees, plants or fields must not dethrone Him who sits upon the throne. God will lend angels to you, to bring out of the deep darkness of despair, into the clear light of a new day. That which has happened in the dark needs to be left there. Why should the fisherman cling on to that which was required elsewhere? If you cling to anything that has happened in the past, then you are robbing someone of a future. There are others in prison, and once you have been delivered there are certain things that *maturity* does not require. The 'walking stick' must be thrown away.[3] What you are leaning on must be left, so that someone who is faint and weary might come and lean and learn.

The Lord knows we are prone to clinging to the past, and it robs us of a future of angelic happenings that He is trying to lead us into. That is why Jesus said to Peter in John 21:15, 'Do you love Me more than these? Fish, fishing boats with their nets, the call of the wild sea, and all that surrounded him as part of the past, are all part of 'these'. Love is questioned when there is no quest in our lives. We are not only dull but blind to future things. Do you love the future more than the past? That is *maturity*, when you love the future much more than the past. When the Lord appeared, Peter put an old familiar thing, a fishing coat, around him and clung to it. (John 21:7.) Do not listen to the 'blast from the past', get a new sound into your heart, the sound of the forthcoming revival.

Old things die hard

Don't cling to that which has blessed you. If you do you will rob it and yourself of a future. The strength given by your Father must not be ministered solely into you but must be taken and shared. You must never be a Judas who took the money because he held the bag, and was a thief. There comes a time when eyes must be taken from the hills and put back where they belong, on the Lord who made the hills.[4] In clinging to some things we restrict our growth and independence. It is good to be helped to walk when you are a child, but later you must walk by yourself. Peter would never be alone because the moment the angel stepped to one side he felt the comfort of the Lord on all sides. Old things must die so that new things can be appreciated. 'Old things die hard.'

Relationship with God will be your relationship with men

Everything has a time and a place. When that time has gone, the place also must disappear, and you must go on to another area, a better man or woman than you were before the angel came. If you haven't changed, the experience has been worthless. Angels have been your companions but men must become your destiny. Your future is with God not the angels, with the church not some heavenly apparition. The angel departed from Mary. (Luke 1:38.) God grants us special times of deliverance, and to walk with angels. We must leave the angels in order to walk with God. What your relationship is to God so it will be to men. 'Love the Lord your God with all your heart, and love your neighbour as your self.'

If this messenger had continued all the days of Peter's life, it would have given him an unfair advantage over the rest of the church. 'Here comes Simon with his angel!' That would have sounded neither sensible nor sane. He said to Cornelius, 'Stand up! I myself am also a man' (Acts 10:25, 26). His manhood and his sainthood had to shine out from him. Angels announced the birth of Christ, and they can be used to announce the birth of new things in your life. Peter had to let the angel go after it had brought him to this place in his spirituality. I operate better when it is just Jesus and me. 'Angels from the realms of glory wing their flight to worlds unknown.'[5] They go back to where they belong, and I must go to where I am being called.

Maturity is not built on angels

Maturity is not built on angels. It comes about when, because of a prison experience, we come through gloriously whether God sends angels or not. We triumph, not because of the messenger but because of the Lord of Hosts. They are but servants even as we are. I must not spend the rest of my days relying on some angel coming to me with strength. I must trust the God of my life, who is my strength. When Jesus could have called ten thousand angels to assist Him, He did not because He relied on His inner strength and the qualities of His *maturity*.

This messenger from God had led Simon so far, training him to walk and to trust in the living Lord. The fisherman must learn that the sent one was just an ambassador for the King, it was not the King. God sends and lends some things, others He gives for us to keep. Now, Simon must take the next few steps into his destiny alone. All that he had received while in that black hole must be revealed on another street in another sphere. There are many more streets for you to walk in the city of God.

If Peter had continued with the supernatural being he might have written an epistle to angels. He is left long enough for all the will of the Master to be revealed and fulfilled. Even when the messenger's ministry had finished, the angel and the man must move on, the keys to the prison be thrown away because the keys to the Kingdom are with Peter. Those keys are not literal keys, they are things God arranges that will open and shut doors, seen in miracles and manifestations.

Circumstances and not miracles make a man

Everything that happens should not leave you in a prison cell with iron gates locked, the key thrown away. It should lead you out of a bad experience. If it doesn't it is not an angel but a devil that has been seeking to control you. When the offer came, Simon took it, binding on sandals, and putting a garment around his body. He was saying, 'Wherever the Father leads me I am ready to go.' He was dressed as one going on a journey with an angel, but that journey came to an end. One moment the heavenly man was there, the next he had gone. Aren't happenings just like that? No two days and no three weeks are the same. We are led so far and no further. The next step you must take. We would all love to have a special agent as seen in the comic strips, suggesting that whenever we have a need, he will arrive on the scene and pulverise all our enemies! There are times when you seem to be alone, yet you are not alone. If the Lord had to respond to your every whim and whimper, assigning a flaming figure to every believer, all would believe, and there would be no walk of faith into the future. I am not sure that having visions of angels really *matures* us. It can be a step in the right direction, it can add a little to us, but it does not add all that we require. What we received must be shared, and can only be shared when we are prepared to move on. While you cling to one thing you let go of another. If you cling long enough and hard enough, then the very thing that was allowed into your life to minister life can choke it, as tares choke the corn. That which was meant for blessing and life can introduce stagnation and death. It will grow stale and old, you will become the same.

Simon Peter was led to a new landscape, to another street, which appeared to be empty. It might have been an old street, but a new man walked on it. This was a man who saw things differently, not because he had been in touch with an angel but because he had been in touch with the Almighty. In prison he received a slap on the side, telling him to get dressed and go on. God can give us a friendly slap or a fiery slap. We all need the Potter's touch. I want something to push me on into the next street of sanctity, like the slap from a special messenger. We all need a 'final push' that will send us to our destination as if loosed from a sling.

Angels come in all shapes and sizes

God sends angels in all forms and sizes. Do not wait for the shining body and the outstretched wings. Have the eyes of your understanding opened so that you can see angel's wings in the many tokens of grace in your life. You will be *mature* when you see ministering angels in everyday things. 'Angels have 'entertained' some unawares.'[6] You have not been aware of the angel, and when you do there is a tendency to worship at its feet. That is why your Father has more than one ministry with which to affect your life. I note that it was the street that led to fellowship and a church meeting in the house of Mary the mother of John Mark. The son of Jonas had been here before, but not with a message of deliverance! People will judge how you walk with men if you have walked with angels. No experience will remove humanity from us. Every spiritual happening should make us more human, but that humanity must operate within the influence of Divinity. The more spiritual and *mature*, the more you will realise that you need other humans to be your companions. Angels have never been where your friends have been. Friends have the same temptations and fears as you. Friends as brothers and sisters are good to be with. Having seen an angel they will not only keep your feet on the floor, they will keep you walking in the right direction, forward not backwards or sideways. Even marriage and children are given so that love might be expanded, and does not become self-love.

Angels are the tools of God

It seems as if the Eternal draws a line, and that is only as far as the deliverer from prison must go. Then only one pair of footprints goes further. All experiences come and go, as the angel did after seeing His work accomplished. As a good workman, the Eternal lays his tool on one side, ready to be taken and used again when necessary. Angels teach us so much about service. This messenger was as delighted to come and stay as to leave and go elsewhere. The angel went, but note how in Luke 24:28 Jesus would have gone further, and that is the difference. Jesus never leaves, while angels and experiences come and go. The messenger can deliver from prison, but he must not be involved in any further acts of Peter. This convert must start all over again. Another messenger might come in a different way and for a different purpose. God proves that He has more than one angel.

Simon Peter has to show to the believers that the God with him in prison is still the same in the world at large. He has millions of ways of deliverance. Do not get religious or traditional in your thinking of how the Almighty will deliver you. If you get glass eyed at the working of God you will miss that which is sent to help you. I hear you think, 'I want to worship the Lord with all of my heart.' How do you worship Him with all of your heart? By giving Him all, not just a part, so not even the feather of a heavenly messenger must come between you and your Lord. He can't only be the Lord of the prison cell. He must become the Lord of your life. Lordship is not for a time or a season, a place or a pleasantry, it is in all areas and at all times. You take what you have made Him, and He takes what you give Him everywhere. It is something we are never free from.

You can be the next angel to be sent

When the Eternal has no angel to send, He might send you. If you have listened and been delivered, that was part of the training for you to take the place of the heavenly being. If you get wrapped up in angels' wings, or hide in their feathers if they have them, there are so many things about God you will miss. Don't get taken up with the service rather than the Eternal you serve. If you do, then your service will be lukewarm and 'half baked'![7] You are not being transformed into an angel, but into the image of Christ. You can arrive in heaven knowing all about angels, but you have to arrive looking like God.

Special happenings are alright for rare endeavours, but there is a level plain on which we must operate for most of our life. When angels are absent, then what I am is in the I Am. It takes more grace to live with an angel than I can describe. In *maturity* the Almighty wants you to be what you are with a special messenger or without one. Trust Him in everyday living, with or without spiritual manifestation. Some say they have angel visitations in the night. Wait until the morning light to see how they live before determining whether that has the ring of truth about it. If the 'ring of truth' awakens you in the morning then you will have a splendid day.

Don't be like a horse that needs a bit and a bridle

You are called and led to face the difficulties of life without the constant help of the supernatural. I know God answers prayer, but there are some things that the Almighty expects you to do for yourself, such as trust Him and have faith. You are being developed, not submerged, by supernatural visions. It is not right that you become the horse with a bridle as stated in the Psalm 32:9, or that you are like a ship with a rudder or helm that turns you this way and that. Choices have to be made, and the choices made will make you what you are going to be. Even the wind blows where it will, but it comes and goes, and so is everyone that is born of the Spirit of God. (John 3:8.)

For you to be content there has to be a variety about your life. It can't be manna every day or you will say, 'Our souls loathe this bread.'[8] The 'common' can soon become the 'unclean'. We get bored, even with that which comes in the form of a heavenly man. In the Lord there is such variety. The only variety angels know is in the work they do. We make the extraordinary so ordinary, the spectacular becomes the spectacle. If staying with the angelic was allowed, when in heaven we would be taken up with angels instead of with the Almighty. What the Lord has allowed taking us from 'A' to 'B' is not necessarily the thing to take us from 'Y' to 'Z'.

Deliverance comes from unexpected quarters

The things that I do for myself contain greater teaching for me than the things others do for me. I learn through experience how to handle situations, rather than situations handling me. Don't let your circumstances become your crown. If you do, it might be a crown of thorns! I can't call upon an angel every time I am in trouble. I can call upon the Lord, and He will determine how to answer. The visitor might depart but the faithful One remains. Deliverance comes from unexpected quarters because I am not expecting it that way.

God has not promised an angel every day to take you by the hand as you leave home, but He has promised that which will be with you forever, His presence and Spirit. If a heavenly messenger is at your right hand all the time, you are not going to do much witnessing or be a real exponent of faith. What Cephas had received from the messenger must be taken and used to help the weak, to make strong the surrendering, and to nerve those who are afraid. No ministry and time spent with the messengers of heaven is wasted. The only wasted hour is that spent thinking of what might have been, instead of concentrating on what is. Peter did not walk in the visitor's shoes or wear its cape; he walked in his own shoes towards his destiny in the Eternal.

In Acts 12:17 when the dust had settled, Peter went from where he was to another 'place'. However deep or enlightening any happening is, when provided by the One above it must lead to a different 'place'. We might commence in one area of faith, but step by step and triumph by triumph we are brought to our destination. The Lord of Glory can see the final step even before the first step is taken. As sheep with dull eyes, we cannot see two steps ahead, and that makes us vulnerable. While we stop to gaze at the mountains which block the way, the Almighty looks through and beyond. If we can see Jesus, then all will be well.

The Lord will always provide another opportunity

When Peter went to another 'place,' having been restored to the fellowship of believers, that word 'place' suggests, according to Dr. James Strong DDL, a figure of a 'new opportunity'. When one fire goes out, let the Lord light another, just as He did in John 21:9, and also when the fire Peter had warmed his hands on in the temple had gone out. (John 18:25.) When one pathway comes to an abrupt end as it falls over a precipice, let the Sovereign turn the earth in another direction to make a path for your feet to tread on. Cephas was presented with another opportunity, and he took it with both feet, one foot following the other in the footsteps of Jesus. The word translated 'place' is the same word rendered 'place' in the Garden of Gethsemane in Matthew 26:52, when the disciple was told to put his sword in its 'place' suggesting 'scabbard', where the sword was held when not in use. It is only there to rest before the next onslaught.

That word 'place' describes where two seas met in Acts 27:41. In the Eternal all roads lead to the throne. In England, whatever road you take, if you follow it long enough it will lead to London. It is good to come where all things meet together for your good. The north, south, east and west all met at the point of his appointment.

God trains His soldiers for triumph in future battles

In prison the son of Jonas received his cutting edge. There would be many a battle before him, and he had to be as a sword in the hand of the Lord. We must not allow fear or faltering, dungeon or danger to make us blunt in our perception of the will of God. Don't blunt the sword by trying to batter steel shutters or locked levers in doors. We must not be blunt in our response to the call into the Battle of Life. When the Lord views you, He needs to view you even as David did the sword of Goliath: 'Give it to me; for there is none like it' (1 Samuel 21:9). It is that which has been produced and forged in the fires of His love for you. David was without a sword on one occasion, and the only sword on offer belonged to Goliath. King David took it, and won the next battle. God's methods are not simply men's.

God has only one plan for your life

There was no other plan for Peter. Your plan is the Peter plan, where the Almighty develops *maturity* in your meanest moments. There must be the heart of God in your happiest days. The Almighty only evokes what He has put into you as you have trusted Him for more light in the darkest night. He has made you into a man of *maturity* through a prison process. The sword would cut and kill, but it would also set free those who were bound. That received in the dark place can be the blade formed in the fires of affliction. Simon had been into the cauldron and now, like Elijah, he must go from the brook Cherith to Zarephath, then on further in the will of God. Your map might show there is nowhere to go. The way out and through might not seem to exist. What you feel may tell you there is nowhere else to operate. It is not what I am thinking but what God is saying that will lead me to another place, to continue where heavenly beings must not tread, because they have received no command to enter that area. The map and the plan that the Lord holds is always unfolding as a script in the hands of the crucified Saviour. There are parts where you have never been and can't hope to understand. He Who reveals it all will take you there. At the end of your journey, pray that you will not be as you were when you commenced. He who commences a race and moves away last is most disappointed if, at the finish, he is still the last. Don't be a Bacchis, a sacred bull that changed its colour every hour of the day. That was part of the old Peter nature, where the term 'petering out' comes from.[9]

This Galilean walked out of prison with a light in his soul, that same light of revelation that he had taken in with him. He used it to take him to his next destination. You need to be a light to help those who are in the tunnel. Don't stand at the other end; be in that tunnel with them.

'The Master has come and He is calling for you.'

When you look into your diary, don't just look at your next appointment, look into your heart and see what the Eternal has written as if with a nail from the cross of Christ. He says to you, 'What I have written I have written.'[10] Then He will ask you: how did you read?[11] What have you read? He is saying: read it through to the end. At the end of the searching of your own heart you will hear a voice saying, 'This is the way, walk in it.'[12] As you read and listen, as you ascertain, so you will act. You become that living word in your *maturity*. You become all that the Lord has said to you. 'The Master has come and He is calling for you.'

Peter became a G.O.M. A grand old man, the title given to Mr Gladstone, who served England as Prime Minister 1881–1885. When anyone in the country referred to the Grand Old Man, everyone knew to whom they were referring. He enjoyed the title because of the Christian life he lived and the conduct that characterised him as one of Christ's men. He was not the 'Grand Old Duke of York', who led men only halfway up a hill and who, when things were hot and difficult, and they couldn't see over the hill, marched them down again! The end of the ditty states, 'When they were halfway up they were neither up nor down.' They concluded where they commenced. Those who experience *maturity* reveal that quality in the ordinary things of life just as this fisherman-disciple did. Walk as Peter walked in the Acts of the Apostles and you will never be far from faith, or left around the corner from Christ.

In all this we might refer to Simon as *Calceos matavit*. He has 'changed his shoes'. He has become a Senator, part of the Council of *mature* men. When Romans became Senators, they changed shoes. These new shoes were not the shoes of sonship or of the soldier; they were shoes of the servant, sandaled across the instep and up to the ankles. Simon took off his old shoes in prison, and came out wearing new shoes. The shoes Peter had worn in the past had taken him into many places, but now as a servant he wears a servant's shoes, and the token of this is obedience that leads to *maturity*.

Notes

[1] Judges 13:19.

[2] Quoted by A.T.Robertson, *Word Pictures in the New Testament*.

[3] Exodus 4:1–10, the Message translation.

[4] Psalm 121.

[5] Part of an old Christmas carol.

[6] Hebrews 13:2.

[7] Hosea 7:8, used of Ephraim who would not stay long enough to be offered as a sacrifice.

[8] Numbers 21:5.

[9] See author's book, *The Growing Pains of Peter.*

[10] Words spoken by someone in supreme authority in John 19:22.

[11] Acts 8:30, 31.

[12] Isaiah 30:21.

Chapter Nineteen

THE MAN WHO SAID
THE RIGHT THING
AT THE RIGHT TIME

It is one thing to 'say' the right thing, but a totally different scenario to 'do' the right thing. Those 'doings' must follow our 'sayings' as day follows night. There are times when debate and strife cease, then Heaven will be inside of us and beside us. Debate and strife needs someone who has sanctified common sense in order to settle a matter and sort it out. The answer must always be the king of the question. The question will bow in worship when the correct answer is given. Any answer, like pills in a bottle, has to be taken and swallowed before a remedy can be produced. The settling of any difference is by prayer, and as you pray the Lord will reveal the heart of another to you. We must learn to walk in each others' shoes; only then will we appreciate the difficulties, and know what to do.

What we have to say must be worth listening to
The words Peter had to pass on to those in debate in Acts 15:7 are worth hearing and receiving. He used every experience he ever entered, and what he learned was passed on. We carry with us the evidences of where we have been. Those things that have blessed us, we need to use to bless others. We need to be able to distinguish the end from the beginning. There is *maturity* in those who see the end of a matter from the beginning. It is good to give advice, but that advice must first be relevant to your own life.

As we journey we collect diversity for the university of life. Through experience, God is making us into a people full of wisdom and knowledge. What we receive today is just not meant for today; we lay it on one side and, like the scribe of the kingdom, bring things out old and new. In any situation of hurt or pain, your doctor will have advised you, and in your recovery you have remembered certain things.[1] God has helped you in order that you might help others.

You can be a ministry of helps

Those in distress need someone to hear their cry. God sends help in time of trouble. You become a ministry of 'helps' as in 1 Corinthians 12:28. You have to be what Christ is and He is the Answer. He is the Yes and Yes to the needs of the heart. We glean as Ruth did, gathering here a little and there a little until we become a repository of love, and learn answers to the many questions which arise in the quest of life. An enquiry can be met out of the abundance of the heart. Every circumstance becomes a teacher that passes on to you the scholar, so that you can pass on to others. C.H.Spurgeon had quaint sayings on these matters: 'I have milked many cows but churned my own butter.' In another sermon he says, 'Burn my weeds and cultivate my flowers.' Paul could write, 'That which you have seen in me, pass on to others.' Through life experiences you can become a dictionary on Divine happenings. Wise people will draw advice from the heart of wise man, and in doing so will build his house on a Rock.

Store up everything that happens to you. Be a hoarder of good things, you will never know when you will need them. See how a squirrel in the autumn gathers nuts, burying them for winter days of fog, hardness, ice and snow. In our house we have a drawer, where everything that seems superfluous is put in. In times of need some have come to that drawer, and taken from it just what was required. Be as the disciples who, after the feeding of five thousand people, gathered up twelve baskets of broken bread.[2] That which was gathered from the miracle could be used in the future. Remember the good things forever. Let the rain of the day wash away the bad things to be remembered no more.

Make room in your heart for vital lessons

Make room in your heart for that which can be used in a future session or season. It is God who seeks to will and do of His good pleasure. You will never stand as a soldier ill clad or without a weapon when facing opposition if you will take into your heart all those things Jehovah has revealed to you. As Peter, you will meet with those who have not had the same revelation as yourself. What you say, and the advice you pass on, will help others to turn from the Jericho Road.

In Acts 15:4–22, a dispute arose over the matter of circumcision. Simeon, as he is called in Acts 15:14, could comment simply because he had passed through so many experiences. This is the first and only time that he is referred to as Simeon. The man's heart is a fountain, one of wisdom that will help with the deep longings of others. When a person is 'as hungry as a hunter', what you say can be the 'quarry' they are hunting for. Peter had to take what Christ is – wisdom, righteousness, sanctification and redemption, which was in Him – and apply it, as the council met together in Jerusalem.

Dark dreary hours do matter —they may not help you, but they will help another, and you do so in Jesus Christ. You will meet with that which speaks of schism, where the Body of Christ seems to be torn apart. It is then that you are able to be the answer and give the answer, and what you say and are will become ointment without the fly (Ecclesiastes 10), which sends out a pure fragrant smell of Jesus. How are you going to become light if you never have to face darkness?

How can you help those who are hurting if you have never been hurt?

How can you exercise a healing ministry if you have never been sick? In the tumble of life you learn to stand on your own two feet so that others can lean upon you. You can only comfort with the comfort that you have been comforted with. (2 Corinthians 7:13). That born in your own affliction becomes a sure word of help for others. There will be times when you will be called upon to be the Daysman,[3] the man who umpires and decides. The best cricket umpires are usually those who have played the game. They have 'been there, seen that, done it and bought the 'T' shirt.'

There are times when we need to lift the lid off, or lift the skin to see what is underneath. We are human, that is why Christ became a Man, so that He might be 'touched' with the feelings of our infirmities.[4] He can be a 'help' in time of need. You can be what the word 'help' suggests, the ropes going under a ship at sea in a storm when the sea threatens to break it apart, the under-girding help that will keep it together and on course. The ministries and servanthood that help the most don't come from your mouth, your foot or your finger but from your heart. Simeon did not 'talk from the top of his head' or simply give an answer 'off the cuff'. There was nothing *ad hoc* 'off the hoof'. It was a reply that would help others in need. Just as Jethro, the father-in-law of Moses, had become eyes to Israel (Exodus 18), Cephas was seeking to be those eyes as someone who went ahead seeking out the land, watching for an 'ambush' that suddenly springs out as a tiger. Peter had passed through those things he spoke about. He was not afraid of shallow waters or a creek; he had been in the deep sea.

Each word you speak can be baptised in experience
If you can take from the pattern that the Eternal has formed in your heart, you can use it as a map to help those who are stumbling. At the edge of the precipice, be as one holding the lamp. The Message Bible says, in Isaiah 26, 'We are content to linger in the path signposted with your decisions. Who you are and what you've done are all we'll ever want.'

The *mature* person will not only be 'streets ahead' but words ahead. When others are thinking, he is speaking. While some are still on their knees you can be on your feet. It was Simon who spoke that which was described as 'golden'. To 'stand out' in a crowd does not mean you have to shout to gain attention. Every question must bow low before the answer. While they are working it out, he has spoken it out. Each word Simeon spoke was baptised in experience. Every time something happened in his life there was a lesson to learn and a story to tell in the future. If you are *mature* you need to ask yourself: What can I take from this experience that will not only help me but help another, to fulfil the Scripture, 'help ye one another'? Billy

Richards was a minister for many years in Slough, Buckinghamshire, England.[5] I often saw him with a notebook in his hand. If anyone said anything worth repeating or he heard a good story, he would write it down, and ask the story teller of its origins.

It is not only reading that makes a man full

It is not only reading that makes a man full, it is listening and ascertaining truth. The truth of the hour can become all that is required in the moment of dire need. To hold some things together you require more than a great psyche and large hands, you need a warm heart. When some people are drowning, so we are told, the last thing they see is a picture of their life as it flashes before them, as if nature has stored up all the views and words, depositing them as gold in the strata. Don't wait until you die to utter a few answers; use what you are in everyday situations, and maybe, just maybe, you will stop Cain killing Abel. In arguments, if you feel that people are 'walking all over you', you have fulfilled the service of Christ as a mediator between man and man. Remember your answer can spell 'sorry' in the hearts of those who need to hear and say it.

In your ministry you can interpret needs

When it seems as if it is Greek or an unknown tongue that is happening to another, do not only pray for the interpretation, be the interpretation. Be the translation of trouble into trust. Simon was willing to take a risk in what he said. He might have been misunderstood or told to keep quiet. He could have been as the oxen with its mouth muzzled as it treads the corn. Daniel is described as one who dissolves knots. We need to know in the mind of Christ how to handle difficult problems. Solve the problem by not becoming the problem. If a person falls into icy turbulent water that will freeze to death, it is ridiculous to jump in after them. A splash might be made, but no rescue will be effected. You must remain warm, reaching out from where you are to pull them out. By throwing yourself into the same problem you will not help but hinder. Peter did not take sides; he stood with Christ Who stood with him. It is little wonder that they said of Jesus and the disciples, 'Where did these get such authority from being unlearned and ignorant men?' There can be a theological college in your home, in your street or the place where you work, where God is training His best to be the best, so that when those around are losing their head you keep yours. When the going gets tough, the tough get going.

Don't let past faults restrict future faith ventures

What made it even more difficult for Simeon to give the correct answer in the debate was the fact that many who had gathered knew all his faults and failings. In some minds they would be ten thousand times ten thousand and thousands of thousands! They had been present when he had spoken 'out of turn', suggesting things that seemed ridiculous. God had not only worked on Peter, He had also been working in the hearts of the other disciples who earlier in their experience had only been there for the miracle bread. That miracle bread was still part of Peter, and is seen in the answer he gave to the enquiry.

Here is *maturity* in its finest colours, like the King's daughter, all glorious within, with clothing of wrought gold. (Psalm 45:13.) 'Wrought' as colours interweaved, formed into squares of embroidery. Such things the Eternal is doing in a life that is to be used by Him.

It doesn't seem as if Simeon's answer was acceptable. Barnabas and Paul had to add to the testimony of Peter by telling what the Lord had done among the Gentiles (verse 12). The answer does not always come from one person, but little by little it is given and received. When the question is married to the answer there is no divorce.

Learn to wait on the Lord for the answer

Later, James takes hold of the words of Peter, applying them as ointment, and a healing takes place. Occasionally your answer may be left on one side, and then later someone else can take hold of it and use it. Some do not take advice on the 'spur of the moment', but wait a while, and later after their heart finds a place of acceptance and the result is peace. They no longer saw Cephas wearing the dunce's cap, but saw him for what he was, or for what the Lord had made him. He was 'full of substance' from the Lord. (Proverbs 16:20), 'He that handles a matter wisely shall find good.'

Simeon did not join in the debate. He simply took what he had, and what he had allowed the ministry of Jesus to form in him, and he used it to the best of his ability. It is not recorded that he said anything before he stood to his feet. After finding his feet in *maturity* he could stand on those feet. 'Every barrel must stand on its own end,' but it depends what is in the barrel. If you look at a problem, see into it, and then see right through it, you will help others who are as the blind leading the blind. That is why it is good to take a step back when, instead of being cocooned in the disturbance, you look at it from the outside instead of the inside. You can see far more looking in than looking out. Looking out you see through an open door or a window, and if it is night you see very little. If you take a humble position as a backward step, you can lift the roof off, and look at the whole thing.

Most advice is just anointed common sense

I don't think that what Cephas said was a manifestation of the word of wisdom, as listed in the gifts of the Holy Ghost, 1 Corinthians 12:8. It was simply anointed, sanctified common sense. It was so simple I think it took them all by surprise! Peter knew it was of the Lord, because he couldn't have worked out this answer using an abacus! We say things that are beyond our years and *maturity*, and have to acknowledge that such advice was given by the Advocate, the Lawyer.[6]

Like this *mature* man, your experience in God is the greatest wisdom that you will ever have. Your words can build up or tear down. In a soft answer you can turn away wrath, you can make an appeal to the heart, or you can enrage the spirit. That which is home-made and home-wrought is better than anything read or taken from another source. What the fisherman was saying was part of his heart, that is why it was acceptable. He spoke the truth, the whole truth and nothing but the truth. Experience can colour our theology. Our failures can be introduced into what we believe and teach.

Learn to share what has been shared with you

Each day should begin as a blank sheet of paper, for the Lord to put something on which can be taken and shared among others, as Ruth shared a full cloak of corn with her mother-in-law. (Ruth 3:15.) As you lie in your bed at night, it is good to think of all the rainbows the Lord has shown you during the day. Count your blessings instead of sheep. Better still, communicate with the Shepherd, drifting into His arms as you fall asleep. There is more wisdom in every seeking heart than the seeker can calculate.

Peter is deliberately called Simeon in Acts 15:14. James makes a glorious pun by using this new name for Simon. The name takes him back to the Old Testament, back to his roots, suggesting someone 'who has heard'. In some Old Testament words three tenses are involved: past, present and future. Peter has heard from the Lord, is listening to the Lord, and will hear the Lord. Hear a promise, hear a story, and hear some wisdom, then pass it on. Simeon means to 'hear intelligently', 'hearing with acceptance' the spoken word. Two ears we have, but just one mouth. Listen to twice as much as you say. Hear the words of wisdom and knowledge and use them to help others. Out of a pound of experience a ton of help can evolve. You can hear all the Lord has to say, but are you listening? Have you heard clearly enough to pass it on to someone so they can act upon it? Peter did not want to add another mistake to those threatening the young church. It was not time to walk on water or raise the dead; the moment of truth had come, it was time to tell it as it is. At the moment when he gave the answer, what he said was the important thing. His words became warriors to work it all out and through. The ear will follow a voice and a word. Let the ear become the disciple of the word. Let what you say, in answer to those in need, be a beat of your own heart.

What you are can be a beam of light

Simon the son of Jonas had passed through so much. As he journeyed, what he heard and understood he was able to use when they gathered together in Jerusalem. There are some things that take place in truth, and you wonder how they can ever benefit you. If you let the Hand that has guided you gather it all together, then nothing will be lost.

Nothing shall pluck it from His hand. (John 10:28.) There will come a moment in your Christianity when, in a dark situation, what you have and are in God will be a beam of light that others can look at and follow.

Acts 15:7 says, 'when there had been much disputing,' Peter stood up. He did not rush in 'where angels fear to tread.' He simply listened to what others had to say, and like a marksman, looked to his target before he spoke a word. That which is born and developed in *maturity* will patiently wait its turn, for part of being *mature* is being patient. Peter as the 'man with the answer' listened to all the questions. His mind became a balance on which he weighed all the 'pros and cons'. Because he knew what he knew, there was no need to shout. This was more a teaching session than preaching. He spoke to the people, so that it would enter into their hearts. When wisdom is flowing it can flow quietly. What this man said in the answer touched their hearts and, because of James, they adopted what Peter had suggested. This was the essence of 'free speech'.

Don't try to get your own way

Simeon was not an angry man trying to get his own way, or force through his own agenda. He was there to help, and in helping and offering advice to one, he offered to them all. This disciple was so different from Mrs Sarah Gamp. She was a nurse famous for her large umbrella, and her often references to Mrs Harris, an imaginary person, who never existed. To get her own way, Gamp would say, 'As Mrs Harris has said, and I agree with her....' She was really following what she herself thought and had decided. All Peter did was to repeat what God had done. It was a time of testimony turned into pure acceptable wisdom.

When the Galilean spoke he was describing the works of the Lord which were embedded in the words; they were a psalm of praise unto the Lord. All his devotion and doctrine are found in these moments of joy. His words and work was to describe the activity of the Lord. The nature of Simon declared His handiwork. Where the Lord did not bind, they should not bind. Where God didn't limit, they should not limit. If the Lord accepted, then they must accept. As Peter talked it through, he was following the Lord as a true disciple. The *mature* man will not put a yoke on people because they are new converts. No list of 'dos' and 'don'ts'.

A dispute can be a 'put down' and a 'knock down'

There had been a 'dispute'Acts 15:7. A 'dispute' is to 'knock down'. It is to be at the funfair, taking aim at the coconuts, seeking to knock them down. Be knocked down, but don't be knocked out.' The word 'quarrel' in the Latin *ob-jacio* is to 'pull against'. 'Fellowship' is to 'pull the same way'. It was Jacob who grabbed at the heel of Esau at birth, revealing the future struggle between the two brothers.[7] This is 'fellowship', two fellows in a ship sailing the same sea and going to the same port. It is not 'fellowship' when sailing in opposite directions to different ports of call and with different captains giving the orders. The Latin *contendo* meaning 'quarrel' suggests 'throwing darts at one another'. The problem with that is that some people are so short sighted, they throw darts that stick in those who were not the intended target and many are hurt. The Welsh *cwarel* means a 'dart'. To 'wrangle' means to 'strain by twisting'. It is not 'wrangling' the church needs; it is 'wrestling' with the Lord as Jacob did, when his name was changed from 'supplanter' to a 'prince with God'. (Genesis 32:24, 25.)

Learn to put your energies into prayer

When the apostle Paul writes about prayer, one of the words he uses is 'conflict', describing two wrestlers in a ring, with different holds and grips on each other. Your greatest power should be reserved for prayer, to take hold of God. Power should not be used to get the better of another. Do as Jesus did when He washed the disciples' feet. He threw in the towel (John 13:4, 5), and that settled all manner of dispute. In the New Testament, two were arguing. They asked Jesus to settle the matter. His reply was, 'who made Me a judge or ruler over you?' (Luke 12:14). The reason he said this was not because he was abdicating his responsibility. The reason He said this was because they had made Him judge and ruler without making Him King! If he is King, the two people arguing come together at the foot of the throne. There is nothing like Lordship to establish relationship with others. It is the King who makes us kind.

A need is not met by ignoring it

Peter was more *mature* at this time than Moses was when he heard two people having an argument, and slew one. (Exodus 2:12–14.) That action at the time seemed to settle the argument, but what it did was to prolong it. Eventually, Moses had to flee for his life. Arguments are not resolved by throwing stones, but by pointing to the Rock, Christ Jesus. Jesus was like a lamb before its shearers,[8] He opened not His mouth when He was threatened. This is some quality of *maturity*. Simon pointed out what Jesus had done, and was saying let us follow Him in word and deed. There is no surer or more pleasurable way of settling an argument than pointing to Christ. If we can lead those who are arguing to the feet of Jesus, we shall be as Mary who sat there to listen. The cross of Jesus Christ ends all arguments with the devil about sin and acceptance, and will end all difficulties with others. What seems to be a crown of thorns in your relationship can appear as budding roses growing among the thorns, if those thorns can get close enough to crown His head.

The last word might not be the final word

We can have the last word, we can be the last to speak, but it doesn't necessarily mean that we have won the argument. One great man, before entering into any argument, would make the suggestion: Go through the letters of the English alphabet. If you can find a word that tells you they were wrong and you were right, then speak, and only then. It is not what Peter said that won over the Pharisees, it was what he had done. He had walked in the shadows. He had seen the dead raised, bodies healed. These things had given him something to say. I can listen to a man who doesn't 'talk his noise', who doesn't want to be seen because of what he has to say. Gentile ministry granted Peter Gentile compassion, because he had been with them.

'The heart of the righteous studies to answer'

In the *maturity* of Peter we see answers to questions. He became that solid rock, prophesied by Jesus Christ, on which others could build. Proverbs 15:28 says, 'The heart of the righteous 'studies' to answer.' It does not come at the problem with a flaming tongue, burning and scorching all before it. The word 'studies' is 'meditate'. Peter listened with his ears opened wide. 'He that has ears to hear let him hear'. A modern translation says, 'He that has ears should use them!' Famous words, when you are *mature* and have the answer are: 'Friends, Romans, countrymen, lend me your ears.' In Yorkshire, England, if mum wanted to teach us a lesson, she would 'box our ears'. You will not be the answer to anyone's problem if you have 'cloth ears'. Before Simeon listened to men he listened to God. If you are in tune with the Lord you will sing His music. If you are listening to the Lord you will speak His words, and they will be as oil over troubled waters. The problem is that many only listen to themselves, and do only those things they hear themselves say. There has to be another, louder voice than yours.

Simeon had to learn to listen more than he talked. Listen to ten times more than you say. That is very difficult for some. We have a colloquial when anybody talks too much, that they are 'rabbiting', like a rabbit scratching its ears! One telephone company in England is called 'Rabbit'. We are called to be sheep, not rabbits! Sheep do not say much, they are trained not to speak but to follow.

Don't become dull of hearing and tired of speaking

The charge against Israel was that they would not listen,[9] because they had wax in their ears, making them 'dull of hearing'. If that is so, the argument is then one way and that is your way. If you have a bee buzzing in your bonnet, get rid of the bee —the wax will go, and you will hear clearly what the Master has to say. In Revelation He has the voice, the sound of many waters.[10] Peter has been to these waters, he stopped, stooped and listened. In him this produced *maturity* —rich, rare and able to reason with the unreasonable. To move people on simply because they don't agree with you is not the answer. The answer is in every problem, it just needs winkling out.

The answer is through your *maturity* to bring them so close together that they become flesh of your flesh, bone of your bone. It is then that we return to Acts chapter 1:14 where they were all gathered together in 'one place' with one 'accord'—heart.

Notes

[1] See author's book *In Sickness and in Health.*

[2] Mark 6:43.

[3] Job 9:33.

[4] Hebrews 4:15.

[5] Billy Richards was a minister with the Assemblies of God. He pioneered a church called 'Slough Full Gospel Tabernacle'.

[6] 1 John 2:1.

[7] Genesis 25:26.

[8] Isaiah 53:7.

[9] Hebrews 5:11.

[10] Revelation 1:15.

Chapter Twenty

THE MAN PETER, A SERVANT AND AN APOSTLE OF JESUS CHRIST

Fulfilled 'ambition' (vote catching to gain office) is not *maturity* achieved. *Maturity* is the end product of a process of sanctification to holiness resulting in honour, glory and dominion. When God commences any great work He usually starts with something small. A seed is planted and great things grow. The acorn produces the mighty oak. From small seeds come great forests. Small beginnings bring great benefits. God commenced this way with Peter. He commenced with some who were casting nets,[1] others were cleaning nets,[2] some were mending nets,[3] and some were using nets to fish.[4] If God wants to take you to the sea, He will usually start with a fish and a boat. Great garments come from little threads and a small point at the end of a needle. The beginning is not important, but it is important to consider the ending.

Jesus commenced working on Peter where He found him
Jesus commenced changing the life of Cephas where He found him. The Lord takes us as we are, takes hold of what we have, and makes it into something that has the handprints of himself all over it. We can be assured that God is *maturing* us when people say, 'The hand of the Lord is in this matter.' This is His work just as much as the evening sky is part of His creation. The ensuing years were spent

putting something into Simon that was of eternal value. Jesus takes it step by step, place by place, experience by experience. As Israel, we are not led straight into the Promised Land. We are shepherds and sheep keepers, but in the ensuing days we are turned into soldiers, being made ready for the fight before us. One figure of *maturity* is that of a fighting soldier fully trained and equipped.

When you read what a man has written, you are reading the man
It you want to know what is in a man, read what he has written. It will reveal more about him than anything he has ever said. When Simon sees miracles, and is in full flow as he preaches, that does not reveal the depth of his heart. We can handle the strings of the parcel without knowing what is inside. What is lacking in speech will be found in reading, as you read what the man has written. By opening the epistles of Peter you are opening the door to his heart. There is a pretence in the spirit world in taking the palm of a hand, and pretending to read the past, present and future from it. When you look at Cephas, see all that he did, you see an enlargement of a man's heart in the grace of God.

To see and hear this apostle is to see and hear Jesus Christ at work. We become an echo of what Christ is, even as John Baptist was the voice of one crying in the wilderness. (Mark 1:3.) The servant must serve, the disciple must be disciplined, and the apostle must be sent. When Simon refers to himself by any name, it is not just the use of a title, he is describing what he is. The shepherd must shepherd as the servant must serve.

Simon Peter, a servant and an apostle of Jesus Christ
In 2 Peter 1:1, Peter himself wrote: 'Simon Peter, a servant and an apostle of Jesus Christ.' That is where Christ had taken him. This was his 'high water mark'. It must become the 'benchmark' for all believers, including you and me. In 2 Peter 1:1 the picture has been completed by the artist, and is presented to us. When an artist paints the latest portrait of Queen Elizabeth of England, she must attend as many as thirty sittings so that the artist might study her from every angle, adding the finest details with shadows and shades. What

Simon is gives his words clarity, authority and acceptability. He is no ghostly apparition, but a real man, who lives among men. His spirituality was apparent whether inside of the home or outside, in his work or at play.

To see Simon from three different perspectives, look first in the Gospels, where he was very much a failure. View him in the Acts of the Apostles as a dynamic man of the Spirit. See his character, sheer depth and fullness in his two epistles. You see Peter for what he is and how he is as you read his two epistles —that the 'pen becomes mightier than the sword'. The sword tells of the quick tempered Peter, who would slash off an ear if it refused to listen.[5] The pen in his writings tells of all the healing virtues that flowed as he began to write. Without knowing it, he gives us a self-portrait. The warts have been witnessed in the Gospel accounts of his deeds, while his epistles give the handsome features of the man. The term 'handsome' was the word describing 'grace' in the beauty of form for Simon.

Read and know the heart of the man

What the Epistle to Philemon was to the apostle Paul, recording the richness, depth, height, length and breadth of his heart, so those writings reveal the same depth in Peter. When he writes, it is no mere swallow approach, skimming over the surface of the water, no walking on water or along the shallow waters of the beach. There is real depth in what is written. As we read, we could say, as Jesus said, 'Go and do likewise!'[6] The Word of God will always be a mirror in which we see a reflection of ourselves and a reflection of the writer. 'He being dead yet speaks'.

When corresponding to suffering Christians, he takes something from every incident recorded in the Gospels and makes it relevant to everyday Christianity. Even when he prayed for the sick, he did it as Jesus did. There is a Christian book entitled 'What would Jesus do?' When you read what Simon wrote, you see what Jesus would do, and what He had done in another man. Some of the words are verbatim of what Jesus began to do and to teach. His writing is the continuation of 'all' that Jesus began to do and to teach, as experienced in life.

From humble beginnings Peter became something

Many of the facts and much of the data in Mark's Gospel came from Mary the mother of Jesus, and also Peter, who became something from nothing. God who hung the worlds on a word is quite capable of doing something with an empty life. Peter was an 'eye witness in the mount'.[7] He describes himself (after he has written one epistle) as Simon Peter, servant, and an apostle. When he commenced his first Letter it was not with a fanfare of trumpets. In a still small way he writes, and as he develops his themes we see Peter appear as a servant. It seems as if he is saying that he has progressed from one stage and state of glory to another, from Peter to apostle.

In order to 'go on' you have to 'get off'; you recognise, as Cephas did, that as any part of creation is the Lord's handiwork, also so are you are in the plan of salvation. You are not a 'rat' in the 'rat race'. You are more than a shovel and a pick to be taken and used when necessary. You are destiny capable of demonstrating the life of God. You are not a number on a computer list, a house, a field, a chattel, or simply an address. You are not what you were, you are not even what you are going to be, and you are what you have allowed the Lord to produce at this moment in time.

Discipleship means design by degrees. The finished article will never appear, unless you allow those degrees and design to work in you. You can have glimpses of the glory of God on the way to the eternal city, heaven. What makes Simon Peter so appealing is that we see him in every turn we take and every decision we make. Every mistake seems to have its root in Peter. He must not become the excuse for our humanity; instead he must become the example for our destiny. As we read his epistles we still look for his shadow that it might fall across our path and heal, thereby bringing us into a greater dimension of discipleship.

God is calling you to follow Him

If you are looking for someone to lean or build all on, he appears as Peter, the small rock that offers shade and sanctuary in time of need. If you need to hear a human voice, read his epistles, and you will hear that voice echoing from the past into the present, calling you into the future. It is not an 'uncertain sound'[8] that will be heard, but a sure trumpet blast calling you to war, and out of a doomed city to follow Christ.

If a great epitaph and a wonderful memory is what you desire to leave behind, then do something worth copying; achieve the impossible because you were willing to believe the Lord. Do something or write something worth reading. When we read Peter's epistles we feel like the Jews of old as they wrote the Name Jehovah. After each letter they would wipe the pen clean, it was such a sacred Name. When we read the Word of God we are sanctified, and Peter is there to ensure the Word is applied to our hearts. Some would read the epistles as a ledger, others for pleasure, but some will see them as a treasure of truth. It is through this written word that we are able to grow. (1 Peter 2:2.) He sees us as 'babes' turned into youths, youths into fathers, and fathers changed into men —*mature* men.

Here are principles that will help you to grow

As Simon Cephas writes, he gives certain principles that will help us to grow in the knowledge of Jesus Christ. As a bean we can grow into the beanstalk in the story of 'Jack and the Beanstalk' taking us into the land of giants, where there is a goose that will lay golden eggs. Sell the cow, get rid of the idol to buy the seeds of smallness which, when planted in your heart, will develop into greatness. You will occupy the land of giants. Though small we grow tall, tall enough to increase our vision of the world to come. If we were not meant to be tall, why did we invent ladders, and why did the Lord create mountains? How is it that you can stand on your tiptoes?

As Peter mentions the 'example' that Jesus left for us to follow,[9] so he places footsteps throughout his writings. If you walk in them, you will grow as Peter grew. Here is miracle seed promoting growth in dirty, poor quality, shallow and dusty soil. Jesus commenced with Peter as a little bit of rock —rough, unshaped and wobbling. A famous proverb of the day was, 'Can any good thing come out of Nazareth?'[10]

Jesus changes us from glory to glory

Jesus took that description of nature, and made it into a palace beautiful seen in the life of Simon Peter, the servant and an apostle of Jesus Christ. Cephas anchors all that he is, all he has been made, to Jesus Christ, giving him all the glory. What Jesus had done with many a broken piece of wood in the Carpenter's shop, He achieved through the life of Peter. He was just 'flotsam and jetsam', driftwood that Jesus made into a Noah's ark that would face many a storm. There had to be a moment when the first piece of wood was chosen for the ark. There was a moment when the first raindrop fell from the skies, leading to a deluge. If you can't be first, be a copy of the First as you emulate Jesus Christ. Paul said, 'You became 'followers' of me as I was of Christ (1 Corinthians 11:1). They became imitators of Jesus. Many have played 'Follow my Leader', a game for children in which you had to do all that the leader did as you followed him.

When passing through darkness, help and hope is given

Peter has given hope and love to help during the dark periods of life, when all we can do is trust. There are things in his letters that become beacons on a dark night, flashing with hope, leading us on to *maturity*. *Maturity* has never meant that we do not make mistakes. It does, however, mean we learn not to make the same mistake forty times. When we fall, we know how to get up and go on. When a child falls, it dusts itself down and goes on as if nothing has happened.

In AD 60–65, the persecution of the church extended from Jerusalem into the provinces, reaching those 'scattered abroad'. It is to this company that Peter writes, wanting to strengthen their faith. 'Faith' is mentioned seven times, and 'trial' referred to seventeen times. Affliction can be the best book in your library. It will teach you far more than anything written by man or machine. Facts about the suffering Saviour are on record in 1 Peter 1:6–9; 4:12–19. We have seven examples of Jesus undergoing suffering in order to help us through. (1 Peter 2:21–24.) These are the things that have taken Simon on to service, sainthood and priesthood.

Peter had passed through much tribulation

Peter understood all about persecution and tribulation. He had been sifted by Satan, as prophesied by Jesus Christ. That tribulation suggests a metal instrument on which corn was rubbed to remove the husks so that the corn could be used to make bread. The word 'Hovis' is the name of a company which bakes and sells bread, and means 'strength.' Ambrosia is the 'food of the gods'. The son of Jonas wrote in response to two challenges in his life. 'When you are converted (strengthened) strengthen your brethren' (Luke 22:32). The other challenge is found in John 21:15, 16, 17, 'Feed My sheep.' A threefold challenge to answer to the three times that he denied the Lord with swearing.

Everything written by Peter must touch us if we are going to be *mature* and strong in every part. Thetis took her son Achilles by the heel and dipped him in the river Styx to make him invulnerable. The water touched every part of him except the heel she held him by! He was slain when a dart entered into his vulnerable point. We need the water of the Word to wash us completely and lead us into new strength.[11]

Peter writes as a father to his children

Simeon writes as a father to his children. (1 Peter 2:2.) He pens the paper as a brother in adversity. (1 Peter 4:12.) He is a pastor (Elder) and a shepherd to the sheep. (1 Peter 5:1.) As a *mature* man he writes to men. As an architect he writes about stones. As a hunter he mentions a lion. As a priest he tells of priesthood —meaning 'bridge builders'. As a failure he writes in order to keep men from falling and failing. As a believer his letters are to believers; as a Christian he corresponds about Christ.

His appeal is made to 'sojourners' and 'strangers'. The Greek word for 'sojourners' is made up of two words: 'contrary' and 'conditions'. If you are facing contrary conditions he is writing to you, to pull you through the tough and the trouble. As 'Evangelist' and 'Faithful' helped Christian in Pilgrim's Progress to come through the 'Slough of Despond', and later from Doubting castle using the Key of Promises, so does this writer.[12] He mentions that they were 'strangers' (1 Peter

1:1), people who were away from home, people from another country, clime and king. People 'down here' that belonged 'up there'. Peter would never be a writer for 'The Times', but he did write for the 'times' he lived in. The New English Bible says of 'sojourners' they are 'those that lodge for a while.'

He is known as the Apostle of Hope. He mentions the word 'hope' four times in his first epistle, in an endeavour to promote hope and expectancy. Everything written in his first letter is added to in the second communication.

Simon son of Jonas has much to say about the purifying of faith. All that which is around you as a burning fire is not to burn you up, it is to prove you are genuine. The genuine is the glory of Christ. The nature of God is your nationality. When the Refiner of gold puts the gold into a pot, and then places it on a fire, he waits until the scum can be wiped, and when he can see his image in the gold, he knows it is purified and ready for pouring. You are the gold of God, the coinage of the Kingdom.

There is a joy that knows no limits

Cephas holds nothing back that will benefit those who follow Christ. One of his themes is that of joy unspeakable and full of glory, joy that knows no limits, has no measure. We have peace which passes understanding; inspiration will always take you to where intellect never can; love which passes knowledge; you can't think it through, you can only work it out. Joy causes stuttering for it is 'unspeakable', beyond your vocabulary. We have such a joy that will take us on. The proverb says, 'He is a poor man that can count his flock.' Alexander Pope called joy 'The soul's calm sunshine'.

To those who are thinking 'how can I keep going?' this *mature* man says you may have 'manifold temptations',[13] temptations of all shapes, sizes, colours and from every quarter. To balance these he also mentions 'manifold grace'. (1 Peter 4:10.) Grace with many folds in as life turns back those folds to reveal help. It is too numerous to be counted. You can count the fingers on your hand but you can't count the fingers on God's hand. Multi-coloured grace to meet the blood red of temptation, the black and blue we feel in our spirits as we are assailed by lusts.

Be ye holy in all manner of conversation

(1 Peter 1:15) 'Be ye holy in all manner of conversation.' Be different, is what Peter is saying. As different as chalk is to cheese is how you must be to those living around you. If a letter was addressed to the holy man or woman, with your street name on, would it find you? Those who are *mature* do not look for excuses to be as near to the world as possible without entering into it. Remember, the 'world' is not a place it is a spirit of pride, lust, envy, jealousy and malice that can dwell in you. The word 'holy' suggests completion; and you are 'complete in Him.' The initial thought is of being healthy with all your spirituality functioning properly.

Cheer up! You have been 'redeemed'. (1 Peter 1:18.) The word translated is 'break' and 'loose', used in Acts 27:41 as a ship is broken by waves. The chains have been snapped to allow you to become yourself, to achieve what you were designed to achieve. Salvation does not restrict you, it sets you free.

Lay on one side those things that would trip you up

You have to 'lay aside' (1 Peter 2:1). The same thought is found in Hebrews 12:1, and is a medical term suggesting the removal of fat. If you are to develop, you must do these things. Do not get fat through lack of faith. Sorrow and trouble will bring overweight to you. Weigh yourself by the Word to determine your true weight. If you are to grow you have to desire the 'sincere' milk of the word. The word 'sincere' is corn without chaff, milk without water, and a figure sculpted without wax filling. A wax filling denotes 'insincere', moving into the word 'hypocrite', pretending to be something it is not.

In everything you do, realise that Christ is 'precious'. He is 'dear', a price that cannot be counted. There is the thought of 'darling' in that word 'dear'. 'Precious' is that which is held in 'highest honour'. The preciousness you give to Him makes you a 'peculiar' people. (1 Peter 2:9.) As a slave, if you wanted to do work for another master, the money or substance you received became known as your 'peculiar' treasure. In Malachi 3:17, the word 'precious' (in the Septuagint Version of the Old Testament) is given as 'jewels'. Cranmer's Bible says: 'A people that are won'.

In your goodness show forth the praises of God
1 Peter 2:9 says we must show forth the 'praises' of Him. The word is 'virtues'. A 'virtuous' person described everything that was excellent in a man, connected to the word 'hero'. It described the practise of duty. The Romans used it to describe a good soldier. Peter had proven himself at home and abroad. He had been in many battles but had come through them all. In Luke 10:3, the word 'virtue' is translated 'lambs'. That is how innocent we have to be. Manliness without weakness, desire leading to duty, will be seen as *maturity*.

We have to have our 'conversation honest' (1 Peter 2:12), not referring to speech but to salt, and what we are in God. The word 'honest' was used to describe a 'beautiful garment'. Let the outward be inward as godly women follow the Lord. (Verse 20), 'This will be acceptable with God.'

Learn to be pitiful through the shedding of tears
Be 'pitiful', i.e. full of pity. Don't let the tears dry on your face, let them enter into the human race to help in a practical way. Don't let your tears be just for you. Don't let the tears that dry on your face only be shed for yourself. Let your handkerchief be stained with tears for another. As you wipe them away you become a sketch of God as in Revelation 7:17; 21:4. (1 Peter 3:15), 'be ready to give an 'answer' to those who ask you about Christ. The word 'answer' describes the evidence given by a person on trial. By his evidence he was declared either innocent or guilty. (1 Peter 4:19), 'commit' the keeping of your soul to Him. Give to God soul welfare even as money might be given to you for safekeeping. Be persuaded that all you have committed unto Him, He is able to keep until that Day.

Learn to cast all your cares on Him
Learn to cast all your cares on Him. (1 Peter 5:7.) A modern translation is, 'Cast all your care on Him because it matters to Him

about you.' The Duke of Wellington would weigh every soldier, to see if he would make a good soldier, by enduring hardness. When he had weighed a soldier, the Duke could ascertain how far he would travel, what strength the soldier possessed, and how long he would maintain his fighting prowess before requiring to be relieved from duty. If the burden they carried was too heavy, he lightened the load by giving them further training before fighting. With care cast aside you can lean on your Guide. 'Casting' your care takes effort. In colloquial language it means to 'slap' on the counter, or to slap the hands when making a bargain, as Gypsies do. Cast your 'care' on Him as those who were brought and left at His feet. (Matthew 15:30.) Let that 'care' be cast as a garment onto the back of an animal. (Luke 19:35.) His breast is large enough to take another aching head. Load it onto Christ as you would load a cart or suitcase. (Acts 27:19.) Cast care away as an anchor thrown over the side of the ship to secure it. (Acts 27:29.) It is not what you keep and deal with yourself that tells of your *maturity*, it is what you commit to the Lord, and what you let God deal with.

Add that which is lacking to your faith

'Grow in grace and in the knowledge of Jesus Christ. Add faith to your virtue, virtue to knowledge, to knowledge temperance; to temperance patience, to patience godliness' (2 Peter 1:5, 6). If these things are in you, there will be no branch without fruit. The end will be 'perfection'. (1 Peter 5:10.) Don't let the word 'perfect' frighten you. It is but another word for *maturity*, suggesting a soldier fully equipped for war as in Ephesians 6. It is a workman with all his tools doing the work he has been trained to do. It describes mending broken nets, in order to use them for fishing again.[14] The 'perfecting' of the saints is the process of putting a fractured leg back into position.[15]

Let Him Who has commenced a good work conclude it

The man Peter, a servant and an apostle of Jesus Christ, has left all these things on record to enable you to allow Him Who had begun a good work in you to complete it. Peter's words have been placed as tools for you to take and finish the job! During the 1940 world war, Winston Churchill said, 'Give us the tools and we will finish the job.' A man was so dispirited, he cried to God, 'I wish You had never made me!' The Lord replied, 'I haven't, yet!' There is a work to be completed, which can be finished as you 'follow on to know the Lord.' The man of God must be 'fully furnished'[16] as a ship with all its crew and cargo ready to sail the seven seas and see the seven wonders of the spiritual world in Ephesians 2.

The Lord is not slack concerning His promises

For our benefit, Simon Cephas emphasises that the Lord is not 'slack' concerning His promises. He is not as those in Hebrews 2:1 who would let things 'slip' as a rope loosed, letting a boat drift from its moorings. The promises of God are not as a slack rope. These promises can take the strain of wind, water, tide and undercurrent. God cannot ever be accused of being 'slothful in business'. (1 Timothy 3:15) The word 'slack' is rendered 'tarry'. (Genesis 43:10) The corresponding word 'slack' is found in the word 'lingering'.

Don't tarry; if it has to be done, do it, and do it now! Adoration is service with alacrity. Worship is being willing to go or to stay. Praise is **P**urpose **R**ealised, as the **A**nswer **I**s **S**ent to **E**ncourage.

The Lord is not slack in anything; He takes it from the beginning through to the end. He constantly goes before you to work out the plan for your life, even if it contains pain. The pain and the ointment in the hand of the Physician blend as one. It is His word and His work along with His will to make you into a *mature* person.

Make the God of all grace your goal

A final appeal for *maturity* is found in 2 Peter 3:18, 'But 'grow in grace' and in the knowledge of our Lord and Saviour Jesus Christ.' Fully use the grace that has been given to you. Grow in it as a plant will grow in the soil. Reach for the light as a flower. Grow in grace which is as that refreshed by gentle breezes and the dew of the morning. Grow in grace, grow because of it, and grow through it until you come into full manhood, when your expression will become His impression. Let us grow up in Him in all things. When you think you are 'growing', measure yourself with Christ Jesus. Grow from a convert to a follower, and on to become a disciple. Don't just be there for the bread and fish as some were in the Gospels,[17] be the bread in your *maturity*. It is then that your *mature* life will declare 'To Him is glory both now and forever.'

Notes

[1] Matthew 4:18.
[2] Luke 5:2.
[3] Matthew 4:21.
[4] John 21:6.
[5] John 18:10.
[6] Luke 10:37.
[7] 2 Peter 1:16.
[8] 1 Corinthians 14:8.
[9] 1 Peter 2:21.
[10] John 1:46.
[11] One of the stories of Homer, the Greek writer.
[12] A Christian allegory written by John Bunyan who was serving a prison sentence because he preached outside of the church.
[13] 1 Peter 1:6.
[14] Mark 1:19.
[15] Ephesians 4:12.
[16] 2 Timothy 3:17.
[17] John 6:26, 27.

Other books by the same author:

Paths of Righteousness in Psalm 23 – on disk
Buried Talents
In Sickness and in Health
Dying is Living
The Growing Pains of Peter
More than Conquerors
Dwarfing Giants

All obtainable from:

New Living Publishers
164 Radcliffe New Road,
Whitefield,
Manchester M45 7TU

Website: www.newlivingpublishers.co.uk